Commodity Advertising

The Economics and Measurement of Generic Programs

Olan D. Forker and Ronald W. Ward

Lexington Books
An Imprint of Macmillan, Inc.
New York

Maxwell Macmillan Canada
Toronto

Maxwell Macmillan International
New York   Oxford   Singapore   Sydney

We dedicate this book
to our supportive wives,
Katie and Geraldine

Library of Congress Cataloging-in-Publication Data

Forker, Olan D.
   Commodity advertising : the economics and measurement of generic
programs / Olan D. Forker and Ronald W. Ward.
      p.   cm.
   Includes bibliographical references.
   ISBN 0-02-910405-X
   1. Advertising—Food—United States.   2. Generic products—United States.
3. Advertising—Brand name products—United States.
4. Advertising—Food—United States—Case studies.   I. Ward, Ronald
W. II. Title.
HF6161.F616F67   1993
659.1′13—dc20   92-38941
                                                                      CIP

Lexington Books
An Imprint of Macmillan, Inc.
866 Third Avenue, New York, N. Y. 10022

Maxwell Macmillan Canada, Inc.
1200 Eglinton Avenue East
Suite 200
Don Mills, Ontario M3C 3N1

Macmillan, Inc. is part of the Maxwell Communication Group of Companies.

Printed in the United States of America

printing number
1   2   3   4   5   6   7   8   9   10

Contents

Figures

v

Tables

Preface

This book has been written to create a better understanding of the purposes, uses, and results of commodity advertising and promotion programs. We hope that it will create a better understanding of their economic benefits and costs and the basis for more and better economic analyses.

We both became active in the economic analysis of commodity advertising programs more than twenty years ago. Ward has been involved in the economic analysis of several advertising programs since the early 1970s; Forker became involved at about the same time. Over the years, we have worked with several of the commodity promotion boards. We both have been active on a national research committee that meets twice annually to discuss and develop methodology appropriate for the evaluation of commodity advertising programs. Those meetings serve as a forum for analysts to interact with practitioners and share ideas and research results. It is from our research, the research of others, and the many meetings with professionals interested in the subject that the ideas for this text had its beginnings. As far as we know it is the first reference book, other than books of proceedings, that specifically addresses the economics of commodity advertising and promotion programs.

Commodity advertising is a multimillion dollar industry. Almost $1 billion is spent annually to promote agricultural commodities alone. The book explores how advertising money is raised and spent by commodity promotion organizations. The economics of commodity promotion in theory and practice is set forth. We discuss the differences between commodity and brand advertising and discuss the unique policy and management issues that evolve from these differences. The legislative authority for state and federal commodity promotion programs is presented, and several of the large commodity promotion organizations are discussed in detail, including those for dairy products, beef, pork, Florida citrus, California raisins, and Washington apples. Case studies of other commodity advertising promotion programs are also included to illustrate the strategies and techniques to promote these products and to evaluate the effectiveness of their advertising and promotion activities.

The authors owe a great debt of gratitude to all who have been involved in doing research in this area over the past twenty years. Special thanks go to the members of NEC-63, the Research Committee on Commodity Promotion Programs, for sharing their ideas and research results with us. Henry Kinnucan, John Nichols, and Michael J. Simpson reviewed early drafts of this manuscript for the publisher and provided many constructive suggestions. Wayne Watkinson reviewed chapters 3, 4, and 5 for the authors. We thank them for helping us improve the readability and accuracy of the text.

Both authors owe a similar debt to the various checkoff boards who have interacted with us as they struggle with the issues of evaluation. In particular, we are indebted to the National Dairy Board, the New York State Milk Promotion Advisory Board, the National Beef Board, the National Pork Board, the Washington Apple Commission, and the Florida Department of Citrus for their continued role in fostering the linkage between agricultural economists and the boards' staff and directors. Without their response, much of our work would probably still be on the shelf.

We thank our respective department chairs and many colleagues who were supportive of this effort. Early in the writing of this book, we interviewed a large number of individuals in the commodity promotion industry, and we have received the benefit of the ideas and suggestions of many other colleagues in government and at various universities. We thank them all, but especially we thank Walter Armbruster, James Blaylock, Tom Cox, George deJager, Bill Diggins, Peter Gould, Tom Hale, Susan Hurst, John Huston, Chuck Lambert, Jong Lee, John Lenz, Donald Liu, Archie MacDonald, Les Myers, Rick Naczi, Lyle Newcomb, Barry Pfouts, Jeanna Sowa, Nancy Sprecher, Tom Swearingen, Stanley Thompson, Bill Underwood, Jay Wardell, and Joe Westwater. We also thank Shirley Arcangeli and Carlos Jauregui for assistance with data and manuscript preparation, and we thank Beth Anderson and the editorial staff at Lexington for their support and enthusiasm about this project.

1

Introduction

"Beef: It's What's for Dinner." "Pork, and Other White Meat." "A can a week; that's all we ask." "Made in America." Slogans such as these are part of the American scene. But why? What is going on, and why are consumers exposed to these expressions? How are such efforts to reach consumers coordinated and funded? Though the slogans and messages are diverse, there is a common purpose to reach potential consumers, with the objective being to change consumption habits. Providing consumers (and potentially new consumers) with information is part of the overall marketing effort as products move from the production level through the marketing channels to final consumers.

This process entails a great number of activities, including pricing, grading, packaging, storage, distribution, exchange, and merchandising. These functions encompass a physical transformation of the product in form, time, and geographical distribution. The product in some form flows through the marketing system. As the product flows through the system, its economic value must be established at each point of exchange and transformation. Pricing systems, accounting practices, government support policies, industry structure, and consumer preferences all influence the establishment of the economic value or price of the good. Finally, along with the product flow and establishing the economic value, there must be a parallel flow of information about the product; otherwise, consumers would not be aware of the product and its attributes. Product flow, economic value, and information are interrelated. The concept of marketing, as it is generally used in the United States, includes functions relating to product flow, pricing, and information. Marketing is viewed as the functions that coordinates the movement of the product through the distribution system.

Where, then, do the general slogans and phrases so often seen for many commodities fit into the overall marketing of commodities? Our purpose in this book is to address this aspect of marketing with the primary goal of

1

providing insight into the marketing activity generally referred to as generic advertising and promotion. Although a formal definition will be given later, the term *generic advertising* is intended to denote three primary activities: injecting information into the marketing system, coordination and funding of the information programs among producers with common goals, and addressing product attributes common to the commodity group.

Individual firms producing commodities and services sometimes feel that if only they could expand the demand for the product category, the industry would be more stable, and the individual businesses would be more profitable. This feeling has led to groups of firms joining together to raise funds for joint advertising and promotion efforts. Because the effort is directed to promoting the generic or common attributes of the products or services being produced, this effort is usually referred to as *generic advertising* or *generic promotion*. In this book we refer to the effort as *commodity advertising and promotion*, as we focus on the efforts of commodity groups. The theory, economic concepts, and evaluation methodology, however, are applicable to any situation where a group of firms collectively advertise and promote their products' common characteristics.

Generic advertising and promotion can be found in almost every U.S. agricultural industry. Generic efforts have grown in importance, and the legal and political base for supporting them has substantially changed since the early 1970s. Understanding commodity advertising and promotion and how it is accomplished is essential if one is to understand the marketing of U.S. agriculture. Although generic advertising and promotion is only a part of the total marketing, it is becoming an increasingly important part. It is important not only because of the additional information flows but because of the coordination among producers of the good involved.

We focus on commodity advertising and promotion because commodity groups have received special legislative authority for producers of a commodity to be assessed for the purpose of underwriting advertising and promotion programs. Since the funds are normally deducted from the payment made by the first handler of the commodity for the producer, the term *producer checkoff* is used to denote the manner by which the commodity advertising and promotion programs are funded. Such commodity promotion programs, while modest in size two decades ago, now have evolved to nearly a $1 billion annual effort. The funds are invested in a wide range of activities, including product and process research, education, public relations, promotion, and advertising. Most of it is invested in generating and conveying information to consumers or users of the commodity in question.

Supply and Demand for Information

Information is the lifeblood of decision making where consumers are faced with a multitude of daily purchasing and consumption decisions. It is usually assumed that the consumer is a rational individual who makes decisions only after having assimilated the appropriate data, analyzed the facts, determined the options, and assessed the constraints. The accumulation of these decisions translates into consumer demand; that is, demand is realized after having the information in hand to judge the product, its value, and the alternatives. Acquiring the necessary information, however, is a major constraint in the purchasing process. As potential consumers, we usually do not have the capacity to review every potential fact that could be germane to making rational decisions. Consumers often draw on their experiences and the experiences of others. Yet in market economies where the alternatives change almost daily, it simply is impossible to be aware of all options, much less experiment with them. Thus, as our need for an increasing variety of products expands, our requirement for information increases proportionally, or possibly at an increasing rate. There is a need for information, and thus a market for such information.

Consumers demand information as a guideline for decision making. Suppliers of information have responded in a variety of ways. In one extreme, buying and selling information may be treated like any other good: the product is defined, the attributes set forth, and a price established. In a growing service economy such as that in the United States, the market for information is a major business where exchange transactions take place in much the same way as consumer or producer goods are sold, with a price negotiated directly for the product. Hundreds of examples can be cited to illustrate the market for information. *Consumer Reports* magazine is probably the best-known example of consumers directly paying for the information closely tied to their normal purchasing habits. Other examples include subscriptions to newspapers, stock reports, and magazines that provide timely information about products and markets, information that would otherwise be impossible to assimilate. Subscriptions to home television shopping are another new mechanism for consumers to receive information on a user-fee basis, and interactive computer networks (such as CompuServe and Prodigy) are even more contemporary examples. Although there are a vast array of user-fee means for dissemination of information, a parallel market exists where no direct user fee is paid. (We emphasize the word *direct*.)

Information in and of itself does not create utility. Consumers do not satisfy their basic needs of taste, hunger, pleasure, and sociological and psychological positioning with the information. Product information is a means to an end for fulfilling these needs. The information allows us to decide which foods to consume, the types of clothes to buy, the vacation to take, or the car to purchase. Even impulse buying is influenced by consumer exposure to product information. Media industries have evolved recognizing that much of consumers' demand for information is simply a means for acquiring the product. Thus, the outgrowth of advertising and promotion as we know it today developed. Much of the advertising and promotion information that consumers receive is not on a user-fee basis. The information appears to be free. Obviously, the free information is intended to persuade consumers in their selection process; the cost of the information is capitalized in the product price.

User-Fee and Nonfee Information

When comparing these two broad forms of information, they can best be classified as either *purchasing neutral* or *purchasing bias*. User-fee information is used to rank alternatives after which decisions are made. This type of information is expected to be factual and informative in setting forth the product attributes in both absolute and comparative terms. These forms of information are usually purchasing neutral, whereas purchasing-bias information is clearly designed to attract or guide consumers in specific directions.

A large part of our daily decision making and purchases are based on habits. Consumption patterns based on past behavior are often referred to as *habit persistence*. If perfect habit were the norm, then decisions would be predetermined from past consumption patterns. Habit persistence simply means that we normally repeat consumption decisions with some slight deviation; this is particularly true for those products that are frequently purchased and for products that have a low economic value. Habit persistence is a very logical reflection of daily activities. It is nothing more than a composite index of our socioeconomic status, our preferences, and our understanding of the current state of the market and alternatives. While consumers follow patterns in their purchasing decisions, there is always some room for experimentation. Thus, there are two major avenues in which purchasing-bias information can change consumer decisions—changing habits, and encouraging experimentation. The essence of advertising and promotion is to guide habit formation and to direct changes in consumption behavior.

Purchasing-bias information can change consumers' state of knowledge about a particular product. This may be new knowledge or a change in perceptions about product attributes. Either way, the knowledge base has changed, and the potential for deviations from the habit persistence pattern is significant. Factual knowledge about a product can have a direct impact on long-term habits; as an example, continued concern with cholesterol and belief in the health attributes of oats has led to longterm habit changes toward eating more oat grain products. This leads to longer-term repeat purchases of the specific product(s).

Consumer habits for many products will evolve because of technological changes. The development of microwave cooking is a perfect example. In such cases, habits are not initially well ingrained and are subject to deviations. For this example, purchasing-bias information provides consumers with information compatible with the evolving technology. The home video market is another parallel example, as even the starting minutes of a rental video include purchasing-bias information that is received on a nonfee basis.

Information and Experimentation

Some products lend themselves to experimentation. Consumers may be receptive to trying a new product when the risks are low. Introduction of a new diet drink, accompanied with considerable expenditures on advertising and promotion, may be successful because of the nature of the product. There is almost no inherent risk in experimenting with a new type of soft drink, whereas, the introduction of a new brand of baby food may face resistance simply because of a perceived higher risk factor associated with changing the diet of a new baby. The chance for experimentation should be considerably greater among those goods carrying little risks if the product does not meet the consumer's initial expectations.

Effectiveness of purchasing-bias information is dependent on the characteristics of the product and the quality of the information. Product characteristics include such factors as appearance, functional use, and nutritional attributes. The information content ranges from factual data about the product's attributes to promotional copy designed to achieve high recall through persuasive appeal. Some advertising and promotion efforts convey little content about the product but are more directed to the consumption experience and the satisfaction from trying the product. Others attempt to achieve experimentation and change through association with activities that lead to high product recall. A catchy phrase such as "uh-huh" used by Pepsi-Cola says little about the product's attributes but is something that potential consumers are likely to recall. In contrast , the phrase "Pork, the other white meat" not only gives consumers a memorable slogan but attempts to change their understanding about the fundamental attributes of the product. Some products can be better differentiated because of packaging, processing, or other ways to expose consumers to the product forms. Alternatives for advertising and promotion increase with the more differentiable products.

Generic Advertising Defined

At this point, we have indicated that information, and specifically advertising and promotion, provides an essential dimension to the purchase of most products. The role of advertising and promotion will differ among the array of products available. Some highly differentiable products are brand specific and are marketed through intensive firm advertising. Advertising and promotion of specific brands or attributes unique to a subgroup within the product category is referred to as *brand advertising*. Other products that are less differentiable may be better advertised through some type of cooperative effort among producers and suppliers. Advertising and promotion for these cooperative efforts is known as generic advertising. We have defined generic advertising in the context of commodities, because that is the emphasis of this book. Clearly, though, cooperative and generic advertising extends beyond that of agricultural commodities to cooperative banking promotions, advertising of environmental issues, and public safety advertising among others. Even "buy American" is generic in that it refers to the common characteristic of a broad range of products with something in common.

For agricultural commodities, generic advertising has taken an increasingly important role. Although generic advertising is still small in comparison with all product advertising and promotion, it is of major importance to the agricultural sector. The purpose of this book is to deal with generic advertising of commodity products. How generic advertising fits within the general advertising theory is shown; then much of the text concentrates on the programs in place, giving a detailed description of major U.S. programs.

Before proceeding further, a precise definition of generic advertising and promotion is useful. *Generic advertising is the cooperative effort among producers of a nearly homogeneous product to disseminate information about the underlying attributes of the product to existing and potential consumers for the purpose of strengthening demand for the commodity.* Within this definition, there are four key terms. *Cooperation* implies a joint commitment where the programs are funded through some type of coordinated effort, with the legal requirements for participation clearly defined. A *homogeneous product* defines the limits of who can participate, what can be said, and the degree of commonality among those underwriting the programs. *Disseminate information* entails a range of activities, all with the purpose of informing and persuading potential users of the commodity; the effort is one of controlling or at least having some impact on the content and flow of information about the commodity. Finally, the ultimate purpose is *strengthening demand* by building a consumer support base for the commodity. This occurs through the efforts to attract new consumers and to increase usage among existing consumers of the commodity.

The Need for Generic Advertising and Commodity Checkoff Programs

For most commodity groups, the implementation of generic programs grew out of the need for producers to have more direct input into the marketing of their products. From a historical perspective, agricultural producers were suppliers with little interest or expertise in dealing with issues beyond the farm gate. As farms grew larger and agribusiness industries became more concentrated, producers became even more distant from the ultimate consumers of their products. Since the producers were and still are small in size and large in number relative to the purchasers of their production, they have considered themselves "price takers" with little influence over the price or form of their products when marketed. Through commodity checkoff programs, they are able to put together enough money to operate rather large information programs to inform consumers of the attributes of their commodity and the products that are produced therefrom. Through regional and national generic programs, producers use television and radio media, supplemented with print advertising, to communicate directly to consumers and others the benefits and value of using their commodity. Most groups also use other means in addition to communicate, such as educational programs, public relations, special events, trade fairs, and newsletters targeted to processors and distributors.

Historically, commodity groups also felt the need to improve the product and process technology. In some instances, nonagricultural products were taking markets from agricultural producers; the substitution of nylon for cotton and wool is a contemporary example. Thus, agricultural commodity producers have felt a need to improve the technology and knowledge associated with the processing and distribution of the commodities that they produce. They used the checkoff programs to raise funds to support research in product and process technology, new product development, and product distribution. Also, checkoff funds are sometimes used to assist marketing firms in the development of domestic and foreign markets.

Types of Commodities

The ability to implement generic advertising and promotion programs can be traced back to the fundamental characteristics of the commodity. Commodity characteristics set the limits on product use, consumer interest, the range of varieties, frequency of use, and product forms. Furthermore, the product characteristics will determine the kinds of competing alternatives that consumers perceive as substitutes for the product(s) being considered.

Product Groups

All agricultural products can be grouped into one or more of four basic classes, depending on what is derived from the commodity. Agricultural commodities may be consumed (before or after transformation) as (1) food goods, (2) fibers and skins, (3) for aesthetic purposes, and/or (4) for feeds and inputs (ingredients). Food goods include both fresh and processed forms. The product may keep the same form through the marketing channels, or it may go through several stages of transformation before reaching the point of final consumption. Some agricultural goods lose much of their original identity at this final point. It is more difficult to design generic advertising and promotional programs targeted to the final consumer when consumers cannot readily see the original product form on the grocery shelf. The linkage between wheat and bread is a typical example where the raw commodity completely loses its identity at the point of consumption. In contrast, fluid milk is a commodity that keeps its identity throughout the marketing channels. Thus, designing a generic program for fluid milk should be easier than for a commodity where consumers see little association between the commodity and the final product form.

While foods meet our demands for nutrition, commodities produced for fibers satisfy such other needs as protection, warmth, security and psychological appeal. Cotton, for example, is one of the agricultural goods used most extensively for nonfood purposes. By-products from live animals supply a large market for skins and hides. When comparing foods to fibers, it is more likely that food consumption is closer to the habit persistence model, whereas fibers and skins are more susceptible to experimentation. Hence, consumer responsiveness to generic advertising and promotion will differ depending on how the commodity is used.

A third set of agricultural goods satisfies primarily aesthetic needs. The growing floral industry produces products that are almost exclusively used for their aesthetic characteristics and environmental benefits. Products used for cosmetics, fragrance, and beauty aids deal with specific needs of consumers; hence, unique types of informational programs are required. Many of these products are used to address psychological or emotional needs. This requires an entirely different advertising and promotion strategy compared to the promotion of basic food goods. In Chapter 2, several aspects of these product characteristics are discussed.

Finally, the agricultural product's primary use may be for nonhuman consumption, such as feeds, inputs, and ingredients. Informational needs still exist, but users of many of these products may be willing to search out the product attributes instead of depending on media advertising and promotion. The audience and message must be tailored to different users than in the case of food goods. The message is probably more targeted than messages used for general food products that have a much wider appeal to consumers.

At this juncture, the fundamental point is that generic advertising programs will differ depending on the primary uses of the commodity being considered for generic programs. One must have a clear understanding of these four basic classifications in order to design and assess the potential success of a commodity advertising program. The type of commodity and its uses will determine the message to be communicated, the media needed for delivering the messages, the targeted audience, and the intensity and degree of coordination needed.

Generic Program Limits and Controls

In later chapters, a complete inventory of agricultural commodity promotional programs is documented. For most commodity groups, the implementation of generic programs grew out of the need for producers to have more direct input in the marketing of their products. Through national and regional generic programs, producers have used the media to communicate their product attributes directly to potential consumers. This communication has predominantly been in the form of electronic media (via television and radio) and complemented with print media. Generic advertising is designed to influence the final consumer to purchase the product category with the ultimate purpose to establish long-term habit persistence patterns for the commodity. For some goods, such efforts have been successful, whereas others have not.

Several factors can be identified that directly or indirectly place limits or controls on the nature of a particular advertising and promotion effort. Some of the more important aspects include (1) the current state of consumer knowledge about the product, (2) the commodity's characteristics, (3) the political structure of the industry, (4) the history of industry and program successes and failures, (5) media availability and creative efforts, (6) government regulations and policies, (7) degree of industry competitive structure, (8) consumer awareness and behavior (including demographic differences), and (9) the industry resource base and structure. Significant problems with one or more of these could prevent having a successful generic program. As the industries are reviewed in later case studies, it is important to keep these nine factors in mind. Though often the discussion does not explicitly note it, the essence of most of the discussions can be put in the context of one or more of these limiting factors.

Putting the Programs in Perspective

In later chapters, detailed descriptions of various commodity advertising and promotion programs are set forth. Before proceeding into the more descriptive analysis, however, it is useful to have an overview of the general scope of most commodity advertising and promotional activities. All commodity advertising and promotion programs can be subgrouped according to three criteria: (1) source of funding, (2) breath of coverage, and (3) control of the message. Four groups responsible for commodity advertising and promotion activities exist: (1) private brands and joint ventures, (2) trade associations, (3) checkoff programs, and (4) direct government participation.

Private firms conduct commodity advertising and promotion efforts with the purpose of increasing the demand for their specific forms of the commodity. While the advertising efforts may enlarge the demand for the entire industry, a firm would also expect to see its own market share increase (or at least not decline). Firms individually or through some form of joint venture control the program design but also pay the costs of the advertising and promotion. They receive direct benefits, but they may also be subsidizing others if their efforts expand the demand for the total good. In any case, the private firms have maximum control over the message but much less control over the total industry's efforts, unless the specific firm can exercise considerable market power over the entire industry because of its place in the market. Tropicana brand orange juice is a good example of a national brand for a product that also has a generic advertising program; Jimmy Dean sausage is another established brand for a commodity with parallel generic efforts.

Programs through a trade association are one step closer to a generic program in that the design is intended to benefit all members. The fundamental problem is that the programs are underwritten through voluntary participation. Although there may be political pressure for groups to participate, legally trade associations are not mandatory. There is always room for the "free rider," the individual who shares in the benefits but is not willing to pay the appropriate share of the costs.

Commodity checkoff programs are a direct outgrowth of the potential free-rider problem. Commodity industries recognize the need to advertise their products but also recognize the need for everyone who benefits to pay their share of the program costs. Thus commodity checkoff programs evolved as a way for groups of producers to promote their products while assuring that everyone shares in the cost according to some agreed-upon assessment. A commodity checkoff program is simply a way for producers to agree on a tax to create a pool of funds to support generic advertising and promotion. Producers pay the costs and have control over the program design. The design is most often directed to the total commodity and not specific brands; that is, the programs must be designed to benefit the entire industry and not selected segments within the industry. Checkoff programs range from regional coverage to national in scope. Recent examples include national programs for dairy, beef, and pork, all funded through national checkoff legislation.

Finally, the states and the federal government have become direct participants in the generic promotion of many agricultural commodities. Most states have programs funded through general state revenues that are designed to promote the state's agriculture. These programs include both domestic and international efforts and are mostly designed to increase consumer awareness about the particular state's commodities. In contrast, federal government programs are not usually commodity specific. Through various formulas, commodity groups can tap into certain federally funded programs to supplement ongoing generic advertising and promotion programs. In almost no case does the federal government become involved in the design and implementation of advertising programs, instead, public funds can be accessed to complement existing programs or potential new programs. These programs usually have an international orientation, where the government becomes a participant in helping various commodity groups to develop foreign markets of their products. The use of federal funds carries with it guidelines and restrictions that must be carefully followed.

In the subsequent text, emphasis is placed on checkoff programs, which support only generic programs. There are not sufficient data to report on private and trade association expenditures.

Commodity Advertising Issues

To understand the issues associated with commodity advertising, one must have a clear picture of the actors in the system. That is, who is involved in funding, implementing, and receiving the nonfee-based information? Figure 1–1 identifies five major groups as significant participants in disseminating and using information through commodity advertising and promotion. One can view the influence of commodity advertising moving through the vertical marketing channels for any commodity.

Firms view commodity advertising and generic efforts differently from the remaining participants. For the firm, four main issues become paramount. Will the advertising create growth for the specific firm, and how will it change market shares? How will generic advertising influence the firm's ability to achieve product differentiation? Is brand and generic advertising at odds when considering brand differentiation objectives? Finally, each firm is usually concerned with how other firms respond to one firm's advertising and promotional initiatives and to the generic programs. Will the advertising simply force competing firms to adopt more aggressive nonprice competition policies? Will generic advertising increase or decrease a firm's ability to differentiate its particular form of the commodity?

Moving from the firm to the commodity group, the range of issues changes considerably. At this level, the impact of programs on the total industry becomes the major focal point. Thus, the more important issues deal with measuring the program impact, acquiring the appropriate funding, developing the correct program strategies, and long term planning and evaluation. The focus is on the whole and not on the individual parts of the industry.

The media and agencies represent the creative node in the system and the conduit for delivering the message. Their issues center around creative design and delivery, audience targeting, and program performance; the criteria for judging may differ from that of the commodity groups and firms. Figure 1–1 is drawn with linkages between the groups, implying some coordination of information flow among the groups. Clearly, the importance and linkage will differ depending on the commodity being studied.

Firms, the commodity groups, and the agencies are all *suppliers* of

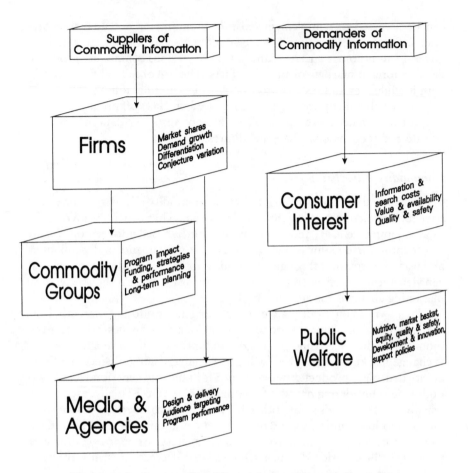

Figure 1–1. Commodity Advertising and Promotion Issues

information in the schematic in Figure 1–1. Consumers and the public as a whole are the recipients or *demanders* of information. Thus, the issues for these latter groups would be expected to differ from those for suppliers of information. Consumer issues about commodity advertising generally lie within three areas: (1) How do the advertising and promotion programs influence search cost and ability to acquire information about an array of products? (2) Does the information confuse the decision-making process, or does it provide useful information for discriminating among goods without first sampling goods? (3) Do the advertising and promotion programs contribute to quality selection and food safety? Does the information facilitate determining product value and availability? That is, does the advertising enhance price competition, or impede it? Can the advertising be judged as a reliable indicator of product quality that can be consistently relied on through time?

Finally, one must view commodity advertising and promotion programs from a broader public welfare perspective. Though a wide range of issues exist, they can be categorized into the following questions: (1) Does commodity advertising enhance nutritional education? (2) Does it facilitate food safety and quality? (3) Does it change the market basket or commodity mix of foods purchased? (4) Does advertising affect the competitive structure? (5) Does it improve marketing efficiency? (6) Does it facilitate product development and innovation? (7) Can it complement or substitute for some agricultural support policies? In the following chapters, we will touch on many of these issues. Dealing with the public issues relating to commodity advertising, however, is probably the weakest link in the state of knowledge about commodity advertising. As the reader proceeds through the various chapters, it is important to refer back to this figure in order to keep a perspective on the discussion of generic programs. Most of our discussions and evaluation efforts will be focused at the commodity group level, for it is at this level that most programming decisions are made and funded.

Evaluation and Performance

Efforts to evaluate commodity programs have received increasing emphasis; some commodity checkoff legislation even mandates an annual evaluation. Part of the purpose of this text is to set forth what is known about the economic effectiveness of commodity promotional programs. In order to evaluate the programs, criteria for judging performance must be agreed on, data on program activities must be available, and the appropriate methods for measuring performance must be adopted. Methods for evaluation are dependent on the time frame for the programs. If assessment of the potential benefits from a new program is being considered, then preprogram methods must be adopted, whereas, if the evaluation is directed to programs with a history of activities, then postprogram methods are appropriate.

The evaluation tools generally fall within three categories: monitoring and testing, case studies, and analysis of market data. Monitoring and testing include collection of data on advertising recall and awareness, media coverage, controlled panels, and opinion profiles. Some of these data points provide clues as to the potential response to actual programs. They often point to needed changes in the copy and design before being used. The major weakness of monitoring and testing analyses is that the linkage between the advertising and actual consumer behavior in the marketplace is not measured.

The second approach is the case study method, in which one learns about successes and failures through intensive case studies of specific examples. This approach's primary merit is that the total industry within which the advertising took place is viewed as a whole. One can draw on economic theory, but one still must set forth criteria for judging the successes and failures. Extrapolating the conclusions from one case to others is an area of concern when trying to use one case model to generalize to a broader group of commodities.

Finally, when historical data are available, one can turn to the deductive and empirical approaches of evaluation. Historical data may occur through actual market exchange transactions or through controlled experiments. Given the historical events (advertising, demand, supply and so forth), then logical models of the actual events can be specified from which empirical models are estimated. Given successful modeling of the advertising and promotion, statistical inferences can be made. For example, the linkage between consumption or prices and the advertising efforts can be measured, and statistical inferences can be drawn. This process is known as *econometrics*. It has been used extensively in the last several years to measure the impact of several commodity programs. In Chapter 6, we will discuss in detail many of the econometric methods adapted to evaluating commodity promotional programs.

Overview of the Book

In this introduction, we have tried to set the stage without going into great detail. The guiding objective of the text is to provide the reader with a perspective on commodity advertising that is both theoretical and practical. Hence, considerable time is allocated to describing the current programs in the United States and then turning to several empirical studies that deal with specific evaluations. The book is organized to provide the reader an understanding of the economics of commodity checkoff programs. In the description of commodity checkoff programs, we describe the basis and reasons for their existence, and we provide a comprehensive description of their activities. The theoretical basic for commodity advertising is discussed in Chapter 2. Generic advertising is discussed within the framework of advertising theory and is differentiated from brand advertising; it is also discussed within the context of the theory of consumer demand. In Chapter 3, the economic issues involved in program planning and implementation are reviewed. We discuss the economic issues associated with planning objectives and promotion activities. A model for better understanding the effects of advertising is presented, and the types of programs and their importance are noted.

In Chapter 4, we cover the basis for supporting commodity advertising and promotion efforts and the rationale for their existence. The evolution and nature of the legislative authority is outlined. Existing commodity promotion programs are detailed in Chapter 5. Programs are described within the framework of the legal structure from which they function.

Methods for evaluation are presented in Chapter 6, where we discuss the concepts of pre-and postprogram evaluation. Emphasis is placed on the economic analysis of programs. The results of several economic studies (postprogram evaluation) are presented in Chapter 7 in the form of case studies, including programs for fluid milk, beef, apples, wool, catfish, citrus, potatoes, soybeans, oils, and fresh tomatoes.

Finally, Chapter 8 provides some insight into policy issues and their economic implications, as well as some general conclusions. In the last half of the chapter, we provide a comprehensive summary of the important points covered in the text, drawing from both theory and empirical analyses. We have tried to keep the materials as up-to-date as possible, although we recognize that commodity industries and their advertising efforts constitute a dynamic process that assuredly will have changed before the completion of this text.

2

Commodity Advertising Theory

ommodity advertising and promotion is an integral component of the marketing of U.S. agriculture commodities. The types of programs are diverse, and understanding of their role and effectiveness is at best incomplete. Promotional programs range from highly structured efforts where most potential beneficiaries pay a prorated share of the cost to programs supported by only a small portion of the industry. The legal authority for the various types of commodity promotional programs can be defined within a small set of alternatives, with much of the legislation based on state and federal market orders and national research and promotion acts. How the authority is used to support various activities, however, is quite diverse among the commodity groups. Diversity is seen in coverage, program intensity, copy design, and timing.

What do we know about commodity advertising? Is there a theory that helps us understand the role of advertising within and among commodity groups? What are the more important dimensions to the economics of commodity advertising? Are there unique aspects of agriculture that somehow make commodity advertising different?

The specific purpose in this chapter is to provide a framework for dealing with commodity advertising. Specifically, we will develop a framework and perspective for understanding advertising theory as it relates to both generic and brand activities. The emphasis throughout the book and in this chapter, however, is directed to generic advertising. It is important to recognize fundamental differences between generic and brand advertising and to understand the roles for both within an industry. An analytical framework will be developed to illustrate how advertising is incorporated into the demand for a particular commodity. This section is important in that it provides the theoretical basis for empirical analyses; that is, the theory set forth in the section provides the basis for directly including advertising in the demand function. We conclude the chapter by setting forth several hypotheses relating to the potential impact that advertising may have on an industry, the consumer, and the producer.

Commodity Characteristics and Information

Advertising and promotion can convey information as well as create or change perceptions. Ultimately the impact is reflected through reformulation of consumer preferences and thus changes in behavior. Changing consumer behavior may generate increased consumption in total or simply cause a redistribution within the bundle of goods consumed. The number and form of products to select from are often a direct function of the ability to advertise. Fundamental to dealing with the effects of advertising on consumers and the impact on the total market basket is understanding the product characteristics to which the advertising is directed.

The Role of Advertising

If we are dealing with an economic system or a commodity industry where information is complete and no uncertainty exists, then there is no information role for advertising. In this setting, the only role advertising could play would be for its entertainment value, because it could not provide any new information. What do we mean by complete knowledge and no uncertainty? From a consumer's perspective, this implies that preferences are established based on complete knowledge about the commodities being considered. Furthermore, it implies that consumers know all information necessary for making current and future rational consumption decisions. Under a state of complete knowledge, consumers would have a total understanding of all nutritional and dietary needs, and they would know the necessary mix of goods and the alternatives for fulfilling these needs. In a world of complete certainty, all present and future knowledge regarding product forms would be known, even by new consumers. Thus, consumers' preference sets for particular goods would be based on being apprised of the full set of alternatives and the merits of each. For example, all possible product forms, such as different types of packaging, would be known. In this fictional setting there would be no room for advertising, since preferences would be set based on complete knowledge. Perceptions would reflect reality in this environment. Brand advertising could not lead to shifts in market shares, since consumers would already have the necessary information for evaluating brand alternatives. In short, there would be no reason to expect advertising, either generic or brand, to lead to structural changes within an industry.

Such a setting is obviously unrealistic. Uncertainties exist, and information is far from being complete. Consumer preferences are not static; rather, they are subject to some degree of randomness and systematic change. New products continue to be developed, as do forms for existing products. Consumers' nutritional needs are never fully understood, as they evolve along with our changing life-styles. The rapid pace of new technology, as one example, has had a profound influence on the dynamics of food consumption, as demonstrated by development and impact of microwave technology.

Information is never complete and is always changing. Humans, by their very nature, are dynamic in terms of their preferences. For many goods, preferences are readily altered and may not be particularly stable, whereas for others the preferences are well defined. Clothing provides an example where preferences are readily changed within limits usually defined by long-established traditions and customs. Consumers respond to new styles and are generally receptive to new fashions and other aspects that improve their perceptions of themselves. The cotton industry's effort to change consumers' perceptions of the attributes of cotton fabric is a good illustration of how preferences for specific types of clothing can be influenced. The fact that cotton in recent years has become more fashionable to wear can, at least partially, be attributed to advertising and promotional efforts by the cotton industry. Changes in new technology and product development funded in part by checkoff funds are obviously other major factors influencing this market, as are changing consumer styles.

One can find other products where consumers are resistant to change. Consumption of certain staple food items may prove difficult to change significantly, simply because of the fundamental importance of the product to good health and because of limited alternatives; fluid milk would be an example of this. The normal human life cycle is such that there are always new sets of consumers entering certain markets where new preferences must be established. For some commodities such entry and exit adds stability in the consumption pattern, with the stability tied closely to changing demographics. For example, consumption of children's cereals is reasonably stable, because as one age group exits this level, a new group enters.

One can simply look at the market for fast foods and see the importance of this industry to different age groups. Another example where preferences change would be with the age group where new families are started. Couples' responsiveness to information on infant nutrition is at its peak during their early reproductive years. Newlyweds may enter this phase with only limited knowledge and almost no preference set for particular infant food groups. Willingness to take risk by experimenting with different infant food products is probably quite low when information is lacking. The potential for influencing consumer behavior through advertising would be expected to be considerably greater among these potential consumers as long as the risks from poor quality are low.

The above discussion illustrates the diversity among and within markets, and the role of advertising in providing information and changing preferences is evident. We assert that advertising can lead to changes in consumer behavior, and that the degree of change will differ by commodity and potentially by the intensity, content, and quality of the advertising effort.

Search and Experience Goods

There are broad general classifications of commodities that provide some initial insight into the potential role of commodity advertising. Nelson's classification of products into *search* and *experience* goods is particularly useful for dealing with commodity advertising (Nelson, 1974). As stated above, knowledge is incomplete and must be collected in order to establish consumption patterns. There is a real cost to acquiring this information. For search goods, the consumer is willing to pay this cost through time and effort spent on searching out the information needed to determine whether or not to make the purchase. The sources for this information are diverse, and the content may not always be factual; however, the consumer is willing to pay the cost to evaluate such information before making the final decision.

Search Goods. Search goods are usually durable products that carry a high market value. The purchase of an automobile or a food freezer falls within this group. Advertising of search goods generally provides factual information about the product's attributes, which can most often be tested before the consumer makes her or his final decision. There are usually standards from which these attributes can be judged. Standards are set for advertised gasoline mileage on new cars, for example, and information is comparable across cars. Most search goods come with detailed product specifications and operation guidelines, and warranties are most often included. For some goods, consumers even have the option to return the product within a designated period if the product characteristics are not as advertised.

Reported standards are often regulated and subject to periodic governmental review. Advertising of gasoline octane ratings is an example where the information is used to define levels of the product and is regulated by governmental standards. Recent reviews of several gasoline outlets nationally have shown several abuses of misreporting the octane rating; such misrepresentation of standards is subject to federal prosecution. Consumers use such reported information on the assumption that it is factual. Thus, search goods in general are characterized by searching out product characteristics before making the final purchase decision. In some situations, the consumer can readily judge the validity of the acquired information, but in other cases they must rely on regulations to assure the quality of the information.

Experience Goods. Experience goods, in contrast to search goods, include those products where consumers are not willing to pay the search cost before making the purchase decision. The product is usually not too expensive, and the risk from making a poor decision is low. Consumers experiment with alternatives and, after developing a reasonable set of experiences, will then potentially develop stable purchasing habits depending on the results from their experiences. The stability of habits may be short-lived, because alternatives are frequently changing: new products are available, as are new forms for existing products. As a rule, experience goods are nonreturnable except under circumstances where major defects or quality differences exist. There are implied warranties assuring certain qualities and attributes, but there generally are no long-term warranties like those for search goods.

Advertising among these experience goods is subject to frequent change. Messages may be less factual and more impressionistic, since the messages are intended to encourage experimentation. Given that consumers are less inclined to search out all attributes, they may be more receptive to implied attributes communicated through advertising and promotion. There are many attributes that are difficult or impossible to evaluate even after experiencing the good; thus, the potential for gains through advertising such allusive and non-substantive attributes may be considerable. An example would be products advertised to prevent skin aging and wrinkles. There is very little that consumers can do to evaluate such claims, and they may not be willing to accept that the product does not work. Consumers' desire to achieve positive results may hinder their ability to judge the actual benefits of the product objectively.

Comparative Message Content. The content of advertising for experience and search goods is usually substantially different. Advertising of experience goods is directed toward achieving repeated purchases through enhanced product awareness and perception, with potentially less factual content about the product (Ward, Chang, and Thompson, 1985). Celebrity endorsement of experience goods is an example of attempting to stimulate high product recall with limited informational content. Having a high recall for search goods is redundant, however, because potential buyers will always evaluate product attributes before purchasing. Given this fundamental difference in the product characteristics, one would expect to see more direct-to-consumer advertising for the experience goods.

Most agricultural commodities fall within the experience goods category, especially when the commodity is transformed into foods, fiber products, or products consumed for their aesthetic value. Though some exceptions can be noted, much of U.S. agricultural advertising lies within this group, where the advertising is directed toward creating images about the product (along with information on nutrition and related attributes). Some of the experience-goods attributes can be immediately evaluated, whereas others must be assumed to be factual. Advertising of calorie level or the statement "free of cholesterol" cannot be directly experienced but are assumed to be true; as with some search goods, it may be necessary to provide governmental regulations over such product claims.

Cooperative versus Predatory Goods

Two additional classifications of experience goods are useful to understanding agricultural advertising. First, all goods can be classified within a continuum with regard to their cooperative or predatory nature. Products that cannot be differentiated are considered *cooperative* goods (Friedman, 1983, p. 143). Advertising for such products may increase total demand, but it cannot change market shares among product suppliers. Generic and brand advertising would have identical effects on consumer behavior among this group. There would be little incentive for one brand advertiser to promote his goods, since all other suppliers would benefit without paying their share of the advertising cost. Brand advertising for a cooperative good would only occur if the benefits accruing to the brand exceeded the costs even when others also benefited.

The other extreme includes goods that can be differentiated but for which expansion in total consumption of the product group is difficult to achieve. These products are called *predatory* goods. Advertising among such brands may cause shifts in market shares but may not increase total consumption. Generic programs may still be effective, however, if there are specific product attributes common to the predatory good. Cigarettes are probably the best example among agricultural products that fall within this group. Predatory goods are defined within the context of brand substitution for a specific product. One could also view a broader category such as foods and then evaluate whether advertising of one food group leads to switching with other categories or to growth in total food consumption. If the argument is that there is a limit to total food consumption, then one food group may be predatory on another.

One would expect an industry to support a generic program for cooperative goods. All producers should benefit equally in any gains, since the suppliers are producing a nearly homogeneous product. Support for a generic program would then depend on other characteristics that influence the success of advertising efforts.

Most agricultural commodities exhibit characteristics lying between purely cooperative or predatory goods. Such commodities can be differentiated within a range but still include many common characteristics; much of the differentiation occurs through minor product forms and packaging while the basic commodity remains nearly identical across suppliers. It is generally among these commodity groups where significant generic and brand advertising programs jointly exist. Florida citrus advertising is an example where both types of advertising programs are important to the industry (Ward and Kilmer, 1989), as is advertising for cheese (Blaylock and Blisard, 1989.)

Convenience and Nonconvenience Goods

Porter (1976) provides the second added classification by categorizing retail goods as convenience and nonconvenience goods. *Convenience* goods are those sold through such readily accessible outlets as supermarkets and large retail chains. Within this group, retailers have little power to differentiate the product. If the manufacturer is successful in achieving differentiation, the manufacturer can increase factory prices to the retailer and decrease the retailer's margin. For nonconvenience (search) goods, the retailer is needed to provide information for obtaining product differentiation using the local outlets.

Foods fall within the convenience goods category. The model implies that most brand advertising for this group is designed to achieve high repeat purchases. Porter (1976) concludes that the consumer of products sold through convenience outlets is swayed by nonobjective factors and advertising appeal, since he is less likely to spend the time and cost of gathering information. This suggests that physical product characteristics may be less important to the buyer's choice for these products; the payoff to superior payoff characteristics is limited and can be overcome through advertising claims. The same argument suggests that the content of advertising messages may be less factual for convenience goods. Where the manufacturer can shift the bias of choice away from price or relatively objective product features, it is in his interest to do so. Price and objective product features are readily imitated, and competition along these dimensions erodes excess profits. In contrast, the advertising message for nonconvenience goods is expected to be more substantive, since the consumer can verify such claims (Ward, Chang, and Thompson, 1985). Most agricultural commodities fall within the experience/convenience goods category, especially when the product is transformed into foods and fibers purchased directly by the consumer. Most commodities that are advertised under a cooperative effort (such as dairy, beef, pork, eggs, citrus, or potatoes) fall within the experience category.

Characteristics and Program Successes

There are several additional commodity characteristics that can directly influence the role of generic advertising to a commodity industry. Generic advertising usually conveys information about the commodity in forms that are closely tied to the production level. For most national generic commodity programs, product identity is maintained throughout the distribution channels from producer to consumer. If a commodity loses its identity at the point of final consumption, then generic programs would not normally be very effective in changing consumers' perceptions and subsequent behavior. When the product maintains a readily identifiable form, however, generic advertising is more likely to stimulate consumer responses.

There are several examples to illustrate the range of product changes as the commodity is transformed at various stages in the market system. Most fresh produce and fruits are readily identifiable at the point of consumption. Fluid milk keeps its identity; although processed cheeses and butter are processed forms of milk, consumers can still relate the products back to the original good. Commodities that are primarily ingredients may lose their identity at the retail level. Many of the grains and some fruits, such as tart cherries, fall within this classification in varying degrees. Generic advertising among these types of goods would not generally have the same impact on consumers as that among goods readily identifiable at the final point of consumption.

The impact of advertising on consumption is achieved through changes in the state of knowledge and perceptions, which in turn translates into consumption responses. The potential success of any program is dependent on the current state of knowledge and the consumer's understanding of the ranges of use and attributes of the good. The advertising response rate would be expected to be lower for those products that remain a staple part of the diet and when consumers already have broad experience with the commodity. Total consumption gains would be limited under such conditions. Similarly, advertising gains would be limited for those goods where consumption is near a saturation level. In some circumstances, advertising may influence the upper level, but there is usually some point of saturation within a given period. Several commodity characteristics that contribute to the success of a generic advertising program are noted below (Ward, 1985); successes and failures relate to both impact on consumers and the ability for a commodity group to fund and implement programs.

- The product must be reasonably *homogeneous*. There must be a high degree of production and marketing commonality among the producers expected to underwrite the generic programs.

- The product must not totally lose its *identity* in the market channels. Otherwise, the potential gains become diluted, with benefits being distributed to all involved in the value-added process and an increasing share going to those not contributing to the cost of the generic efforts. It becomes more difficult to communicate about product attributes when the consumer cannot directly purchase the good except as an ingredient.

- The product must have clear *standards* that can be perceived by consumers, and these qualities must be reasonably stable after purchasing. Generic programs are designed to identify significant product attributes that the consumer can expect to continue to experience. Products with considerable variation in quality may completely negate any efforts to entice consumers to increase their demand for the good. The importance of standards points to the need for a coordinated marketing effort, for which generic advertising is one dimension.

- The distribution system and product *availability* must be acceptable. High levels of out-of-stock items and poor product distribution can easily negate efforts to gain long-term repeat purchases.

- There must not be an excessive number of *substitutes*. Generic programs that must also entice consumers to switch from alternatives can expect a generally slower response to the generic efforts.

- Consumption potential must exist, and the market for the good must not be *saturated*.

- There are a variety of potential *uses* for the commodity among consumers. The range in variation expands the potential clientele to which advertising and promotional signals may be successfully directed.

- Producers must have *common objectives*. Programs are designed around meeting common objectives and assuring a reasonable degree of equity to all required to contribute to the funding of generic programs.

- Industry structure must not be *monopolized* by a few firms.

- Geographical *distribution* of production and relative size of producers can cause problems. The coordination problems are likely to increase exponentially with the geographical dispersion of production.

- Low *barriers to entry* can reduce long-range effectiveness. If programs are highly successful, the result may be an eventual increase in supplies.

- *Supply response* (including imports) to rising prices may at least partially offset promotional gains. As a general rule, imports must be subject to the same advertising and promotion taxes as the domestic product. Otherwise, inequities would assuredly arise because of the "free riders."

- An *administrative structure* must exist to support the programs.

- *Funding levels* must be adequate (and reserve funds available) to assure program continuity.

How Does Advertising Work?

As indicated above, advertising can convey knowledge and change perceptions. Messages are directed to existing and potential consumers within the purpose of enhancing sales and bringing about changes in consumption behavior. Linkages between knowledge, perceptions, and consumption are not always apparent.

How does advertising work? Sheth (1974) identifies four separate mechanisms through which advertising produces a potential change in consumer behavior: precipitation, persuasion, reinforcement, and reminder. *Precipitation* encourages consumers to experiment and to become buyers of a product category. Consumers' motivation levels are increased, and desires and understanding are enhanced. Precipitation would generally be most pronounced among new potential consumers who have limited experience with (and even misperceptions about) the product. Recent national advertising of prunes is a good example of precipitation. Per capita consumption of prunes is relatively low, and only limited understanding of the attributes of the product exists among most potential consumers. Hence, advertising the high fiber content of prunes provides factual and important information that may precipitate consumption that would otherwise not take place. Introduction of new products or new forms of existing products also falls within this classification.

Advertising can be *persuasive* either by communicating desirable attributes or, through association. Persuasion is intended to influence consumers' preferences for particular brands within a product group. Persuasive efforts may be achieved by communicating attributes, but also by appealing to the consumer's desires and perceived needs for satisfaction and recognition. Product endorsements by celebrities can be used to appeal to consumers' desire to be associated with those characteristics thought to be embodied by the celebrity. Sometimes there can be a subconscious linkage between endorsements and quality; a professional athletic endorsement of a product can imply superior quality whether or not such quality exists. Endorsements are most often used to achieve immediate high recall value and may be short-lived.

Advertising can *reinforce* consumers to become repeat purchasers. Reinforcement is particularly important for those goods facing several substitutes. It is essential for those goods that are not necessarily part of the staple food group; that is, if consumption is nonessential and there are alternative sources for acquiring similar attributes among other products, then the consumer needs to be reinforced. If the product is not normally associated with more staple foods, then reinforcement is particularly important. Reinforcement consists of constantly reassuring the consumer of the highly desirable attributes of a specific product or brand. Generally, precipitation and reminder functions are more likely to increase total industry sales, whereas persuasion and reinforcement are usually associated with maintaining or increasing market shares (but may also increase total industry sales).

Advertising also can be a *reminder* encouraging consumers to become a repeat purchaser of the product category and to be continually aware of the essential nature of the product group. Together, reminder and precipitation are associated with generic advertising, which is directed toward establishing a long-term understanding and preference for the product category.

Generic and brand advertising can bring about changes in consumption behavior through any or all of these four mechanisms. The importance of each is dependent on the products being advertised and the prevailing market structure among producers. The effects of the advertising relate to how each of these mechanisms brings about changes in the consumption behavior. Consumer behavior and preferences can be altered, and in turn, market structural adjustments may take place. Markets can become more, or less, competitive. Advertising can facilitate entry of new firms, or it can create major barriers to entry. For either effect to occur, it must be that the advertising has affected the demand for the product category or a specific brand.

Advertising and Demand for the Commodity

Demand depends on the prevailing price and the prices of substitutes, the resources needed to make the purchase, and the attributes of the product. Consumption also depends on consumers' knowledge and perceptions about the product's attributes. Consumers' purchases are intended to produce a set of characteristics. For example, characteristics satisfying nutrition, sweetness, and flavor are part of what are generated with food consumption. Embedded in each good are attributes that contribute to consumers realizing the desired sets of characteristics; once consumed, the goods are transformed into these characteristics. This transformation process is influenced by consumers' knowledge and perceptions about the product. The characteristics consist of factual attributes (including product form, quality, and services), as well as images consumers have about the product.

Consumers' perceptions may be more important than actual attributes. Consider the example of Häagen-Dazs ice cream. Consumers evaluate some attributes of this product through repeated purchases, but the product name creates a certain type of image that may have little to do with actual product attributes. This image likely has a profound effect on demand. Grey Poupon mustard is another example where the product image can be as important as the actual physical attributes of the good. The characteristics set of such food products includes nutritional attributes, flavor, color, and quality, but may also include such aesthetic characteristics as the desire to appear in style or the desire for acceptance.

Advertising can provide information about certain real attributes and can create the image associated with other consumer desires. One can think of a household production process where consumers produce a set of desired characteristics from the input of the primary good. The term *household* should be viewed as the unit where all information is assimilated and used to identity product characteristics and where consumption decisions are made; information and consumption produce characteristics, thus leading to the term *household production*, with the product being the characteristics. Through advertising and the subsequent change in knowledge and perception, this household production process is changed. Figure 2–1 illustrates this linkage of advertising and consumption.

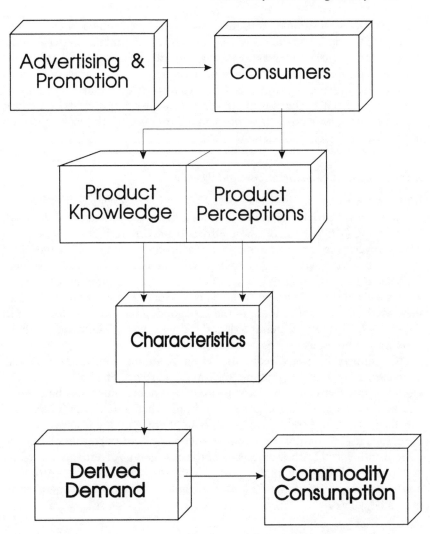

Figure 2–1. Linking Commodity Advertising and Demand

The accumulation of knowledge determines the extent to which consumers understand the product form and quality. Experience with the good enhances consumers' understanding of the associated attributes. In contrast, product images flow directly from perceptions. Advertising and promotion can play a major role in influencing the state of knowledge and perception (and hence consumption). Consumers' purchases depend on their preferences for specific sets of characteristics, and these characteristics are produced through the consumption of the base product.

Advertising changes consumers' perception of what is produced with the commodity. For example, through advertising a consumer may become aware of nutritional attributes of the base good. The linkage between these attributes and the good was already there; advertising simply made the consumer aware of the attributes. Furthermore, if the advertising changes preferences and images, then its role extends beyond that of conveying knowledge. Finally, the consumption of the attributes yields a derived demand for the base good. It is this demand that is typically measured with advertising included in demand modeling.

Advertising and Consumer Demand Theory

Initial work by Stigler and Becker (1977) and subsequent results from L. Nichols (1985) provide a framework for linking advertising and demand; Julio Chang (1988) built on these efforts to incorporate both generic and brand advertising into the demand for a product group. The concept of utility is central to linking advertising with the actual product consumed. Embedded in a commodity is a set of characteristics desired by consumers having a given state of knowledge and perceptions. The set of characteristics depends directly on the amount of the base good purchased. As illustrated in Figure 2–1, the set of characteristics includes factual knowledge about product attributes, as well as perceptions.

Consumers receive direct satisfaction from the consumption of the characteristics, with satisfaction measured in terms of consumer utility. Utility or satisfaction is generated from the consumption of the characteristics flowing from the base good and from other goods; the amount of satisfaction is directly related to the amount of both goods consumed. At this point, it is useful to think of the other goods as products consumed but not directly influenced by the advertising of the base good. Advertising enters the above model through an explicit form, as shown in equation 2–1. Although a range of specifications could be considered, one reasonably general form would be where

$$C = kX^{g(A)} \qquad (2.1)$$

with C = the characteristic set,
  X = the quantity of the base good,
  A = advertising,
  k = a scalar adjustment between X and the C,
  $g(A)$ = a function showing the effects of advertising on the household production function.

This specific function states that there is a direct mapping between the consumption of the base good (X) and the realized characteristics (C). If advertising conveys considerable information and greatly improves perceptions, then the characteristics flowing from the base good will be increased;

that is, C increases even if X remains fixed for some goods. The linkage between the consumption of the good and the resulting characteristics is established with the function $g(A)$. For each level of X consumed, there exists a level of C forthcoming as determined by $g(A)$. For the abbreviated model in equation 2–1, this response implies that $g(A)$ is a positive number normally expected to be close to a value of one. If it were equal to one, increases in the consumption of the base good would always generate a proportional increase in the accompanying characteristics. In contrast, if $g(A)$ were near zero, the perceived characteristics flowing from the base good would remain small over a wide range of levels of the good consumed. In other words, when $g(A)$ is near zero, advertising has little to no impact on the linkage between the good and the forthcoming characteristics.[1]

Illustrating the Characteristic Model. A few examples may be helpful at this point. Suppose that consumers have been purchasing orange juice and receive levels of satisfaction associated with the characteristics flowing from the product. New advertising suggests that the product now supplies an important source of calcium. For the same quality of juice, consumers now perceive that they receive a higher level of desirable characteristics because of the new knowledge about a calcium source. The beef industry's contract with Paul Harvey as a spokesperson provides another example. Consumers' association of beef with the quality and integrity of Paul Harvey should add to the perceived characteristics generated with consuming the product. In both examples, advertising has increased the value of $g(A)$ in equation 2–1, where the characteristics are linked to the base good via the levels of advertising.

The value of the advertising function $g(A)$ is symbolic of both consumers' product awareness and the effects of advertising. If the function is small or near zero, then regardless of the level of advertising, the amount of characteristics generated from consuming the base good remains small. Without advertising, there exists some linkage between the characteristics and the good; consumers already have some basic knowledge and perception about a product. If this initial state of understanding is already quite high, then one would not expect a significant response to any level of advertising. With little initial understanding of the product attributes, then the effects of advertising in bringing about additional change will depend on the product and what can and cannot be communicated about its attributes. For example, even without any advertising, the current state of consumers' understanding of the attributes of fluid milk is already quite high. If calcium is part of the characteristic set, then consumers will know something about the calcium content of milk without any advertising. With the introduction of a new product (such as new packaging of dried fruits), however, the consumer may have little perception of the product attributes. Through advertising, consumers' product awareness is improved, perhaps translating into increased consumption.

There are few cases where the characteristics consumed remain nearly fixed over all levels of the base good. Generally, consumers will increase their consumption of the characteristic set along with the base good. Consumption of one glass of milk provides a level of calcium, a desirable characteristic; two glass of milk provide a proportional increase in the level of calcium. Candies are purchased to satisfy the desire for sweetness, again part of a desired characteristic set. Increasing the consumption of candy meets the needs for sweetness; however, the degree of sweetness will not increase proportionally with more candies. This is partially true because part of the sweetness is based on perceptions and tastes and not nutrient intake.

Another example could be consumption because of an associated "snob appeal." The purchase of a $500 bottle of wine will, in addition to the actual quality, create an image generated by letting everyone know of your purchase. The purchase of two, three, or more bottles may also contribute to the image, but the amount of snob appeal likely levels off quickly with additional action. This is generally true when the created characteristic is dependent on others' perceptions of your purchase. Part of the decision to purchase a particular make of car is similarly based. One buys the car for its mechanical and aesthetic looks, yet the purchase is also dependent on your perceived appearance while driving the car, as well as how you feel when driving and talking about your new car.

One should not confuse the characteristics created with satisfaction. Satisfaction and utility come from the consumption of the characteristics. Satisfaction from the snob appeal or from the pleasure of being in a new car leads to the demand for these characteristics. The characteristics flow from the base good, and this flow is likely nonproportional to increases in the actual good consumed.

Characteristic Responses. Two interesting aspects of the car example are worth noting. Satisfaction from adding more amenities to the car probably increases at a lesser rate with each new amenity. Furthermore, satisfaction from being seen driving a particular type of car decreases over time, and thus the desire to make a new purchase surfaces. Such changes in positions will occur even though the physical attributes of the good may have remained fixed; perceptions are dynamic.

Preferences for different styles, changes in eating habits, and so forth can contribute to a reduction of the characteristics flowing from the base good over time. This deterioration of satisfaction is an important element leading to a continued change in demand and thus the opportunity to achieve gains through advertising and promotion. Also, the deterioration in satisfaction suggests the need for continued reinforcement through some types of advertising and promotion.

In the limited circumstance where $g(A) = 1$, there is a perfect linear relationship between the characteristics and the good. Increased consumption will continue to increase the level of characteristics. Consumers may get tired of the particular characteristics; if so, satisfaction will decline. The linkage between the product and the generated characteristics remains intact, even though consumers may change their desires for particular characteristics.

The most likely situation is that $g(A)$ lies between some minimum and one. Here the level of characteristics received increases, but at a decreasing rate. Products are consumed because of their attributes, which might include color, taste, odor, and aesthetic value. Increased consumption continues to provide these attributes, but the perceived attributes do not increase proportionally with the good. For example, the initial taste of a steak generates a level of desired characteristics associated with taste and hunger. Additional steaks still provide positive attributes, but the marginal gains in fulfilling the desired taste needs usually decline. Thus, the first steak produces a level of characteristics, whereas the second steak produces a somewhat lower level.

The relationship between the characteristics and the product is illustrated in Figure 2–2. When $g(A) = 1$, the linkage between the consumption and the resulting characteristics is linear: increases in the good produce a proportional increase in the characteristic set. For some products, the slope of this line may be large, implying several desirable attributes created with the good. For other goods, $g(A)$ may still equal one, but the slope is considerably less; that is, the amount of characteristics flowing from the good is much smaller. Consider two goods both providing a source of protein. The linkage between the goods and the amount of protein may be linear, as suggested by $g(A) = 1$, but the absolute amount of digestible protein from the first good is higher than for the second. The two linear vectors projecting from the origin in Figure 2–2 denoted by (1) and (2), capture these differences.

For other goods, the levels of characteristics increase but at a lessening rate, as reflected in curves (4) and (5). The use of goods satisfying the desire for sweetness probably falls within this category, as does the purchase of goods to fulfill the demand for being stylish or for aesthetic appeal. Finally, in some circumstances, the level of characteristics generated from consuming the good increases at a growing rate. This situation may occur with early or initial consumption; however, in most circumstances, one would not expect the same proportional increase in the characteristics with continued consumption of the good.

An example corresponding to curve (3) in Figure 2–2 could be the consumption of flowers, or specifically roses. A husband's purchase of one rose for his wife will produce certain characteristics cherished by the wife. These characteristics include not only the beauty and smell of the rose, but the expression of love it represents. The purchase of a dozen roses may greatly enhance the perceived beauty, fragrance, and expression; this rapid

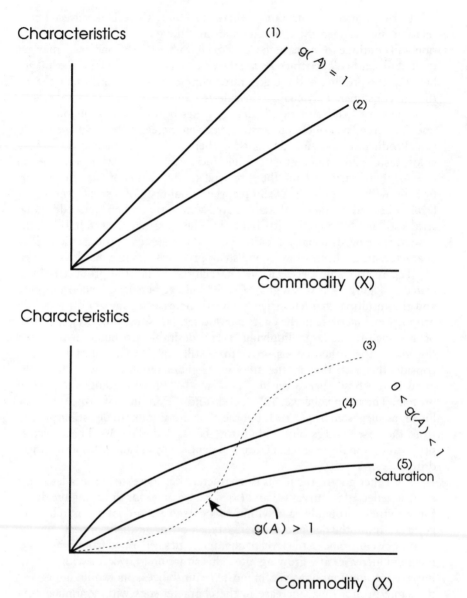

Figure 2–2. **Linkage between Product and Characteristics**

increase in the characteristics produced is reflected in the initial values of the curve. If six dozen roses were purchased, however, it is doubtful that the same incremental gains in the characteristics would be forthcoming for the last dozen roses. Most of the expression of love has likely been achieved with

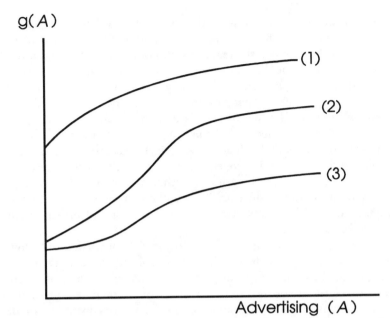

Figure 2–3. Advertising and the Household Production of Characteristics

the first dozen roses. In fact, the curve could turn down because of "over-kill." Curve (3) thus levels off rapidly to demonstrate this possibility.

Figure 2–2 shows that characteristics flow from the consumption of a base good, yet the quantity of the generated characteristics is not necessarily proportional to the product consumed. Furthermore, advertising can directly influence the process of generating characteristics from the consumed good.

Incorporating Advertising into the Model

How does advertising enter the argument? Advertising provides consumers with information and changes their perceptions. If, through advertising, consumers are convinced that particular characteristics are desirable and can be realized through consuming a specific product, the linkage between consumption and the perceived levels of the characteristics is established. Consider the earlier example of prunes. Initially, the level of perceived characteristics from consuming prunes was probably reasonably low because of consumers' incomplete knowledge about the fiber content of prunes. Consumers have a preference and understand the need for fiber in their diets, yet they may have failed to perceive the fiber source from prunes. Through generic advertising, factual information about this attribute of the product was conveyed to the consumer.

In Figure 2–3, advertising contributes to the linkage, shown by the function g(A) in equation 2.1, between the consumed good and the characteristics. The extent of the shifts in g(A) will depend on the existing state of knowledge about the product, the real attributes of the good, current levels of consumption, and the quality and intensity of the advertising. Three cases are illustrated in the figure, with advertising intensity expressed on the bottom axis and its effect on changing the characteristics on the left axis. With curve (2), the initial value of g(A) is quite low without advertising. Consumers have little knowledge of the product attributes and have almost no initial image of the good. With advertising, g(A) may rise rapidly, and a strong linkage exists between the consumed good and subsequent characteristics. Curve (1) illustrates the situation where consumers have nearly complete understanding of the product attributes without any advertising, that is, g(A) is quite large without advertising. Little gain from advertising such goods would be expected.

Finally, curve (3) represents the case of low initial knowledge and a low response to advertising, which may be attributable to the quality of the advertising or to the limited attributes of the good. Introduction of a new product that receives almost no consumer acceptance would be represented by this curve. A classic case of this situation is Ford Motors' introduction of the Edsel. Initial knowledge was low, and the perceived attributes of the car were even lower. The product ultimately failed despite considerable advertising efforts.

What is being implicitly assumed about advertising in this model? Specifically, advertising is assumed to be a vehicle for conveying information and changing perceptions. There is no direct satisfaction from the advertising; satisfaction comes from consuming the characteristics. The benefits of advertising are through changes in the actual and perceived characteristics, as expressed in Figure 2–3.

Advertising can have entertainment value, but those benefits are only peripherally related to its effects on consumers' perceptions and knowledge. If the entertainment value leads to subsequent recall about the product, then the entertainment is one vehicle for capturing the consumers' attention and improving subsequent understanding of the product attributes. The risk from advertising with high entertainment value is that consumers receive the entertainment satisfaction but do not respond through changes in their consumption behavior for the advertised product. For example, recent national advertising of raisins would score high in its entertainment value, and one can see the "raisin figures" in stores that have little to do with food or raisin consumption. Whether this success in achieving a high entertainment score translates into increased sales of raisins, however, is an empirical issue.[2]

Properties of g(A). Linking advertising to the demand for the characteristics and the consumed product occurs through the function g(A). The properties

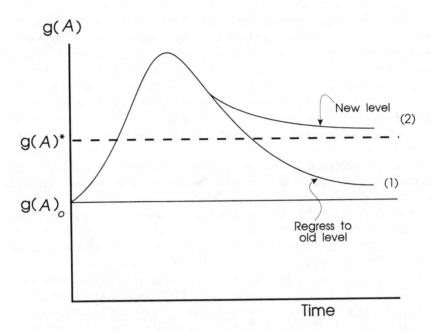

Figure 2–4. Impact of Advertising on Product Characteristics Over Time

of g(A) provide direct insight into why advertising is often diverse, repetitive, and short-lived. The relationship between the characteristics and the good is dynamic in several ways. First, improvements in production and processing technology can lead to changes in the characteristics realized with the base good. New aseptic packaging, prolonged shelf life, or enhanced quality standards are examples where consumers, through experience, can judge such improvements. For these types of adjustments, the new characteristics should be permanent, with the permanency depending on technology. In Figure 2–1, these types of changes relate to attributes noted with the conveyance of knowledge.

Second, g(A) is dynamic because of the image-creating capacity of advertising. Advertising may cause improved images of the product, but over time its value may adjust back to some base level. The decline in g(A) after some initial increase is what is referred to as the *carryover effect* of advertising. Figure 2–4 illustrates a hypothetical adjustment process in which major advertising initiatives stimulate responses via increases in consumption and satisfaction associated with the generated characteristics. Consumers continue to respond by purchasing more, but the rate of response most likely declines over time.

In Figure 2–4, the advertising initiative at time *t* stimulates an increase from g(A)$_o$ to g(A)*. After ample time and the initial advertising effort, g(A) gravitates back toward the level g(A)$_o$. If the advertising shift to g(A)* is due to images alone, then eventually $g(A)$ will revert to the preadvertising level. If the advertising conveys permanent knowledge along with the image dimension, then $g(A)$ may eventually approach a level exceeding the initial $g(A)_0$, as shown with curve (2) in Figure 2–4. An example of this case could be the gain in potato consumption achieved through dispelling consumers' image of the high calorie content of potatoes (Jones and Ward, 1989). If the initial advertising purposely misleads consumers, the $g(A)$ may eventually fall below the initial level of $g(A)_0$ because of lack of consumer confidence in the product.

Introduction of a product with claims of having new attributes will demonstrate these potential responses. Assume that a product is advertised as "new and improved," and consumers respond because of the perceived new set of attributes. If, after experiencing the good, the consumers perceive the attributes as real, then a permanent higher level of consumption is achieved (that is, $g(A)$ will not regress to the original level). If the advertising claims prove only temporary and more fanciful than real, however, then the likely scenario is that without additional advertising stimulants, consumers will revert to near the original preadvertising levels. As already suggested, misleading advertising could eventually force $g(A)$ to levels below its initial value.

Advertising Carryover and Dynamics in g(A). Carryover effects in Figure 2.4 differ by commodity and according to the quality of the initial effort. Analysis of several generic commodity programs show an advertising carryover response extending up to several months (Ward and Dixon, 1989). Fluid milk advertising, for example, has been shown to extend up to approximately twelve months. Other programs are intended to have little or no carryover effect. These types of advertising programs are often tied to temporary specials or product attributes that will not continue. The expectation is to achieve an immediate response without gaining any particular consumer loyalty to the product.

As a rule, generic advertising falls within the category of advertising directed toward achieving longer-term responses. In contrast, in-store advertising and promotion (often tied to price discounts) is intended to generate a temporary consumer interest, with little expectation of realizing prolonged consumer loyalty to the product.

The patterns for $g(A)$ in Figure 2–4 illustrate the need for continued consumer reinforcement through advertising. If $g(A)$ declines after a given advertising effort, new programs are designed and implemented to keep $g(A)$ from dropping below a given minimum level. If this decay phenomenon did not exist, there would be little reason for follow-up advertising after an initial effort. Clearly, consumers forget so much advertising and have so many options that the decline in $g(A)$ is the norm. Recent efforts by Pepsi-Cola using major celebrities to promote the consumption of its product illustrate this point. These messages have little informational content but are designed to achieve a response via the image aspects of the advertising effort. That new multimedia advertising efforts occur quite frequently provides some evidence that the carryover effect likely is low.

There are unique risks associated with using celebrity endorsements. The recent news that Michael Jackson does not drink Pepsi-Cola even though he is a major celebrity spokesperson for the company created considerable skepticism among consumers for this product. The beef industry's use of James Garner, who experienced a heart attack during the same period that he was promoting beef, provides another example of the underlying risk of using celebrities. Although there was no established linkage between the product and his health, the message sent to the public was clearly the wrong one.

Even with the expected carryover effects, there is additional uncertainty about what can be achieved with advertising. A precise form of $g(A)$ is seldom known when advertising programs are being designed. Preliminary market testing can give some clue to the potential success, but uncertainty is always prevalent. The fact that $g(A)$ entails considerable risk along with high potential payoffs further illustrates why the use of advertising is so dynamic.

Why, though, would $g(A)$ be dynamic among agricultural goods? One would generally not expect the generic advertising function for well-established foods to be as dynamic as for less essential items. The image-creating aspects of many staple food products should not be as strong as for selected "faddish" foods. As a general hypothesis, the potential gains from advertising among the staple food group is likely less than for less staple goods. The risk in the potential payoff, however, should be greater for the nonstaple products; that is, $g(A)$ is likely lower for some food groups, but is probably more stable in comparison to other advertised products.

The magnitude of response via $g(A)$ and the level of uncertainty can be traced back to the product classifications noted earlier in this chapter. An experience good with little potential for differentiation would be expected to have a lower $g(A)$ index than for a similar good that is more differentiable, yet the variability in $g(A)$ would also be expected to be greater for the more differentiable goods. Similarly, the success through $g(A)$ depends on the existing state of knowledge about the product. The level of $g(A)$ would be expected to be lower for fluid milk, as an example, than for goods where consumers have less experience with the product.

Product Demand and Advertising

The function $g(A)$ reflects this transference linking consumption and characteristics. How, then, does advertising enter the demand model? Julio Chang (1988) sets forth the analytical relationship between advertising and product demand. Using the characteristic mapping noted above, where $C =$

$kX^{g(A)}$ and the utility function U = u(C, Y), the demand for the characteristic can be derived as initially implied with Figure 2–1.[3]

Consumers maximize utility with respect to the amount of characteristics perceived to be consumed. From this maximization, an implicit value for the characteristics can be derived. This implicit value is called the *shadow price*. Since the characteristics are derived, the goods are linked through the advertising effects, as shown in Figure 2–2. The demand for the base good can also be related to the levels of advertising, that is, X = f(P_x, A). Advertising would be expected to cause shifts both in the demand and in consumers' sensitivity to price changes, as well as in other variables entering the demand model. If, through the advertising, consumers are convinced of the essential nature of the attributes of the good, then they may not be as concerned with price changes when making their consumption decisions. That is, the advertising could lead to a reduction in the price elasticity of demand, along with absolute shifts in demand. Shifts in demand imply that consumption increases for the same price, holding other nonadvertising variables fixed.

Advertising in the Demand Model

The basic argument for including advertising directly in the demand for the primary good is as follows. Characteristics are produced through consumption of the commodity. Actual characteristics are influenced by conveying knowledge about the product and changing consumers' images and perceptions. The linkage between the primary good and the set of attributes produced is referred to as a household production function, as explained earlier. This function can be influenced by advertising, depending on the circumstances discussed previously. With this process, advertising's role is through transferring information and changing perceptions and preferences. No direct satisfaction is received from the advertising; that is, utility is not generated from the advertising, presuming that any entertainment value from the advertising has been excluded.

Analytically, advertising is directly included in the demand function for the primary good used to produce the characteristics. One seldom finds models dealing directly with the characteristics, primarily because of measurement problems. The theory, however, points to the role of advertising influencing the characteristic set, which in turn affects demand for the good. Although there is nothing wrong with this procedure, it is important to understand the logic for placing advertising directly in the demand function. When advertising is included in the demand function, it is representing the composite effects of all those characteristics and satisfaction noted earlier.

Generic and Brand Advertising

Up to now, the discussion has concentrated on advertising without making any particular distinction between generic and brand efforts. The model set forth relates to total demand, not that for any specific brand. Generic advertising calls consumers' attention to the product group, emphasizing the aggregate product attributes. Such emphasis may convey knowledge and create new product images. One consistent element to the generic effort is its focus on the total product. Although brand advertising may convey much of the same information about product attributes, it is more focused on attributes and images that can be associated with a specific brand within the commodity group. There is nothing inherent in brand advertising that would prevent such advertising from expanding the total market, yet the emphasis on specific attributes unique to one segment of the product market may cause growth in that segment relative to others (for example, promotion of brand A versus the total product category.)

Brand advertising can lead to shifts in market shares (because of a redistribution of purchasing habits) without expanding the total set. Similarly, brand advertising can cause shifts in market shares while expanding the total level of consumption. Gains in sales may or may not negatively influence other segments of the market, depending on whether total demand is growing. Other firms' sales could increase, even with a decline in their share of the market. The effects of brand advertising relate back to whether the commodity is a cooperative good, a predatory good, or somewhere in between.

Generic advertising should not lead to shifts in market shares. By its design, there should be no information embedded in the message that leads consumers to believe one brand is different from another; the attributes common to all brands should benefit equally. The only time that one brand may benefit over another would be if a particular brand has some unusual market advantage. Such advantage could include having favorable shelf space, an efficient distribution system, a strong market support organization, and superior quality and attributes that immediately become apparent to the consumer when they first decide to purchase the product group. These advantages have nothing to do with the advertising. One other case could be when the industry includes both brand and private-label products, which are generally considered more generic in form and attributes. An argument can be made that generic advertising favors the private label, since it potentially negates some of the brand claims to differentiation. In this case, private labels could gain at the expense of major brands. The extent of such shifts becomes an empirical issue that would have to be measured to draw definitive conclusions.

How does generic and brand advertising enter the model discussed earlier? Both generic and brand advertising influence the set of characteristics flowing from the consumption. Thus, advertising initially expressed with A in the $g(A)$ function could be defined to include generic (G) and brand (B) efforts. The characteristics specified conditioned on $g(A)$ then would become $g(G, B)$. Julio Chang (1988) developed the demand models where both G and B are incorporated into the demand for the base good via the utility for a set of characteristics.

Three Cases of Generic and Brand Impacts. Figure 2–5 gives a simplistic representation of the effects of generic and brand advertising. For Case I, the inner circle represents aggregate consumption and the distribution of consumption among brands (shown as A, B, and C). If generic advertising is effective, then growth in demand should be forthcoming, as drawn with the outer circle. Note that the market shares remain fixed in this case. If the product were a completely cooperative good, the distribution of shares would not change with brand advertising, even though the total market would grow. In Case II, brand advertising takes place within a class of predatory goods. The total does not grow, but brand A's share of the market increases. Brands B and C both lose shares to brand A. Finally, in Case III, brand advertising contributes to total demand but also changes the market shares. Such a case would be expected from products that lie somewhere between cooperative and predatory goods: there are many common product characteristics, but some brands can still achieve differentiation.

An example of Case III is worth illustrating. Consider the case of Tropicana Pure Premium orange juice, a particular brand of orange juice that has been heavily advertised and whose share of the market has grown. Empirical evidence points to the fact that the brand's advertising has substantially contributed to growth in total demand for orange juice. (Ward, 1988a); that is, consumers drink more orange juice because of the advertising. Furthermore, the image created with the advertising, that the brand is "made from fresh oranges," provides a strong source for product differentiation. Consumers buy the differentiated brand in part because of the freshness characteristic.

Generic and Brand Effectiveness. The realized effects of both generic and brand advertising clearly depend on the attributes that can be emphasized. If there are unique and desirable characteristics identifiable with a specific brand, then such brand advertising may be successful. The success of brand advertising to attain product differentiation depends on both the actual product attributes and how easily these attributes can be measured. For many foods and fibers, attributes such as taste, quality, and packaging can be judged (Ward, Chang, and Thompson, 1985). There also exists a list of attributes that cannot be readily judged. If generic advertising emphasizes certain attributes common to all brands within a brand group, then brand differentiation will likely be more difficult to achieve.

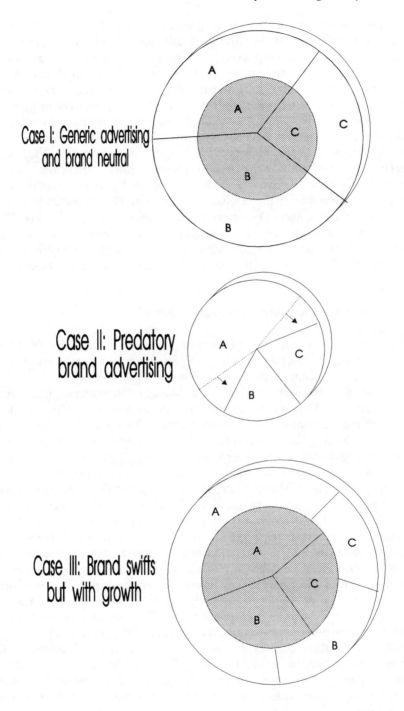

Figure 2–5. Generic and Brand Advertising Effects on Markets

One could then argue that generic promotions force brand advertisers to focus on those attributes that are more difficult to evaluate. Under these conditions, brand advertising would be expected to be directed more toward enhancing perceived differentiation rather than toward actual attributes. The brand emphasis is on characteristics that are more difficult to evaluate objectively. A recent television endorsement of a high-fiber cereal by two well-known comedians provides a good example of attempts to achieve differentiation through association with attributes difficult to measure. The message is that the product has high fiber, yet the message implies "fun and pleasure" through the association with the well known celebrities. Many cereals may have nearly equal fiber content, but they may not have the fun attributes achieved with the celebrity association. This brand advertising may convince consumers to buy more cereals to meet the need for fibers. The message may also increase the particular brand's share of the market. Generic and brand advertising are interrelated and any conclusions about the effectiveness of either effort must be conditioned on this interrelationship.

The Conditions for Commodity Advertising

Advertising has been directly incorporated into the demand for the base good. What conditions, then, would be expected to have a significant impact on whether advertising is effective in changing consumer behavior? Broad descriptive categories were noted earlier, including if the commodity is a search or experience good and if it is a cooperative or predatory good. More detailed properties can be identified that should condition how advertising influences consumer behavior. These properties can be subdivided into three basic areas: (1) product attributes, (2) consumer knowledge, and (3) product use and form. These distinctions can overlap, as will be seen in the following discussion.

Product attributes should generally be viewed as those characteristics that exist within the product regardless of consumer action or perceptions, these attributes do not necessarily require the consumer's response for them to occur (for example, the level of vitamin C). Consumer knowledge is generally self-evident. The distinction between attributes and product use, however, is not clear. One should view use and form as conditions requiring consumer action and product transformation. For example, in how many ways can the consumer utilize a particular commodity? Does it have a wide array of uses in the diet, or is it quite limited? Two commodities may have similar protein content, for example, but one may have many more uses and forms than another. Both beef and peanut butter share the attribute of protein content, but the uses and form are dependent on consumer applications. Although these distinctions are not essential, they can be helpful when explaining the various roles of advertising and why the level of effectiveness could differ.

Product Attributes

The most important dimension in determining the effects of advertising relates to the product's inherent attributes, which will differ depending on the class of agricultural goods (food, fibers, aesthetics, or inputs). For the food group, product attributes relate to what aspects of nutritional needs are fulfilled with the particular product. Fibers include cotton, wool, lumber and other fiber products, along with animal hides and skins used in apparels; materials such as lumber are used in the production of consumer goods that often fall within the search category. Aesthetics include those goods consumed for the pleasure received from viewing, smelling, and feeling the product, but generally not from eating. Flowers and ornamental goods provide beauty, fragrance, and environment complements that are consumed via our perceptions versus direct taste and satisfaction of hunger and through the indirect benefits to other goods consumed. Finally, some agricultural goods are used as inputs into the production and manufacturing of other goods. It is within this last group that much of the initial product identity is lost.

In recent periods, nutritional attributes probably have provided the greatest opportunity for conveying new information to consumers. Consumers, at least in the more developed markets, are much more nutritionally conscious and concerned with calories and cholesterol levels. Increasing emphasis has been placed on maintaining a balanced diet. Such nutritional concerns have led to a whole spectrum of new product development as well as changes in exiting products. Many commodity groups have tried to change old perceptions about existing products. Florida's orange juice commercials ("it's not just for breakfast anymore") provide an example where the primary emphasis was to change old preferences about orange juice only being consumed at breakfast time. In the case of the beef industry, consumers are concerned about high cholesterol in the product and have shifted to white meats. The industry has developed new product forms (such as "lean beef") and has spent millions of dollars promoting these changes. Much of the advertising effort for beef has been driven by the need to counter perceived negative attributes and to deal with increasing consumer awareness of substitutes for the product.

Most food attributes are quantifiable, and many attributes must be reported directly on the package. In contrast, aesthetic attributes are more subjective and probably are prone to greater randomness in consumer preferences. Such randomness can decrease the potential gains expected from generic advertising efforts. One can look at the national advertising of flowers to see the difference. National promotions of flowers, while noting the specific product attributes, concentrate on what can be expressed with the flowers. The range of expressions is almost unlimited, but the potential gain from broad generic efforts may be more difficult to achieve because of the array of choices the consumer has to satisfy these expressions. In contrast, the ways to express the attributes of milk are considerably more limited, but the alternatives consumers have to substitute for milk are equally limited. Consumers' desire to satisfy aesthetic needs must usually be filled with several alternatives. These needs can be changed through advertising. Given the diversity among the flower attributes, however, it is less likely that national coordinated promotional programs would be successful among this class of goods versus others.

The essential nature of a good to consumers can have a profound effect on the success of proposed advertising activities. If promotion activities are intended to achieve a switch to alternatives for the essential good, then little success can be expected. For example, fluid milk is generally considered an essential part of our daily diet. Thus, it is doubtful that one could design a promotion program to persuade consumers to substitute, for example, grapefruit juice for milk.

There are few goods that are considered essential, for those that are, one would not expect competing products to have much impact on the demand. If the good is essential, then it is likely that consumption is already at a reasonably high level. There may be little room for additional consumption growth beyond that associated with increased population. Fortunately for most agricultural industries, there are few commodities that exclusively satisfy a particular need. Salt was at one time such a good, but now there are even salt substitutes. Product attributes are a matter of degree; there is almost always some degree of promotional activity that can be expected to be successful. In principal, however, it is important to recognize that this essential nature of a product can have a significant impact on the payoff from promotional activities.

Consumer Knowledge

It is equally important to assess what the consumer already knows about the good. If the product is new or represents a significant change in an existing good, then one might expect both generic and brand advertising to be potentially successful relative to products that have existed for some time. If the state of knowledge is already quite high, there is likely less that can be gained with additional intensive promotional activities. Much new product development is a direct result of recognizing that consumers are approaching a near-saturation level and have considerable knowledge about the product. Hence, new product forms, alternative packaging, and expanded uses all provide new avenues for reaching consumers. Some goods lend themselves to change, while others do not. Thus, the potential longer-term gains from advertising and promotion are likely to be in direct proportion to the ability to communicate new ideas about the product to the consumer.

Advertising programs can play a major role in dealing with misperceptions about a product. Many product attributes, such as cholesterol level, have taken on increasing importance to the consumer. Sometimes misperceptions about the product must be overcome or alternative forms of the product must be developed to counter real negative attributes. Thus, new product development and advertising and promotion must be coordinated to assure that consumers do have knowledge about product attributes and new product developments.

Consumption habits have a major impact on the potential success from both generic and brand advertising efforts. Purchasing habits can be tied to cultural, ethnic, and socioeconomic differences among consumers. Product availability and the knowledge base influence consumption habits. Habit persistence exists among all consumers; such persistence can be both beneficial and detrimental to maintaining and/or expanding the demand for a specific commodity. A high level of habit persistence assures repeat purchases of a product. The level of advertising needed therefore may be substantially less when consumption is primarily derived from habit persistence. If there is perfect habit persistence, then no level of advertising would be successful in creating change.

Unusual events can have a profound effect on well-designed advertising programs that may have been ongoing for some time. News about alar (a pesticide used in apples) or the EEC import ban on growth hormone in beef are recent examples where advertising programs and subsequent demands can be negated almost overnight. Given the mass media network and the politicalization of world trade in many agricultural goods, almost every commodity is subject to demand "scares," regardless of the ongoing efforts to convey factual information to consumers. National generic programs may provide the immediate vehicle for dealing with such potentially damaging events when and if they occur. The programs can be readily used to correct misinformation or to communicate when needed adjustments within the industry have taken place.

Product value reflects the implicit characteristics of a good. Advertising and promotion can increase the value by both communicating the characteristics, as noted earlier, and by changing consumers' perceptions. Relative values across commodities, however, are usually quite apparent with or without the advertising effort. As a rule, as the per-unit price increases, consumers are more willing to invest in search time before making the final purchase decision; this is often referred to as "comparative shopping." Thus, one would in general expect less response to generic advertising for high-value goods versus those of lower value.

Product Uses and Forms

As different generic programs are visualized, the expected impact must depend on the primary uses of the commodity. For some commodities, the uses provide an array of alternatives for advertising and promotion through generic and brand efforts. For others, though, the end form greatly limits the use of direct product advertising, because much of the initial product identity is lost in the transformation.

The success of commodity advertising is clearly dependent on the product uses and forms. As stated earlier in this chapter, if the product maintains its product identity throughout the distribution system, then generic advertising is likely to be more successful. Also, the audience to which generic advertising is targeted depends on the product form at the point of final consumption. It makes little sense to advertise grains to the consumer when the product is not recognizable at the point of consumption. Possibly some of the advertising should be directed to those points where the transformations are taking place, such as manufacturers. This clearly is a research question and depends on the commodities being analyzed.

One would usually expect a greater payoff from commodities that have a number of uses and a reasonable range of product forms. This is generally true because of the wider range of consumers that can be reached with a diversity of messages; however, the base product must still be readily identifiable. Other characteristics having an impact on the role of commodity advertising include the storable nature of the product after purchasing, and maintenance and convenience requirements. Convenience is particularly important. Consumers have increased their demand for ready-to-serve orange juice because of its convenience, among other things. Some of the gains in the ready-to-serve market, though, have been at a cost to the frozen juice market. Analyses of the effect of generic and brand advertising on both product forms clearly show a differential return to advertising. Similarly, the number of substitutes has a direct negative impact on the extent of gains expected from commodity advertising.

Maintenance of product quality must be central to any long-term commodity program. A consumer's experience with poor quality can have a lasting impact that far outweighs any effort to communicate positive attributes. Commodities that are prone to have misuse at the consumer end are likely to show poor advertising performance. Fresh tomato storage is a classic example. Consumers place their tomatoes directly in the refrigerator before they are ripe; this stops the ripening process. When consumed, the tomatoes may be perceived as having poor quality. This, in turn, can discourage repeat purchases, irrespective of advertising efforts.

Another interesting quality example can be found with the grapefruit industry. The Florida citrus industry advertised fresh grapefruit and the Florida seal of quality. An early-season variety of grapefruit used to be marketed in October, well before the season started. The product was generally bitter and undesirable to the consumer, yet it was the only product available at that point in the season. Bad experiences with this preseason grapefruit had a potentially damaging impact on the forthcoming season.

Advertising could hardly be expected to offset these experiences. Without some type of restrictive controls on this early-season variety, it is doubtful that any generic promotion efforts would have been successful.

Advertising and Market Structures

Up to this point, we have said little about the market structure dimensions to advertising. Industrial organization literature is rich with studies about the role of advertising in bringing about changes in the degree of competitiveness within the marketplace. The literature deals almost exclusively with firm advertising and its influence on market shares; it says little about generic activities. The traditional argument is that advertising is a form of persuasion that creates product differentiation and allows firms to exercise market power at the consumer's expense. Alternatively, advertising can be viewed as an inexpensive means for conveying information to a number of consumers, thus stimulating competition and diminishing market power (Ekelund and Saurman, 1988). The focus on industrial organization research has been on the industry, with emphasis on refining the analysis of the form and behavior of the group of competitors within an industry. Dealing with the array of industrial organization issues is beyond the scope and focus of this book. We will end this chapter, however, by briefly detailing some of the structural dimensions as developed by Ward, Chang, and Thompson (1985).

If advertising brings consumers closer to understanding the true commodity characteristics, then this advertising is informative. Any resulting market power is not from the advertising, but from real differences within the commodity group. If the advertising creates perceived attributes that are not necessarily real, then the advertising can contribute to market power. Gains from perceived differences may continue even with repeated purchases if the perceived attributes are difficult to measure.

Market power is gained through barriers to entry. Barriers exist when established firms have an economic advantage over potential entrants (Bain, 1972). Most analytical research addressing entry barriers shows that although advertising encourages repeat purchases, it is used more to obtain markets than to hold them (Conner and Ward, 1983). Given the dynamics of the marketplace and the continued influx of new consumers, existing firms, like potential entrants, must communicate with these new buyers. New products tend to be advertised more than old ones. Advertising is used to create disloyalty more than loyalty, and some evidence suggests that there is less consumer loyalty in the heavily advertised markets.

Generic advertising can have some impact on market structure. Generic efforts should reduce barriers to entry, since they are designed to expand aggregate demand and do not emphasize brand differences. As long as potential entrants can supply the commodity qualities emphasized through generic messages, entry should be facilitated. Consumers should generally gain from more competition among suppliers and potentially benefit from relatively inexpensive information sources. Producers gain by expanding the demand for their commodities.

Ward, Chang, and Thompson (1985) state that generic advertising and brand advertising are interrelated. They set forth hypotheses and generalities about the relative roles of generic and brand efforts:

- Generic advertising encourages consumption and repeat purchases of the product category.

- Generic advertising provides information about product groups and would generally be expected to be less persuasive (and less deceptive) relative to brand advertising.

- Generic advertising probably has more factual information than brand advertising, but it is still more oriented to high recall than the kinds of messages one would expect from promoting search goods.

- Generic advertising should have a negative impact on product differentiation, thus reducing barriers to entry and excessive profits (and margins) among first handlers beyond the farm gate.

- Generic advertising is likely to force brand advertisers to concentrate on product attributes (where real or fancied) that are more difficult for the consumer to verify.

- Generic advertising may provide producers and smaller firms with a mechanism for benefiting from any economies to scale from advertising if such economies exist.

Summary

In this chapter, we have set forth a theoretical and practical framework for understanding the role of commodity advertising. A general framework for classifying commodities was given, along with an analytical linkage between advertising, utility, and demand. The potential role of commodity advertising was then shown to be directly linked with product characteristics. Product attributes, consumers' knowledge base, and the range of produce uses were emphasized. The chapter concluded with a brief overview of the relative roles of generic and brand advertising in bringing about structural changes.

In the next three chapters, we turn to the application of theory and to actual ongoing generic programs in the United States. Emphasis is given to program type and details of the working structure for various advertising and promotion programs.

3

Planning Objectives and Commodity Promotion Program Activities

T he theory of commodity advertising was discussed in the previous chapter. But what about reality? How does the practice of advertising relate to theory? For example, what level of expenditure will maximize sales or producer returns? How does one maximize returns within budget constraints? How important are awareness, beliefs, attitudes, and consumer intentions? And even more important, are there relationships between the advertising effort and consumer behavior, as set forth in Chapter 2? An understanding of the economics of these relationships will be useful in considering alternative planning objectives and alternative program activities.

The focus in this chapter is on economic and practical issues. Our desire is to connect theory to reality and to provide an explanation of the economic issues involved. It is neither our intent nor our desire to provide a set of guidelines for a particular promotion organization to follow; each promotion organization's planning objectives and program activities will be unique.

For discussion purposes, we specify that the process of strategic planning on commodity promotion involves the delineation of organizational objectives and program objectives, the identification of commodity attributes, recognition of budget constraints, the development of an implementation strategy, and the creation of an evaluation procedure (Figure 3–1). The process is normally considered sequential, going from the establishment of objectives to evaluation. It is also often considered periodic; after an appropriate lapse of time, the process is repeated. Ideally, strategic planning is continuous and iterative. Information at any one phase is used to make adjustments in any other phase. In this chapter, we will limit our discussion to economic issues associated with the selection of alternative objectives and alternative advertising and promotion activities common to checkoff programs. The economic issues discussed here provide the conceptual framework for the economic analysis presented in chapters that follow.

Program Planning Objectives

In a survey of the managers and directors of U.S. agricultural commodity organizations, 62 percent of the respondents listed "increase commodity sales" as their first or second objective.[4] Fifty-six percent ranked "maximize producer returns" as their first or second objective, and "change consumer attitudes or beliefs" was ranked first or second by about one-third of the respondents.

Linkage between advertising expenditures and producer returns is depicted in Figure 3–2. Producers or processors contribute to the promotion fund through an assessment on gross returns. Funds are allocated to various advertising and promotion activities designed to alter consumers' behavior by providing them with useful information. If the information directed to consumers creates a positive response, the result will be an increase in total revenue at the retail level. Increases in total revenue will result from some combination of price and volume increases as a direct result of positive shifts in demand.

Improvement at retail will result in increases in demand at the wholesale and at the processor and producer levels. The magnitude of the increase in producers' derived demand will depend on the size of the demand increase at retail and the extent to which it gets passed through the system. The extent of the pass-through will depend on two factors: the nature of competition at the intervening levels of trade, and the extent to which the producers respond by increasing supplies. If there is little competition at the intervening levels, only increased retail and wholesale margins will result; producers will receive only a portion of the benefits.[5] If the competition is keen, the producers' benefits will depend on the speed and cost at which the intervening levels adjust production capacity. In addition, it is possible that some of the increased demand at retail will be for marketing services.

To set the stage for planning, we ask the question, how does an advertising-induced increase in demand affect industry revenues? This is an application of consumer demand theory. In the very short term, the total supply of a commodity such as beef or milk is fixed. Assume, looking at Figure 3–3, that advertising results in an increase in demand from D to D_a. Total revenue is increased by the shaded area, which is the increase in price multiplied by the total quantity available. With supply fixed, an advertising-induced increase in demand can result only in an increase in price, although some net movements out of storage might occur. The appropriate objective in the short run is to increase price and thus total revenue.

In the long run, the appropriate objective is to increase both sales volume

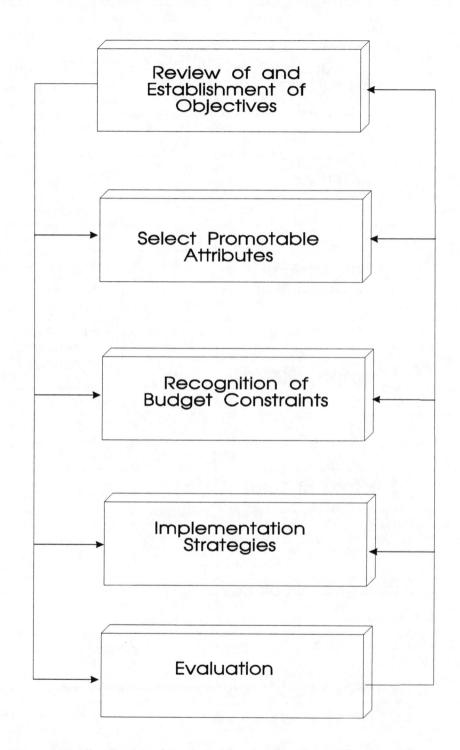

Figure 3–1. The Process of Strategic Planning for Commodity Promotion
Organizations

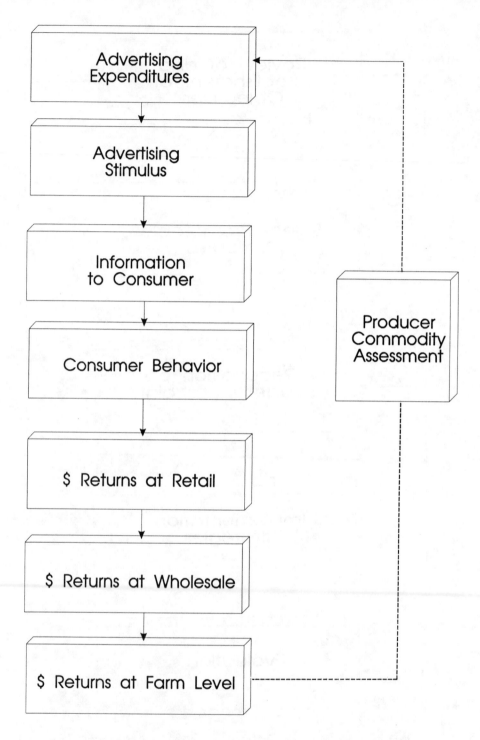

Figure 3–2. Linkage between Advertising and Return to Commodity
Producer Groups

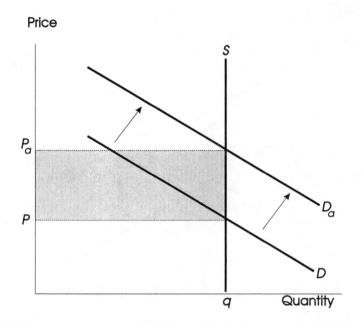

Figure 3–3. Impact of Advertising on total Revenue, Short-Run Case

and price above what they would have been without the advertising effort. In the context of dynamic adjustments, the product supply will expand in response to higher prices, and a new equilibrium price and volume will be realized (Figure 3–4). The supply response is represented by the curve S. Without a supply response, the price would rise to P'_a; but with a price increase, one would expect a supply increase. The increase in supplies will result in a lower price than existed before the increase in supply. Unless the industry overresponds, though, the new price will be higher than the price before advertising took place. The size of the increase in total revenue (depicted by the shaded area in Figure 3–4) will depend on the magnitude of the advertising-induced increase in demand and on the relative shapes of the supply and demand response functions.[6]

The Objective of Maximizing Return on Advertising Investment

From the producer's perspective, as indicated above, a prime objective of commodity advertising could be the maximization of return on the dollars invested in advertising and promotion by the group providing the funds. This objective has two possible dimensions: how much should be invested in commodity advertising, and how does one get the most out of the money available? That is, how far to the right will different levels of expenditures

Price

Figure 3–4. Impact of Advertising on Total Revenue, Long-Run Case

shift the demand curve? A hypothetical advertising response function is depicted in Figure 3–5. In this example, no response occurs until advertising expenditures reach a_1. From a_1 to a_2, the rate of return increases at an increasing rate. Since over this range the marginal returns (MR) are greater than the average variable returns (AVR), total revenue can be increased further by increasing expenditures beyond a_2. Beyond a_2, returns are still increasing, but at a decreasing rate, to a_3. Beyond a_3, the advertising has a negative effect on sales. This last position is seldom if ever observed in normally operated commodity programs. In economic terms, returns are maximized when the revenue from the increased sales is equal to the cost of the last unit of advertising. This economic optimum level of advertising expenditure will occur somewhere within the area of decreasing marginal rates of return (a_2 to a_3). If marginal cost of advertising (MC) is as depicted, the optimum economic level of advertising expenditures is at the point where MC and MR cross.

If the maximization of producer returns on investment from advertising is the objective, then one needs to know the shape of the advertising response function, as well as the marginal cost of advertising. The shape and level of the advertising function depend, of course, on the quality and effectiveness of the advertising effort. But given a particular type and quality advertising program, the shape of the curve is fixed for some time period, and the economic optimum can be determined. As can be seen in Figure 3–5, the size

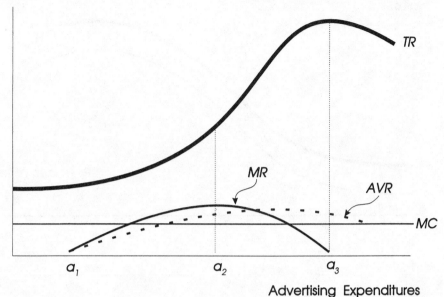

Figure 3–5. Conceptual Advertising Response Curve

of the impact and the rate of return to producers are dependent on the level of advertising investment. Also note that the shape and level of the response function can be influenced by the type and quality of the advertising and promotion effort.

How does this relate to the theory? The advertising response function in Figure 3–5 is the reflection of the new equilibrium price/quantity relationships as consumers respond to advertising messages. It is the trace of the intersection of the demand and supply curves as the demand curve shifts to the right in response to increasing levels of advertising expenditures. The advertising expenditure purchases an advertising effort that influences consumer behavior and, in turn, patterns of purchases at the retail level.

Advertising response functions at the farm level are likely to be different than those at the retail level. In Figure 3–6, the top curve represents the advertising-induced increases in retail sales. The lower curve represents the value at the producer level if all of the increased value from advertising is retained by the marketing firms. Alternatively, the producer level curve could be an exact image of the retail level curve (line PL' in Figure 3–6), indicating that all of the increase is passed through to the producer level.[7] A response function someplace between these two extremes is most likely.

An important qualification is in order. The discussion above involves aggregate demand and total returns to the pool of funds available. Net

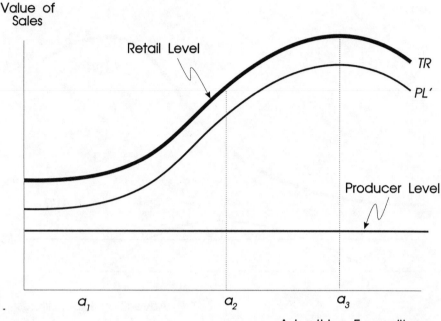

Figure 3–6. Relations between the Retail and Farm Level Advertising Response Curves when Processors and Distributors Retain the Benefits

benefits to individual contributors will be equitably distributed only if the assessment (contribution) and price increases are uniform across all units of production of the contributing producers. These conditions are likely to hold only if the commodity is competitive across all markets or points where transactions take place and if the attributes of the commodity are uniform across producers.

Maximizing Returns on Investment with a Fixed Budget

If the promotion budget is fixed, which it usually is in the short term, then the appropriate objective is to maximize the returns to that fixed budget. Knowledge of the advertising response function will be necessary here as well, but now we need to know the shape and nature of the response function for each of the various possible advertising and promotion activities. Conceptually, the objective of maximizing the returns from a fixed budget can be achieved by equating the marginal returns across all of the possible advertising and promotion activities. The rate of return at the margin from TV advertising should be the same as that from radio which should be same as

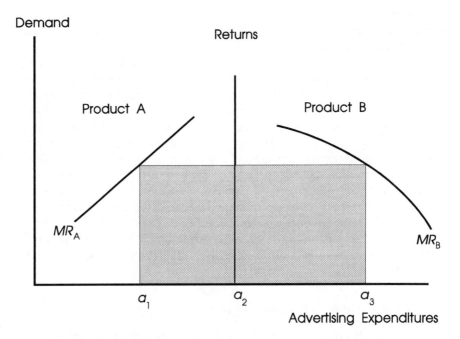

Figure 3–7. Maximizing Returns from Advertising Investment with a Fixed Budget, 2-Product Case

that from print, etc.. A similar rule holds for multiple products from the same commodity. For dairy, the marginal return from advertising fluid milk should be that same as that for cheese and butter. Similar rules would hold for allocation of advertising expenditures across markets.

A two-product example is given in Figure 3–7. Assume a total available budget is represented by the range from a_1 to a_3. The allocation that will maximize returns is a_1–a_2 for product A and a_2–a_3 for product B. Returns are maximized when the marginal returns (MR) are equal across the two program options. The same logic applies to multiple products, multiple promotion activities, and multiple markets. Conceptually, such multiple dimension solutions are straightforward, but empirically, they are very complex.

Obtaining the maximum return possible from a fixed budget is an objective that is generally well understood. Program management, advertising agencies, and other contractors work together to create commercials and promotion activities that are the best possible. Managers need to try to allocate funds across all possible known programs so that the marginal returns are equal across all possible activities. The challenge is to obtain enough information about market response relationships so as to make informed allocation decisions. In the case of a fixed budget, the producers have already made their decision to invest a certain amount of money; the producer benefits will be maximized (given the fixed budget) if funds are allocated appropriately.

It is important here to make two points. First, an objective to minimize costs is not appropriate. Revenue maximization is appropriate. If costs are quite different in two or more advertising activities, then the net marginal returns should be equal to achieve maximum returns. Second, the available funds have to be large enough to be in the area of positive but diminishing returns (a_2 to a_3 in Figure 3–5) in order to achieve a maximum return objective. But how does management know in advance, a priori, the nature of the advertising response function? The answer is that a degree of uncertainty exists, depending on staff experience and research investments. At first, decisions must be based on experience and the creative minds and talents of the staff. But once a program has begun, ex post economic analysis of the kind discussed in this book can provide useful insight into program effectiveness, This insight can also provide guidance for program adjustments toward economic optimum.

The Objective of Increasing Retail Sales

As indicated above, increasing retail sales of the commodity in question is a common objective. Just observing changes in aggregate sales volume, however, is not a satisfactory measure of the effectiveness of an advertising program. Many other economic and social factors also influence sales volume. Consumers respond to changes in the relative price of the products, to changes in the level of their disposal income, and to the amount of advertising for competing products. In addition, the ethnic makeup, age distribution, and life-style of the consuming population have an influence on consumer behavior. All of these economic and social factors must be considered in measuring the net effect of the advertising effort. Methods used to estimate the net relationship will be discussed in greater detail in later sections.

Assume that retail sales are increased as a result of the advertising. Will this benefit the commodity group? The relationships between the retail sales increases and the producer returns have their linkages through the relationships between consumer demand and the demand for the commodity at the producer level. This is a derived demand; the extent to which benefits at the retail sales level are translated into benefits at the producer level is a function of processing and distribution technology and the nature of competition. In economic terms, it depends on the relative price elasticities of demand and supply at the two different levels of trade (Figure 3–8). If a supply response is possible, indicated by S_f at the farm level and S_r at the retail level, the advertising-induced shift at retail (D_r') will result in an increase in retail price to R_r' and an increase at the farm to P_f'. Since we assume that the market will

Figure 3–8. Relationship between Retail Level and Farm Level Advertising-Induced Demand Increases

clear, the sales volume increase will be from Q to Q_1, and it will be the same for retail and farm level. In the situation depicted in Figure 3–8, the increase in total revenue at the farm level is the advertising-induced increase in price (P_f' to P_f) times the advertising-induced increase in sales volume (Q_1 to Q) less the cost of producing the added volume. The increase in total revenue or the benefits to producers is depicted as the shaded area in Figure 3–8. The supply response function S_f reflects the cost of producing the additional volume.

Increasing Processors' and Distributors' Demand

In the marketing channel between the producers of a food commodity and the consumers of the food products made from the commodity, several important groups can be identified: food processors, wholesale distributors, food service establishments, and the technical research and new product development units. Each of these groups has an important influence on the way a commodity is handled and marketed. In turn, the kind of job each does in creative and efficient marketing has an important bearing on the demand for the commodity at the producer level. New products or line extensions of existing products can result in an increase in demand at retail and strengthened aggregate demand at the producer level. Such induced increases in demand have the same impact as advertising on shifting the demand curve as depicted in Figure 3–8. Producers of soybeans, for example, have invested in the promotion of new soybean oil extraction technology. This increases extraction efficiency, decreases marketing costs and margins, and increases the demand for soybeans.[8] Improved efficiency has made soybean oil more competitive in domestic and foreign markets and has expanded the world demand for soybean oil and its products.

The cotton industry has invested in the promotion of new fiber technology that has improved the performance of cotton fibers in the manufacture of textiles.[9] This means that cotton has become more competitive against other fibers; as a result, cotton is used in a greater variety of products. The improvement in quality of cotton textiles has also improved the fiber's image and utility at the consumer level. By promoting the use of new processing technology, the cotton producers have helped create added value and reduced marketing costs. Demand for cotton products at the consumer level has increased. A stronger demand for cotton fabrics, coupled with decreased costs, benefits cotton producers through a stronger demand for their raw commodity.

The dairy producers' promotion organizations have employees who contact food service establishments to encourage and help create new ways to use dairy products. They also conduct training and educational programs for the managers of the dairy sections of grocery stores to help increase sales volume through more effective merchandising. This helps the retailer earn greater profits. With a greater profit incentive, retailers increase their merchandising efforts, and this increased effort expands demand. The stronger demand provides benefits for the producers of the commodity.

The promotion of new technology and of new product uses by processors and distributors is a legitimate objective for a commodity promotion group to pursue. The effort can be targeted to certain technologies and certain segments of the industry. Success can be measured directly in terms of the number of new uses, the extent of adoption of new technologies, and cost reductions associated with adoption.

The point of this section is that promotion-organized improvements in processing technology and new product development can be used to increase demand for the commodity. Techniques to improve efficiency can supplement, and possibly even replace, consumer advertising as a way to increase demand. For some commodities, this approach is likely to be more beneficial. Funds should be allocated to this type of activity until the marginal return equals the marginal return from all other activities. At the same time, it is important to recognize that with sufficient change in quality or other commodity attributes, we may no longer be talking about the demand for the same product.

Advertising and Promotion Activities

The advertising effort of a commodity promotion organization is partially controlled by the board and management through an allocation of funds for advertising. These funds are used to buy advertising and promotion stimuli. Most commodity groups have a small staff to plan and implement programs; they usually contract with ad agencies to create and recommend advertising copy, the method of delivery, and the target audience. The various staff work together to develop strategies. The advertising stimulus can be designed merely to make the consumer aware of the commodity attributes, or it can be designed to persuade and thus alter beliefs or attitude. Intentions can be influenced by advertisements designed to precipitate action, or the message can be written merely to remind and thus influence behavior indirectly. But advertising is not the only factor to consider. Culture, consumer demographics, economics, and price also influence awareness, beliefs, attitudes, intentions, and behavior. Although this is not the only view of how advertising influences behavior, it will provide a basis for the discussion that follows.

Activities to Influence Consumer Behavior

Influence on consumer behavior can be direct or indirect. A person not already consuming can be influenced to at least experiment with the good; persons already consuming can be influenced to increase frequency of purchase, increase the volume of each purchase, purchase additional new product forms, use new recipes, or handle and store the product differently. In reality, a large number of ways can be used to alter consumer behavior. Most of these involve information to consumers upon which they can act. If they react positively to the information provided, then it is safe to conclude that the advertisements have some positive value to them.

Some examples are as follows. Consumers have normally stored tomatoes in refrigerators to prolong life and to prevent rotting. Tomatoes will continue to ripen and taste better, however, if stored at room temperature. The Florida tomato producers advertised to inform consumers of the proper way to store tomatoes. Once consumers adopted the proper method of storage, they became more statisfied consumers, who thus are likely to make purchases more frequently or in larger quantities. In this example, behavior was influenced by altering beliefs and perceptions.

Cheese advertising has been used to encourage more frequent purchases by those who are already consumers. The promotion organization has utilized commercials to provide examples of a large number of possible uses of cheese; in addition, they developed commercials to remind consumers of availability. In this example, advertisements were used to inform so as to make consumers aware and to persuade them by altering beliefs about uses.

Pork advertisements have focused on the theme, "Pork, the other White Meat." Pork has been considered a red meat for many years. The theme is designed to disassociate pork from red meats and associate it with chicken, which is a good strategy as long as white meat is considered a healthful food. This strategy is also designed to alter beliefs.

Activities to Influence Consumer Attitude

Consumers have predisposed attitudes toward most commodities or consumable products. An objective of a promotion campaign thus might be to change existing consumer attitudes. Consumers may have preconceived notions about a product because of tradition. For example, consumers once viewed orange juice as only a breakfast drink. The Florida Citrus Commission mounted a campaign stating that "orange juice isn't just for breakfast anymore." Now more consumers view orange juice as a beverage and not just as part of the breakfast menu.

Attitude changes can be measured through consumer surveys. A change in attitude, though, does not necessarily mean a change in behavior, nor a change in sales volume. We often assume that consumer attitude is linked to behavior, but it does not necessarily follow. Consumers might develop a negative attitude toward a product because they believe it is bad for their health but still continue to consume it. For example, butter contains saturated fats and cholesterol, thus users have a negative attitude toward butter with respect to health. They like the taste of it, however, and the taste factor more than offsets the negative attitude. This offset, in turn, mitigates the change in behavior.

The taste dimension of butter could be the focus of advertising to exploit the positive attitude. Alternatively, the promotion organization could sponsor research to develop ways to remove the cholesterol from dairy products, or perhaps to show the negative connection between cholesterol and health is wrong. In some situations, it might be appropriate to support research to confirm or deny negative health connections and concentrate on the appropriate levels or portions to consume. It might be possible in this way to increase consumption of a product above what it would otherwise be.

Activities to Influence Consumer Beliefs

Consumers generally know a lot about the food products they consume. Some product characteristics are observable, such as consistency, color, or taste. Other characteristics or attributes (such as the nutrient content) are not observable. In either case, consumers have some belief about the nutrient content and other attributes of the products. In some instances, the knowledge is incorrect or incomplete; the purpose of advertising and promotion then is to inform consumers of the correct factual information. It may be necessary to identify the attributes that are important in the consumer's knowledge base and to promote those in order to make sure they know that the commodity carries these attributes.

As discussed in the previous chapter, when consumers purchase a product, they purchase a unique set of product attributes or product characteristics. Food commodities or food items are made up of a complex set of attributes that includes flavor, color, texture, and nutrient content, just to name a few. Consumer beliefs about a particular commodity might be influenced more by advertising one particular attribute over another. For example, calcium is known as a necessary mineral for good health. Focusing on calcium content of dairy products has been used as a way to encourage increased consumption of these products.

Influencing Consumer Awareness

In an environment where every consumer faces many alternatives, it is possible for consumers to forget or ignore the fact that certain commodities or products exist. Advertising may be designed to increase awareness, and through increased awareness to remind consumers to purchase the commodity. To make a consumer aware is to inform. Advertising can be used to inform consumers of the existence of new products or new uses.

Most studies that we have seen indicate a positive relationship between the level of advertising expenditure and consumer awareness of the advertisement. But awareness does not necessarily mean that the consumer's beliefs have been altered, nor that they will develop a more positive attitude concerning the commodity. It might be that those who consume the commodity are more likely to remember seeing a commercial promoting it than those who do not normally consume it.

Market research indicates that consumers prefer certain colors of apples. The Washington apple growers have invested heavily in publicizing the color of their product with the view that consumers prefer that color; therefore, consumers are aware that Washington apples are a deep shiny red. The assumption is that if they are aware that Washington apples have a bright red color, they will purchase larger volumes or be willing to pay a higher price. The selection of an appropriate promotable attribute is a complex process and involves a substantial amount of market research, including consumer surveys and focus group interviews. Promotable attributes can include product color, taste, aroma, texture, appearance, nutrient content, storability, package color, and availability.

Selection of Attributes to Promote

Perhaps one of the most difficult aspects of planning is the selection of the attribute or product characteristic to promote. The choice should be based on solid market research, a thorough knowledge of the product attributes, and a clear understanding of what the industry can deliver to consumers.

Market research should provide information about the consumers' or buyers' perception of the commodity and product attributes. Do knowledge and perception match with facts? If consumer perceptions are inconsistent with the facts as viewed by the commodity group, are the commodity groups' statements of the facts creditable or supportable? Unless the information delivered by the commodity group is supported by some third-party authority, the information might be in question. Also, some attributes can be confirmed through experience, whereas others cannot. The selection of an attribute to promote is usually accomplished concurrently with the selection of a target audience. At times, some attributes are more fashionable to promote, such as "light," "fat free," and "all natural."

Selection of Target Audience

Different consuming groups have different perceptions of a commodity and might react differently to a particular promotion message. Thus, a campaign will usually be directed to a particular target audience. Very few media systems deliver exclusively to a selected target audience, but it is conventional wisdom that a message will have a greater impact if focused on an audience. If focused, the message can be more clearly stated as to the product's benefits. The selection of the target audience, as for the selection of attributes, should be based on sound market research seasoned with intuition and sound judgment. Trade-offs of reaching a selected audience and the costs of doing so must always be weighed.

Certain attributes are best conveyed, and target audiences reached, by different media. A discussion of the different promotion activities and their appropriateness for reaching different audiences and conveying information is presented below. The most appropriate or effective media mix, however, is usually determined by experimentation and past programs. The optimal mix is probably unique for each commodity group and each time period under consideration.

Influencing Those Who Influence Others

Food purchase decisions by individuals are often influenced by the action of other individuals. For example, medical doctors prescribe diets to ensure good health and correct certain diseases or body malfunctions. Dieticians in institutions develop menus based on their understanding of proper balances in nutrition and appeal. Some professionals are well informed in the nutrition science; others are not or have incorrect information. By advertising to these professionals, the commodity promotion organizations can influence those who influence others.

Most of the commodity organizations that promote food have comprehensive programs of this kind. They advertise heavily in diet, health, and medical journals, and in magazines. They also develop and distribute educational material on good nutrition to school systems. The education material is professionally prepared, and every attempt is made to assure its factual content. Most surveys indicate heavy use of the material and consideration of the material as professional and unbiased. The premise is that if the health professionals and teachers are well informed concerning the proper role of various food products in the diet, their clients' behavior will be influenced toward consuming more of their products. In addition, nutritional education programs for the schools are built on the premise that good nutrition habits and beliefs established in childhood will result in similar consumption habits as adults. Many commodity groups' nutrition education programs, however, do not actually promote the commodity. Critics argue that as a result they do little to increase sales. Although the program might improve consumer knowledge of nutrition, if it does not increase demand it provides little benefit to those providing the funds. Others argue, though, that this is a justified public service and builds goodwill for the industry.

Influencing Export Sales

Many commodity organizations are involved in export promotion activities, and public funds are often used to assist them. The objective of commodity export promotion is generally viewed as one of increasing sales volume. If some portion of the volume can be exported, even if at a lower or subsidized price, the domestic price is strengthened, with a resultant increase in total revenue to the commodity group.

The success of an export promotion program probably depends on success in product differentiation. Many agricultural commodities are relatively homogeneous, at least in natural form, and thus differentiation may be very difficult to accomplish. Often, however, countries do produce commodities with identifiable attributes. For example, California raisins and California walnuts have quite different quality characteristics than do raisins or walnuts produced in such countries as Italy, Spain, and Morocco. In addition, a well-organized industry can add value to the commodity by further processing and packaging, and by imposing high quality standards. The objective is to add value that may be unique and of interest to consumers in the target country. Collective export promotion activities can be used to convey some forms of information to potential foreign customers more effectively than if each exporting firm independently promotes their own products.

Earlier discussions about the selection of objectives and the implications apply to generic export promotion as well as to domestic commodity promotion programs. There are unique differences in implementation and evaluation, however, that will be considered later.

The Use of Media

Media advertising is used to expose a large number of people to a message at a relatively low cost (per person reached) in a relative short period of time, but costs vary dramatically by media, coverage, and scheduling time. For example, the cost of a thirty-second commercial on network TV during 1991 ranged between $13.00 and $15.00 per thousand (CPM) twenty-four to forty-nine-year-old adults reached. A thirty-second TV spot commercial in the New York City area averaged $16.40, whereas in Boston the CPM was $28.00, and in Watertown, New York, $43.00. Radio costs for a sixty-second spot commercial averaged $3.53 CPM in New York, $8.10 in Boston, and $6.53 in Watertown.[10] Because of changes in relative demand for network versus local TV and radio spot time, this cost relationship will not stay constant; therefore, media plans must be continually reviewed. As relative costs change, media strategies will need to be adjusted accordingly.

The decision process to determine which media to use, when and how often to show a commercial, and the commercial content is a combination of economics, scheduling, and creative art. Professionals in the advertising and promotion business are best qualified to make some of these judgments. But the advertising agency and the commodity promotion organization employing an agency need to have in place objective methods of determining whether their advertisements achieve the desired results.

Media advertising includes broadcast media (television and radio) and print media (magazines, newspapers, and billboards). In addition, other new and innovative ways of reaching consumers are now available, and more will be developed. Most commodity groups use a mix of several media and nonmedia promotion means as a part of their strategy. Media time is purchased according to the target audience (for example, woman eighteen to thirty-four years of age), the number of viewers to be reached within that target audience (for example, 90 percent), and the frequency at which they would be exposed to the commercial (for example, three times each four-week period). Media objectives are usually specified in terms of gross rating points (GRP), reach, frequency, and continuity.[11]

Reach refers to the number of different persons or households exposed to a particular commercial at least once during a specified time (usually a four-week period). *Frequency* refers to the number of times within that specified period that a portion of the population might be exposed to the commercial. The *GRP* is a number that represents both reach and frequency (that is, GRP = reach × frequency). Thus, GRPs represent the total weight of advertising derived from a media buy. If the reach is 80 percent and the frequency is 2, the GRP is 160. *Continuity* represents the way the advertising is scheduled over a period of time. Thus, the advertisement might be scheduled uniformly each week over some specified time, or 50 percent might be delivered the first month of campaign, with the balance spread evenly over the next five months. Media purchases will be made with all of the media objectives specified. Ex post audits are made to determine that the actual plan was delivered. If the plan is not delivered, credit is given for subsequent times. Actual delivery might deviate from planned delivery because the number of actual viewers fell below (or above) the expected number during the specified time.[12]

A 1990 survey indicated that agricultural commodity promotion organizations invested 43 percent of their budget in media (TV, radio, and magazine) advertising (Lenz, Forker, and Hurst, 1991). Small budget organizations (budgets under $500,000) invested only 15 percent in media advertising; large budget organizations (over $25 million budget) invested 51 percent.[13] A more detailed breakdown of how different-sized promotion organizations invest their funds is presented in Table 3–1. The selection of the appropriate media mix is quite often made on the basis of available funds, relative cost, and the cost efficiency involved in reaching the target audience. A detailed breakdown of the amount of dollars invested by commodity classifications is presented in Table 3–2. The role of major media alternatives in generic advertising is discussed below.

Television. The dairy, beef, citrus, pork, cotton, raisin, almond, avocado, prune, and grape commodity groups rely heavily on television advertisements to deliver information about their products' characteristics directly to consumers.[14] All of these commodities have some common characteristics. They have relatively large budgets and an affective way to collect promotion funds from growers of the commodity, usually under the auspices of state or federal legislation or market orders. The commodity also is easily indentifiable by consumers. That is, the products that consumers buy in the food store or restaurant have been changed little from their original raw form, or if processing has occurred (as for cheese, cotton, and concentrated orange juice), the products can still be clearly identified and associated with the raw commodity sources.

Each commodity has one or more unique characteristics that can be described in a fifteen- or a thirty-second commercial. For example, dairy products are rich in protein and calcium, beef products are rich in protein, and cotton is a unique natural fiber. Thus, dairy products use themes such as "Nature's Health Kick" and "Every Body Needs Milk." Cotton promotes the idea that cotton clothes breath naturally. Beef claims to be the "Real Food." Pork, because of its past image as a fatty product, is trying to change its image by identifying itself with the low-fat image of chicken through the theme of "Pork, the Other White Meat." California raisins used animation

Table 3–1
Percentage of Commodity Promotion Funds Allocated to Various Budget Items

Budget Item	Organization Budget (million $) (Average Percentage Allocated to Each Item)						
	< 0.5	0.5–1	1–5	5–10	10–25	> 25	All
TV	4	11	11	33	27	39	32
Radio	5	3	5	2	6	2	3
Print	6	2	5	11	6	10	8
Billboards	0	0	1	2	1	0	1
Trade advertising	3	6	5	5	2	4	4
Point-of purchase	6	9	4	10	10	6	7
Coupons	0	0	1	0	0	0	0
Sweepstakes	0	4	2	4	2	0	1
Nutrition education	7	16	16	5	5	4	6
Nutrition research	4	1	1	1	0	3	2
New product development	2	4	2	2	2	8	5
Public relations	19	20	9	10	15	4	8
Evaluation	1	1	2	2	2	3	2
Contributions to other organizations	6	3	13	0	2	1	2
Administration	24	15	12	8	5	5	6
Other	12	5	11	5	14	12	12

Note: Totals may not add to 100% due to rounding. One organization with a total budget of $11 million did not report any budgetary allocations and is not included in this table.
Source: Lenz, Forker, and Hurst (1991).

technology in their TV commercials to change the image from dried, wrinkled, and unexciting to one of happiness and excitement. California table grapes try to emphasize the unique characteristic of being a product that is convenient as a snack food, natural, and nutritious.

Finally, most consumers already are relatively well informed about the products and their potential uses. Television is used as a way to remind a large number of consumers continually that the products exist and remind them of the products' unique characteristics. This is especially true of milk, cheese, beef, citrus, and grapes, and to some extent is true of all the commodities listed above.

Table 3–2
Total Commodity Promotion Expenditures Budgeted for Various Items

Budget Item	Grains & Oilseeds	Dairy	Fruits & Nuts	Livestock & Poultry	Vege-tables	Fibers	Other	Total
TV	7.1	89.8	71.1	48.8	1.7	17.5	0.0	236.0
Radio	0.1	9.0	8.5	7.2	0.0	0.0	0.0	24.8
Print	3.8	15.2	10.4	23.6	7.0	1.7	0.1	61.9
Billboards	0.0	3.0	1.4	0.5	0.0	0.0	0.0	4.9
Trade advertising	2.8	3.2	7.9	9.2	2.7	2.3	0.2	28.3
Point-of-purchase	3.7	8.2	18.0	20.3	1.3	0.3	0.3	52.2
Coupons	0.0	0.2	1.3	0.0	0.1	0.0	0.0	1.7
Sweepstakes	0.0	3.3	4.4	0.1	0.7	0.1	0.3	8.9
Nutrition education	2.3	21.3	5.1	12.5	0.7	0.0	0.1	41.9
Nutrition research	0.4	5.5	2.1	6.5	0.2	0.0	0.0	14.7
New product development	4.5	8.0	1.8	8.1	0.9	14.8	0.0	37.9
Public relations	2.8	9.4	32.7	11.9	2.1	0.8	1.2	61.0
Program evaluation	1.9	4.5	4.3	6.2	0.3	0.3	0.0	17.6
Contributions to other organizations	3.8	6.3	3.0	0.5	0.0	2.2	0.1	15.9
Administration	3.4	7.9	17.1	8.9	3.8	5.8	0.7	47.6
Other	11.5	13.9	28.8	18.5	2.3	10.5	0.1	85.7
Total	48.0	208.9	217.9	182.9	23.9	56.4	3.1	741.0

Commodity Category (million $)

Note: Totals may not add to 100% due to rounding. One organization with a total budget of $11 million did not report any budgetary allocations and is not included in this table.
Source: Lenz, Forker, and Hurst (1991).

Radio. Radio is primarily to capture a different audience or a specific target group that cannot normally be reached by television. Radio scheduling is usually in combination with television and print advertisements. The audiences that are reached best by radio include commuters, teenagers, and vacationers; also, radio is listened to more during the summer months than during winter. Organizations with relatively small budgets are likely to use radio rather than television, and some research indicates that this is a very rational decision. See especially the discussion on the evaluation of the Washington Apple Commission's advertising program Chapter 7.

Print. Print is used when the message is more technical or too complex to squeeze into a fifteen- or thirty-second broadcast commercial. The dairy group has used magazine print heavily to inform females of the value of calcium in dairy products. They have also used print to reach health professionals to remind them of the health value of dairy products. Print is the primary media used to inform processors and distributors of new product ideas or new process ideas, as well as to remind them of the unique positive characteristics of the commodity.

Other. Many other ways are also available to send messages to consumers. Advertisements can be shown on video screens with rented video movies, placed in grocery stores, and as part of an on-line computer information system. Billboards (or other forms of outdoor advertising) are also frequently used. Information can be conveyed through free samples at the retail store or by mail. Inserts, perhaps the fastest-growing tool of advertising, can be placed in newspapers or magazines. Many new and innovative means will probably be developed in the future.

The Use of Brand Advertising Rebates

Some commodity promotion programs provide rebates to private firms for the brand advertising that also promotes the use of the commodity. Rebates are rational when brand advertising contains information that enhances aggregate demand for the commodity. Thus, it is argued that the use of pooled funds of the industry benefits the whole industry in addition to increasing the sales of the brand being advertised. The other justification for this arrangement is that the assessment is against the volume sold by this handler; if it increases the sales of the company's brand, it also benefits the producers supplying that company. This argument fails if the effect is to shift market shares without increasing the aggregate sales of the commodity. The Florida Citrus Commission for several years reimbursed part of the costs of brand advertising that included the use of the Florida citrus logo. The almond promotion program in California authorizes credit to brand advertisers for the costs of advertising that meets criteria specified by the Almond Advisory Board. The maximum credit to an almond handler is equal to the amount of the promotion assessment on the volume of almonds handled by the firm. If the assessment amount is not utilized by the firm, the funds go to the Almond Advisory Board to be used for generic promotion.

The raisin group in California also has an arrangement where promotion assessments can be used to support brand advertising. A processor or handler can obtain reimbursement for 50 percent of advertising costs associated with the promotion of raisins. The limit here is the amount of the assessment paid by the handler. (In the raisin program, the handler is assessed an amount equal to the amount assessed against growers.) This arrangement provides a multiplier effect in that it requires matching funds. Whether or not a rebate program is appropriate depends on the characteristics of the commodity and the extent to which the brand advertising affects the product category demand.

The Use of Other Promotion Activities

In-store or point-of-sale promotion is used in one form or another by most commodity groups that have a promotion program. This involves the preparation of brochures, shelf markers, mobiles, aisle displays, or any other method to attract the shopper and encourage them to make an immediate purchase. In-store promotions are often used to introduce new products and new usage ideas to remind the shopper to purchase now. In-store promotion can also involve demonstrations, samples, audio announcements over the stores' loudspeaker systems, or presentations over video systems. It is expected that in-store promotions will provide an immediate response by some portion of those exposed to the activity. It is considered relatively expensive in terms of cost per number of consumers reached, but it does provide information to potential consumers at the time and place where they can take action on the information received.

Some promotion organizations conduct training programs for personnel of grocery stores and other food establishments to encourage them to use merchandising techniques that will place their commodity in a favorable position in the store. For example, the American Dairy Association (ADA) conducts seminars for personnel that manage the dairy case. The seminar draws on research conducted by the ADA that demonstrates the best merchandising techniques to use to maximize turnover and profit from the space devoted to products in the dairy case. The California Table Grape Commission has personnel that visit grocery stores to advise the produce manager and personnel to display California table grapes properly. The Washington Apple Commission has a field staff that works with grocery store produce managers and restaurant chefs.

The Use of Coupons

Coupons, used by only a few commodity promotion groups, are in effect a form of price reduction. But coupons also have an advertising effect.[15] Coupons are used to obtain a quick response or increase in sales volume. Coupons are used primarily by retail stores and brand advertisers to increase market share. A commodity group uses coupons as a way to increase primary demand, to introduce a new product line, or to obtain a quick increase in aggregate sales volume. Coupons can be targeted to a particular audience. Most coupons are distributed through newspapers, but they can also be delivered by direct mail or through displays in grocery stores. Generic coupons could also be delivered on packages of a product if done in cooperation with one or more distributors.

The Florida Citrus Commission issued over 1.7 billion coupons from 1965 to 1978; about 6.3 percent were actually redeemed. This level of redemption is considered good. The commission concluded that consumers showed a significant increase in consumption when they redeemed the coupons, but they also concluded that the effectiveness of the coupons depended in part on the retail price of the product (Ward and Davis, 1978a). This case is discussed more fully in Chapter 7.

The Use of Educational Programs

Many of the commodity promotion organizations devote substantial resources to educational programs directed to specific target audiences. This is especially true for those commodities that have nutritional characteristics or components that are essential in the diet. The dairy industry first established its nutritional education program in the early 1900s with the establishment of the National Dairy Council. The program was supported by voluntary contributions from dairy farmers and processors. All agricultural commodity promotion organizations invested $41.9 million in nutrition education in 1990, representing 6 percent of all expenditures for that year. One-half of that amount ($21.3 million) was accounted for by the dairy industry; the meat commodity groups accounted for $12.5 million.

The National Dairy Council prepares educational material for mass distribution to media, to health professionals, and to the local dairy councils for use in their local seminars. Some of the material is designed for use in schools as part of a nutrition curriculum. The local dairy councils work with local school districts to get them introduced. And over the years, the staff of the dairy councils has developed a great deal of acceptance and the material has been used extensively, having been deemed professionally and objectively prepared. Thus, the dairy industry's strategy was to develop professional status and to influence behavior in youths to be more positive toward dairy products.

Nutritional education programs are designed for long-term results. They attempt to change a basic attitude about the product so that the products made from the commodity will become an integral and continuing part of the diet. In their work in the school systems and with health and diet professionals, they attempt to get the professional to recommend the commodity to the patient or client. In some instances, the desire is to discourage negative advice; for example, the dairy industry attempts to counter the negative impact of the cholesterol content of butterfat in dairy products. The beef commodity groups attempt to counter the negative image of animal fat.

Educational programs are generally labor-intensive and involve a great deal of personal contacts. They are usually considered expensive in terms of the number of people reached. This approach, however, is generally believed to have longer-term positive impact if successful in changing basic attitudes and beliefs about the commodity.

The Use of Public Relations

Commodity promotion organizations have long been active in organizing special events to attract attention and gain favorable publicity. This has been especially true for low-budget programs; the desire is to obtain free publicity through the news coverage obtained. Dairy farmers recognize talented young women by staging dairy princess contests. Many other commodity groups stage similar events: thus we have county, state, and national dairy princesses, peach queens, orange blossom queens, and others. All such programs are designed to gain free media coverage and, by having the winners speak for the industry at special occasions, to put forth a favorable impression.

In some ways, food is a natural for free publicity. Food products can be used in an endless variety of recipes, and so commodity promotion organizations often employ individuals to prepare special recipes and articles about the ways the product can be used for release to the press and to magazine editors. Food products are also the source of nutrient requirements. Thus, commodity groups can prepare timely news releases that remind consumers of the health benefits and nutrient values of specific products. To be effective in obtaining free publicity, the writing staff must be talented, considered professionally competent, and able to maintain good access to the appropriate media outlets. This is perhaps the most cost-effective means of promotion for commodity groups with relatively small budgets.

The Use of Research

The research conducted by or for commodity promotion organizations is of three types. First is product or process research. The intention here is to identify an ingredient or characteristic of the product that can be used as a hard-sell item in promotion activities. For example, the dairy industry supports research on the unique value of the calcium in dairy products for strong bones and good health. With positive research results and the great concern that has arisen about osteoporosis, calcium has been used extensively by the diary organizations in their promotion efforts. Additionally, the intention of product research is to identify new uses or processes that can be adopted by processors or distributors to expand their market or to reduce costs. The Lenz, Forker, and Hurst (1991) survey discussed earlier indicates that a relatively small percentage, about 2 percent in 1990, was invested in nutrition research. About 5 percent was invested in new product research.

Market research is conducted to determine barriers to or opportunities for expanding demand. Focus groups surveys or telephone interviews are used to identify negative attitudes or incorrect beliefs that might be changed or positive attitudes that might be exploited. Such research should yield results that can be used by the commodity organization and the ad agency or public relations firm in the development of a promotion strategy. The results could also be useful in the development of creative material or promotion themes and the media plan. Market research is also conducted to pretest and posttest commercials to determine the effectiveness of the advertisements in achieving desired objectives.

Economic research is conducted to determine the effectiveness of the promotion effort in achieving the economic objectives of the commodity group. Results of economic research can be used to assist in allocation decisions, in the determination of appropriate assessment rates, and in decisions about whether or not to continue the program or parts of the program. The latter two are important components of the evaluation process in planning.

Recognition of the Marketing Functions of Individual Firms

One of the biggest differences between generic advertising and brand advertising is the separation of the functions of advertising from other marketing functions. Generic advertising and promotion activities are planned and implemented by one organization, jointly funded by producers. Other marketing functions, including new product development, quality control, and brand advertising, are arranged mostly by individual private firms that do processing and distribution for the commodity. It is possible and advisable to coordinate the activities of the two groups; however, the final responsibility for generic advertising rests with the commodity promotion organization. In this operating environment, the commodity promotion can focus only on those product attributes that the individual firms deliver. The challenge, then, of the commodity promotion organization is to identify the existing product or commodity attributes that are generic to the set of products produced from the commodity being promoted. The generic promotion campaign is limited to these attributes. In the commodity promotion arena, joint decisions about product quality and generic advertising are desirable, but not always possible. Several commodity promotion groups (such as beef and pork), however, do conduct surveys and studies of consumer preferences and have aggressive programs to inform the industry, producers, and processors about how the product's current attributes differ from those desired by consumers. These studies suggest ways to change the attributes to be more consistent with consumer desires.

The Importance of Economic Evaluation

Evaluation should be—and is, in most promotion organizations—an important element of planning and implementation. But evaluation can take many forms. In 1990, U.S. commodity promotion organizations invested about 2 percent of their budget on evaluation. The largest organizations, with budgets over $25 million, invested about 3 percent (Lenz, Forker and Hurst, 1991). Both market research and economic analysis are included in most evaluation budgets. Consumer surveys are used to determine the extent to which perceptions, attitudes, and beliefs are changing. Changes in the sales volume are monitored through either consumer surveys, tracking studies, or secondary sources of published data. Economic analyses are conducted to determine the economic importance of the advertising and promotion efforts to the group providing the funds. The latter are necessary to determine the impact of the advertising and promotion efforts apart from the influence of other factors.

Many factors influence consumer behavior with respect to an advertised commodity beyond the influence of the advertising message: the price of the product, the purchasing power of consumers, quality changes, the amount of advertising by competing product categories, and the availability of and price of all other products that one might purchase. In addition, the number of consumers changes over time, as does their ethnic and age distribution, and these also influence aggregate sales volume, price and total revenue. Because of the many factors that influence sales, it is not possible to determine the economic impact of the advertising effort unless one can also account for the influence of these other factors. Merely observing the changes in aggregate sales from one period to the next will not provide an accurate measure of the economic impact of the advertising effort. Aggregate sales volume might actually decrease because of price increases or because of decreases in the available supplies, whereas the advertising effort actually may have caused prices and sales to be higher than they would have been without the advertising effort. Or, an observed sales volume increase might be the result of a substantial increase in available supplies and lower prices, whereas the advertising effort had no impact at all.

If one wishes to measure the effect of advertising on sales, then one needs an analytical tool that will identify the factors that affect sales and then estimate their relative importance. Methods for evaluation are outlined in Chapter 6. Economic models, if statistically valid, can then be used to simulate alternative advertising expenditure policy and thus estimate the economic impact. In the simulation, both the price and volume influences can be measured.

Additional steps are required to determine the economic benefits to the commodity groups that provide funds for the collective advertising effort. As discussed earlier, a positive impact at the retail or consumer level of trade might or might not result in an economic benefit to the provider of the advertising funds. Such an analysis needs to consider the factors that influence the demand and supply conditions at the various levels of exchange. The analysis also should account for the degree of competitiveness that exists; the degree of competitiveness will determine the extent to which the benefits at the consumer level get passed on to the suppliers of the commodity.

Econometric models are frequently used to estimate the economic costs and benefits of a commodity advertising effort. Such models simultaneously account for the most important factors that affect demand. A review of the economic analyses that have been completed on commodity advertising indicates that it is possible to develop econometric models and use them to estimate economic benefits. The case studies presented in Chapter 7 will describe the nature of econometric modeling and provide examples of their application to evaluating commodity advertising and promotion programs.

Summary

In this chapter, we have discussed the economics of alternative planning objectives and alternative advertising and promotion activities. In economic terms, the primary objective for commodity promotion organizations, according to the boards and management, is an increase in sales revenue above what it would have been without the generic advertising and promotion effort. Some would expand on this and state that the objective is to maximize producer returns from the funds available for commodity research and promotion programs.

The determination of the extent to which objectives are met requires information about the relationship between the level of expenditure and the impact on sales revenue. To measure this relationship, it is necessary also to account for the effect of changes in other factors, including the commodity's own price, the price of other potential substitute products, consumer income level, and any other factor that is determined through analysis to influence sales of the advertised commodity. Ideally, one estimates an advertising response function accounting for every possible form of promotion and research activity. Even though this is not practically possible, it is possible to develop estimates of such relationships for some components. Also ideally, the attributes to promote and the implementation strategy would be selected with the knowledge of the expected impact on sales of all of the alternative strategies available. Only in this way can one be certain that the objective of maximum returns is being realized. Methods of evaluation with a focus on econometric modeling will be discussed immediately after we discuss the manner in which commodity promotion programs are funded, the legal basis for the programs, and an inventory of the kinds of commodity advertising and promotion programs in existence.

The advertising and promotion activities conducted by the various checkoff programs are extensive and diverse. In this chapter, we described most of those used and discussed some economic issues associated with each. We discussed activities to influence consumer behavior, consumer attitude, consumer beliefs, and consumer awareness, as well as to influence those who influence others. We discussed the process and the activities used; the activities used include television, radio, print, promotions, education programs, public relations, and research.

Because generic advertising and promotion activities under the control of the commodity promotion organization represent only a small subset of the marketing activities, it is necessary to recognize that the commodity checkoff programs have the ability to have only a partial impact on sales. Most of the other marketing functions, such as pricing, sales volume, quality, product form, and brand advertising and promotion, are under the control of private firms. Coordination of the collective activities of the commodity promotion organizations is desirable but difficult.

4

Support For Agricultural Commodity Advertising and Promotion Programs

Having reviewed the theory of generic advertising and its application to program planning and promotion implementation, we will now turn to how generic promotion programs come into being and how they are funded. In the United States, almost all of the funds for domestic agricultural commodity advertising and promotion programs are collected under the authority of federal or state legislation. The enabling legislation specifies that a regulatory research and promotion order be written, reviewed in public hearings, and voted on and approved by a majority of producers, by volume or number.[16] Some state or federal agency is assigned oversight responsibility. That agency is responsible for holding the hearings, writing the final version of the order and the rules and regulations, and conducting a referendum as required. The federal or state agencies are usually (but not always) reimbursed for all direct costs associated with oversight responsibilities by the commodity group.

A board of directors is usually established as prescribed by the specific promotion order with the authority and the responsibility to develop and implement an advertising and promotion program. Board membership is normally representative of the group being assessed. The boards hire their own staff and contract with existing commodity organizations for some services.

Once a national order for a particular commodity is approved by referendum, every domestic producer of that commodity must pay the assessment. The assessment is levied on a per-unit basis against the volume marketed or as a percentage of revenue. Under the provisions of most promotion orders, the first handler of the commodity is required to collect and remit the assessment to a specified promotion organization. The first handler is authorized to deduct the amount from payment to the producer, so that in effect the producer pays directly for the generic promotion program. Because this assessment is similar to a tax, it represents an increase in the cost of doing business for all producers. For the individual producer, it is a business expense.

Some promotion orders authorize refunds. Under those orders, producers who do not wish to support the promotion program can ask for a refund of their assessment in accordance with procedures specified in the legislation or order. This is another way to ensure that the program has the support of the producers involved. State-authorized programs generally do not allow refunds. Until 1983, federal policy was that a refund provision had to be included in all promotion orders; in 1983, Congress passed legislation that authorized a generic promotion program for dairy that did not authorize refunds. The legislation also prescribed that the program become effective without an initial referendum. A referendum, however, was required at the end of twenty-two months from the passage of the act. The vote was affirmative from 87 percent of the dairy farmers who voted, and 90 percent of the dairy farmers voted. Here, as for all other commodity checkoff programs, block voting by cooperatives is authorized. Farmer marketing cooperatives can represent all members by voting on their behalf. In effect, the board of directors of the cooperative make the vote decision. In all instances a member can ask for a ballot and submit a separate vote. With the dairy legislation as precedence, promotion programs with delayed referendums were legislated for beef, pork, soybeans, limes, and pecans.

Although domestic promotion programs are funded almost entirely by the producers of a commodity, export promotion and market development programs are often supported, at least in part, by public funds. The federal government currently operates programs that use public funds to encourage commodity groups to conduct generic export promotion programs for foreign market development. A commodity organization that wishes to obtain federal support must use some of their own funds to match those provided by the government. Several states, especially those with a large agricultural sector, also support generic export promotion programs with public funds.

Legislative Support for Programs

The motivation for mandatory checkoff legislation came from producer groups or cooperatives that had voluntarily started generic promotion programs and quality control programs using producers monies. Under the voluntary arrangements, however, it was impossible to get all producers to contribute to the promotion program or to comply with quality control programs. Arguing that all producers benefit from generic programs that are successful, producers made their point with various state legislative bodies. Thus, enabling legislation was put in place that allowed producers of a particular commodity or group of commodities to establish a quasi-public agency to assess a levy on all marketings of the commodity. In this way they assure equitable support of advertising, promotion, and other market support activities that, in concept, benefit everyone marketing the commodity.

The first federal legislation to provide authority for mandatory assessment was the Agricultural Marketing Agreement Act of 1937. Several state governments passed similar marketing order legislation in the 1930s. But states also passed separate "stand-alone" laws establishing assessment and program authority for a specific commodity. Some stand-alone federal legislation was approved in the 1950s, but most such legislation at the federal level came about in the 1980s.

Government involvement in marketing or in assisting in the marketing of agricultural products has substantial historical precedence. During the early part of the twentieth century, many state governments established legislation for state marketing orders that provided authority to regulate the flow and quality of products from farm to market. Provisions for the establishment of grades and standards, for inspection, and for research and promotion were authorized. Authority was also granted to collect funds from the farmers to support the marketing programs. The federal government has been actively involved in reporting commodity prices, establishing grades and standards, and supporting the prices of agricultural commodities since the depression era of the 1930s. The passage of the Agricultural Marketing Agreement Act of 1937 and the evolution of agricultural commodity promotion programs represents part of an evolving response by government to real and perceived agricultural marketing problems of the twentieth century.

State Promotion Program Authority

Most of the program proliferation and the funding increases for generic promotion programs from the 1930s to the mid-1980s came about under the authority of state enabling legislation. State involvement in generic promotion, however, probably began over a century ago. Several states encouraged producers of their important agricultural commodities to expand their markets in the late 1800s. The state legislatures appropriated public funds to state commodity organizations to promote farm commodities. To make it legal to spend public funds, these producer organizations were made quasi state agencies, which made it easier to defend the constitutionality of the state-legislated checkoff programs that followed. This legal precedence, which has been upheld by the courts, allows producer organizations, under proper legislative authority, to "tax" themselves for promotional activities (Armbruster and Frank, 1988 and Armbruster and Myers, 1985).

Florida was the first to pass legislation that provided for mandatory assessments without refund provisions. The 1935 Florida citrus advertising tax was levied on all marketings of oranges, grapefruit, and tangerines produced in the state of Florida. This law was challenged, but in a landmark

1937 case, the Florida Supreme Court upheld the advertising tax as constitutional. This case has been used to uphold constitutional challenges in other states.

By 1940, advertising checkoff programs had been established for four specific states' commodities: Idaho vegetables (1937), Michigan apples (1939), Washington apples (1939), and Iowa milk (1937). By 1986, 316 state promotion programs were being funded by producer checkoffs authorized by state legislation, compared to 241 in 1979 (Armbruster and Frank, 1988). With this growth, the amount of money that farmers invest in advertising, promotion, education, and research has increased significantly over the initial efforts at the turn of of the century.

The problem with the state-by-state approach is that most commodities are not produced within a single state's boundaries. There are, of course, exceptions; several specialty crops such as olives, dates, orange juice, kiwi fruit, and avocados are produced almost entirely in California and/or Florida. Others are produced in only one or two states. Most of the major agricultural commodities, though, are produced in several states (including soybeans, corn, beef, pork, wheat, milk, and eggs).

For some commodity groups, the solution to the state overlap was to establish national promotion organizations. Each state organization would share in the cost of the national promotion programs according to the volume of the product marketed. For example, the United Dairy Industry Association was formed following the development of several state and regional promotion organizations and the separate establishment of the American Dairy Association, the National Dairy Council, and Dairy Research, Inc. The American Soybean Association was formed to serve the needs of the various state soybean associations.

Some state commodity groups developed mandatory assessment programs that required participation of all producers, while other important commodity groups did not. Some states with mandatory assessments supported the national promotion organizations, whereas others did not. Also, states often had different rates of assessment, which resulted in perceived problems of inequity. This is often referred to as the free-rider syndrome. Thus, the stage was set for commodity groups to request federal legislation to require all producers of a commodity throughout the United States to share in the costs of promotion and market development.

The Agricultural Marketing Agreement Act of 1937

Federally legislated generic promotion programs for agriculture were first authorized by the Agricultural Marketing Agreement Act of 1937.[17] This act authorized marketing orders and agreements for a specified group of commodities. The orders authorized mandatory assessments to fund activities, and they could include various provisions to provide orderly marketing of the commodity. Promotion, the least important provision at that time, was initially limited to a very small number of fruits and vegetables. In the 1970s and early 1980s, however, the legislative authority was expanded to several other commodities, including milk in 1971 and eggs in 1983.

Initially, the promotion provision of the federal marketing order program was used by commodity groups only in a modest way. The other provisions of the orders, such as market coordination or allocation, minimum prices (for milk), grades and standards, and various market-facilitating mechanisms were considered more important. The focus of attention was on supply (both volume and quality), with little attention or concern given to influencing consumer behavior directly through advertising and promotion. Since the 1930s the number of orders and the dollars devoted to advertising and promotion have increased dramatically. In 1986, twenty-two of the forty-five nondairy federal marketing orders contained promotional authorization. But for many the funding levels were still small: In 1989, thirteen federal fruit and vegetable marketing orders with meaningful levels of funding had advertising and promotion budgets totaling about $12.6 million. In addition, there were five promotion programs for milk operating under this legislation; however, these dairy programs were being phased out, since they had been superseded by separate federal legislation authorizing the establishment of a national diary promotion program. Although this legislation provides the authority for selected commodities to establish self-help commodity promotion programs, stand-alone federal or state legislation has become the most common vehicle for establishing and funding commodity advertising and promotion programs.

Federal Legislation for Domestic Promotion Programs

The growth in commodity promotion activities during recent years has come from stand-alone federal legislation (Table 4–1). Commodity groups tend to prefer stand alone legislation over the AMAA of 1937 because it provides for a more informal rule making procedure and the program can be tailored more to their specific needs. The National Wool Act of 1954 was designed primarily to support wool producers' income. The act provided authority for a portion of the federal government's price support money that otherwise would have been paid to wool producers to be set aside to promote wool, mohair, sheep or goats, or the products thereof in domestic and foreign markets.[18] A prorated charge was authorized against all producer payments.

The Cotton Research and Promotion Act, passed in 1966, included promotion authority as one component of a comprehensive research and market development program. Funds were to be raised by a one-dollar-per-bale assessment plus a supplemental charge of 0.6 percent on all upland cotton marketed in the United States.[19] This legislation was developed

Table 4–1
Research and Promotion Programs Authorized by Federal Legislation

Commodity	Status (Date Implemented)	Authorizing Statute
Wool	(1955)	National Wool Act of 1954 [Title VII of the Agricultural Act of 1954, 68 Stat. 910, Aug. 28, 1954]
Cotton	(1966–67)	Cotton Research and Promotion Act of 1966; amended in 1990 to terminate refund authority [Pub. L. 89-502, 80 Stat. 279, July 13, 1966]
Wheat	Inactive terminated 1986	Wheat Research and Promotion Act of 1970 [Pub. L. 91-430, Stat. 885–886, Sept. 26, 1970]
Potato	(1972)	Potato Research and Promotion Act of 1971; amended in 1990 to terminate refund authority [7 U.S.C.A. 2611–2627, 7 C.F.R. 1207 (1988)]
Eggs	(1976)	Egg Research and Consumer Information Act of 1974; amended in 1988 to terminate refund authority [7 U.S.C.A. 2701–2718, 7 C.F.R. 1250 (1988)]
Flowers and plants	Rejected in referendum 1983–84	Floral Promotion Act of 1981 [title XVII, Pub. L. 97-98, 95 Stat. 1348–1358, Dec. 22, 1981]
Dairy	(1984)	Dairy Research and Promotion Act of 1983 [Subtitle B, Title 1, Pub. L. 98-180, 97 Stat. 1136, Nov. 29, 1983]
Honey	(1987)	Honey Research, Promotion, and Consumer Information Act of 1984; amended in 1990 to modify refund authority [Pub. L. 98-590, 98 Stat. 3115, Oct. 30, 1984]
Beef	(1986)	Beef Promotion and Research Act of 1985 [Title XVI, Subtitle A, Pub. L. 99-198, 99 Stat. 1597, Dec. 23, 1985]
Pork	(1986)	Pork Promotion, Research, and Consumer Information Act of 1985, [Title XVI, Subtitle B, Pub. L. 99-198, 99 Stat. 1606, Dec. 23, 1985]
Watermelon	(1990)	Watermelon Research and Promotion Act of 1985 [Title XVI, Subtitle C, Pub. L. 99-198, 99 Stat. 1622, Dec. 23, 1985]
Seafood	Law expired without vote	Fish and Seafood Promotion Act of 1986 [Pub. L. 99-659, 100 Stat. 3715, Nov. 14, 1986]
Soybeans	(1991)	Soybean Promotion, Research, and Consumer Information Act of 1990 [7 U.S.C. 6301–6311, 56 F.R. 31048–31068]
Fresh mushrooms	Pending	Mushroom Promotion, Research, and Consumer Information Act of 1990 [7 U.S.C. 6102–6112]
Pecans	Pending	Pecan Promotion and Research Act of 1990 [7 U.S.C. 6501-6513]
Limes	(1992)	Lime Research, Promotion, and Consumer Information Act of 1990 [7 U.S.C. 6201–6212, 57 F.R. 2988–2997]
Fluid milk (processors)	Pending request from processors	Fluid Milk Promotion Act of 1990 [7 U.S.C. 6401–6417]

primarily to provide the cotton industry a means to compete with synthetic fibers and to reverse the very rapid decline in cotton sales. This program has been considered very successful by many observers; until the refund authority was terminated in 1990, however, 35 percent of the producers (by volume) requested refunds. The 1990 legislation also authorized the addition of an assessment on cotton textile imports. These two amendments to the cotton promotion legislation provide that all cotton marketed in the United States, whether domestically or foreign produced, share in the cost of promotion.

Promotion programs were authorized for wheat in 1971, potatoes in 1971, eggs in 1974, and floral products in 1981.[20] The potato and egg promotion programs were developed to counter the very negative image consumers had of the two products. Potatoes were considered fattening; eggs were high in cholesterol and considered by many to contribute to heart diseases. The potato industry's promotion program has been considered successful by many, while the egg promotion has been only partially successful. Both programs had only partial support from their producers. Eighteen percent (by volume) of the potato producers asked for refunds, and 45 percent (by volume) of the egg producers asked for refunds before the refund provision was terminated in 1990.

The wheat program relied on assessments of the end product user and not the wheat grower. Because end product users had interests other than the survival of wheat producers, the program had a short life. With the dispersal of all funds in 1977, the program was later terminated.

Leaders of the floral industry convinced Congress to pass enabling legislation. Two referendums were conducted, but the support for a floral promotion program was too weak to gain a majority vote. The industry produces a great variety of products that are distributed through a diverse set of distribution networks; this diversity of interests is considered the reason for the lack of uniform support. But the legislation authority still exists.

Important developments occurred at the national level between 1983 and 1990 to provide the basis for assessments for more commodities. Federal authority for a national dairy promotion and research program was granted by Congress in 1983.[21] Authority for a honey research and promotion program was passed in 1984.[22] The 1985 farm bill contained authority for promotion programs for beef, pork, and watermelons.[23] A federally funded promotion program for seafood was established in 1986. The 1990 farm bill provided legislative authority for assessments on soybeans, fresh mushrooms, pecans, limes, and fluid milk (processor assessment).[24]

The Dairy Promotion Program was born out of crisis. The cost of the federal dairy price support program had reached unprecedented and burdensome levels. Congress and the dairy industry were forced to consider all possible ways to reduce the cost of the federal programs. The promotion part of the Dairy Production Stabilization Act of 1983 was part of a comprehensive plan to try to reduce the volume of cheese, butter, and nonfat dry milk powder that the government purchased under the dairy price support legislation of the preceding three years. The act contained provisions to reduce milk supplies and at the same time expand the demand for dairy products. To curtail supplies, provisions were included to reduce cow numbers and lower the level of price supports. The promotion program was to increase demand. A fifteen-cent per hundredweight assessment was levied against all commercial marketings of fluid milk to pay for the program. This assessment became effective in May 1984 and the program began in September 1984; a referendum to approve the program was conducted in 1985.

The beef and pork promotion acts were also born of very specific industry problems. Both industries have cyclical price movements, and the demand for red meats has been declining. Pork producer organizations had been pushing for checkoff programs to support promotion and market development programs for several years. The original legislation for a beef promotion program was passed in 1976, and at least two referendums failed. The federal legislation of 1985 authorized the secretary of agriculture, after holding hearings, to issue a promotion order for each commodity, appoint a board, and enforce mandatory assessments. Referendums were to be held twenty-two months later for beef and twenty-four to thirty months later for pork. Both programs received the necessary support to make the programs permanent at the time of the referendums.[25]

The legislation and subsequent promotion order for honey were developed when the cost of the agricultural support program was considered a major contributor to the federal deficit. The honey price support program had resulted in burdensome supplies of honey in the hands of government; at one point, the government owned 70 percent of the domestic honey stock in storage. In addition, large volumes of honey were being imported. The honey promotion program thus was one way for the industry to help itself. The funds were to be invested to expand the commercial use of honey and honey products.

Export Promotion Programs

Generic export promotion activities, unlike domestic promotion activities, are funded in part by public funds.[26] Some states appropriate funds for this purpose, and the federal government appropriates funds for three program efforts: the Export Incentive Plan (EIP), the Cooperator Program, and the Market Promotion Program (MPP).[27] Management of these programs is the responsibility of the Foreign Agricultural Service (FAS) of the U.S. Department of Agriculture.

The FAS Cooperator Program and the EIP were authorized in 1954 under legislation commonly known as Public Law 480 (PL 480). These two programs provide an incentive for commodity groups to support voluntary or mandatory industry checkoffs that can be augmented with FAS funds. From 1955 to 1990, the federal government provided $151 million to help commodity groups develop markets for grains, grain products, dry beans and dry peas, oilseeds and oilseed products, wood products, horticultural products, livestock and animal products, cotton, seeds, tobacco, and high-value products (Henneberry, Ackerman, and Eshleman, 1992).

The recipients of the Cooperator Program funds are mostly nonprofit U.S. agricultural trade or commodity groups that have industrywide membership and scope. Funds are obtained by submitting a detailed marketing plan and sharing in the cost of implementing the plan. The recipients of the EIP funds are private U.S. firms or agricultural cooperatives selling products under a registered trademark.

Funds can and are used for a great variety of market expansion activities, including trade servicing, technical assistance, and consumer promotion. *Trade servicing* activities could include hosting trade conferences, issuing trade press announcements, advertising in foreign trade journals, distributing promotional material to foreign food buyers, and bringing study teams to the United States to learn about U.S. production capacity and reliability as a supplier of agricultural commodities. *Technical assistance* programs are generally designed to stimulate long-term demand for U.S. commodities. The assistance is usually to existing or potential foreign buyers and may take the form of seminars, research, short courses, or training programs, all designed to show how the commodity can be effectively utilized by the foreign buyer. *Consumer promotions* can be direct advertising to consumers, demonstrations, or consumer education seminars. Public funds for brand advertising are only available from the EIP.

The Targeted Export Assistance (TEA) program, established in the 1985 farm bill, was terminated in 1990. During that period, the federal government invested $495 million.[28] The TEA program provided assistance to firms or organizations that had been adversely affected by subsidies, import quotas, or other "unfair" foreign trade practices. The commodity had to be in adequate domestic supply, and commodity organizations had to submit a market development plan targeting countries that were guilty of unfair trade practices. Also, matching funds equal to at least one-third the amount requested had to be provided by the requesting organization. In contrast, MPP funds differ in that they can be used in any country. MPP is to be funded at a minimum level of $200 million annually, according to the 1990 farm bill.

Rationale for Promotion Legislation

The legislative bodies of the federal government, as well as state governments, first justify the establishment of generic commodity promotion and research programs by concluding that the production of the commodity is important or essential to the nation's or state's economy. Second, they determine expansion of the market is vital to producers' welfare. Third, they conclude that the commodity in question is a valuable part of the human diet, a basic natural fiber, or important to consumer satisfaction. Finally, the commodity must involve interstate and/or foreign commerce. It is Congress's power to regulate interstate commerce that is used to justify this form of involvement in commodity marketing. The declaration of policy in the preamble of the enabling legislation normally will cover the above points. But in order to get this far in the legislative process, there must be some perceived economic benefit to producers and perhaps to society that will result from the advertising and promotion activities to be funded by the checkoff program. These economic benefits could include an increase in the volume of commercial sales, an increase in the price of the commodity, an increase in farm revenue, and a reduction in the cost of a government price support program. The economic benefits could flow from an advertising and promotion induced increase in demand for the commodity. It could also flow from providing information to producers and processors to improve the marketing and distribution efficiency of the commodity in question.

Declaration of Policy

The legislation that authorizes commodity promotion programs always contains a declaration of policy in the preamble. In this declaration of policy, one will find the required rational to justify the act. The findings and declaration of policy in the Dairy Promotion Program provide an example:

SEC. 110. (a) Congress finds that (1) dairy products are basic foods that are a valuable part of the human diet; (2) the production of dairy products plays a significant role in the Nation's economy, the milk from which dairy products are manufactured is produced by thousands of milk producers, and dairy products are consumed by millions of people throughout the United States; (3) dairy products must be readily available and marketed efficiently to ensure that the people of the United States receive adequate nourishment; (4) the maintenance and expansion of existing markets for dairy products are vital to the welfare of milk producers and those concerned with marketing, using, and producing dairy products, as well as to the general economy of the Nation; and (5) dairy products move in interstate and foreign commerce, and dairy products that do not move in such channels of commerce directly burden or affect interstate commerce of dairy products. (b) It, therefore, is declared to be the policy of Congress that it is in the public interest to authorize the establishment, through the exercise of the powers provided herein, of an orderly procedure for financing (through assessments on all milk produced in the United States for commercial use) and carrying out a coordinated program of promotion designed to strengthen the dairy industry's position in the marketplace and to maintain and expand domestic and foreign markets and uses for fluid milk and dairy products produced in the United States. Nothing in this subtitle may be construed to provide for the control of production or otherwise limit the right of individual milk producers to produce milk.[29]

Note that this declaration of policy limits the program to market expansion activities. Other subtitles authorize supply reduction activities.

A Marketing Tool for Group Action

Almost all agricultural commodity promotion organizations operate as autonomous or semiautonomous governmental agencies, and their authority is usually limited to advertising, promotion, and research activities directly relating to market expansion. In many cases, however, the authority has been granted in conjunction with provisions to regulate the flow of the commodity to market or to establish uniform grades and standards; the desired combined effect is orderly marketing of the commodity. For commodity groups that use the Agricultural Marketing Agreement Act of 1937, the range of authorized marketing functions are in one act. Separate acts are passed for the different regulatory functions in stand-alone legislation.

Promotion activities and uniform grades and standards are designed to expand the market, with the intent to increase total revenue to producers of the commodity. Supply reduction activities and the regulation of flow-to-market activities are designed to restrict the supply of certain grades in specific periods and markets, thus increasing prices. Market flow regulations are also intended to prevent gluts in the marketplace that can subsequently lead to quality deterioration. Such changes in quality can have long-term negative effects on demand and can readily negate advertising and promotion efforts. If the demand is inelastic for those markets, then producer revenue will be enhanced by the market flow regulations.

The point here is that advertising and promotion programs are only a part, perhaps even only a small part, of the government's attempts to improve the welfare of farmers by providing instruments with which the latter might influence the demand for and/or prices of their products. As an example, a study of beef promotion concluded that the use of checkoff funds accounted for around 3 percent of the change in demand for the period studied; other factors accounted for the balance (Ward, 1992a). The justification for providing commodity groups with this authority has been that it is in the public interest to do so. Although advertising and promotion programs are only one of several policy tools, they are an important part and are growing in importance. They can be viewed as one way to reduce federal subsidies. As indicated in Chapter 1, they provide information to users on a nonfee basis and can be an excellent source of nutritional education.

Political/Economic Environment

The political and economic environment must be right to obtain checkoff legislation. Public policy is dependent upon the attitude of the legislative and executive branches of government; but their attitudes are influenced by the attitude of their constituencies and the lobbying efforts of the agricultural and commodity trade organizations. These, in turn, are influenced by the economic conditions of the time. "The 1930–32 depression," according to an economist of the time writing in the *Journal of Farm Economics*, "made farmers all over the nation . . . resort to advertising . . . notably after 1935, as one means of stimulating demand" (Wolf, 1944). Authority to assess oneself for promotion has been granted at the time of bad economic conditions for the commodity group affected. It has been one way for the government to help without incurring a direct cost to the government tax base.

The conventional public wisdom states that advertising is not as important to producer welfare as the regulation of quantity and quality. Because most food and fiber markets are price inelastic (that is, a small decrease in market supplies will result in a much larger percentage increase in price), the supply-control argument has held sway in public policy for years. Generic promotion thus was viewed as a nonproductive investment by many. But with the passage of time and increased disenchantment with price support programs, public pressure against supply control developed. With a more complex marketing system and the availability of more sophisticated advertising and promotion methods, generic advertising and promotion have come to be viewed as an important and politically acceptable action. Thus by the mid-1980s, public policy had become generally supportive of commodity checkoff programs.

In considering the importance of a generic commodity promotion program, one also needs to understand the objective of the legislation. In part, the object of much program legislation has been to provide the producers, who are many in number and usually somewhat removed from the consumer, a voice in the way their products are marketed. The program can be considered successful if the producer groups mount an effective advertising program, influence the quality of the product, or change the consumers' image of the product. In other instances, the object is to require the producers to carry the cost of a program to expand demand and to move more of the commodities through commercial channels, thus (it is hoped) reducing the cost of a government price support program. The Dairy Promotion Program is a good example. The dairy promotion program can satisfy the legislation if it does nothing more than increase the commercial sales above what sales would have been without the program.

An important point to remember is that most of the large generic commodity promotion programs that now exist came about because of political pressure from the affected commodity group. In addition, there has been a shift in the willingness of legislative bodies to pass the appropriate laws and of the executive branch to oversee the programs. It is now acceptable public policy to have legislation that will, in effect, place an excise tax on production, the money to be used specifically to influence food consumption practices.

Changes in public policy can and will influence the number and type of commodity groups that will have generic promotion programs in the future. Without the authority to tax, the programs can only be modest in size or importance. With such authority, the generic promotion activities can be larger. Of course, however, the size of the program will depend on the size of the assessment, the size of the industry, and the existence of a refund requirement.

With few exceptions, a major commodity trade organization provides the funds and the lobbying effort to enact legislation for commodity promotion programs. For the dairy legislation, the National Milk Producers Federation represented the industry, and the United Dairy Industry Association provided funds. The National Cattlemen's Association spoke for the beef industry, with support from the Beef Industry Council of the National Livestock and Meat Board. The Beef Industry Council is now responsible for most of the national promotion effort.

Oversight

For a promotion act to be constitutional, Congress must declare that the act is in the public interest, that the commodity is involved in interstate commerce, and that the government has regulatory control over the operation of the program. It is the commerce clause that Congress uses to impose regulatory control. Regulatory control is accomplished by giving the U.S. secretary of agriculture authority over the appointment of the various boards and by requiring that all legal actions, budgets and contracts have his or her approval.

The Dairy Research and Promotion Act of 1983 requires that the Secretary of Agriculture submit to Congress an annual report describing activities conducted under the promotion order. The report must account for the receipt and disbursement of all funds and must include an independent analysis of the effectiveness of the program. The other federally legislated promotion programs specify oversight responsibility but do not require an annual report to Congress.

Procedures for Determining Producer Support

Just because legislative bodies pass legislation to give commodity groups authority to assess themselves does not necessarily mean that the producers are also in support. Congress can be influenced by the special interests of existing commodity promotion organizations whose motive is to increase the size of their programs. It may also believe that a particular program should be put in place because it is the right thing to do. Usually, the legislative authority contains provisions to determine whether the commodity group being assessed is in support of the program and the assessment.

Proposals, Hearings, and Referendums

In every case, the legislative authority establishes procedures for the promulgation of a promotion program. The procedures will require that the Secretary of Agriculture place an announcement in the *Federal Register* calling for proposals for program provisions as specified in the enabling legislation. Specific terms of a promotion and research order are then suggested by organizations representing the interests of the producers that will be affected by the order. Usually, the commodity group will hire a consulting firm with experience in such matters to write the proposed order. The Secretary of Agriculture will then write, based on the suggestions, a proposed order that will establish who will be assessed, the size and composition of a board of directors, the duties of the board, and how its members will be elected. Also specified will be the powers of the board and how members will be compensated. The size of the assessment may be specified, or limits may be established on the authority of the board to establish the size of the assessment. If refunds of the assessment are authorized, the order will specify the procedures for obtaining them. The order may also specify how the board and its staff are to interact with other and preexisting promotion or trade organizations representing the same commodity. In some cases, the order will specify that some of the preexisting state or regional organizations are to receive a portion of the assessment. In addition, the order will contain details on administration, accountability, and oversight.

The proposed order will be published in the *Federal Register*, and a time and place will be specified for public hearings where any and all interested parties will be given an opportunity to comment. Actually two types of rule making exist. One is formal which requires a hearing on the record. The other is informal and does not require a hearing on the record. After the hearing and the publication of the transcript, individuals and organizations can submit briefs stating their views about the proposed order. After a specified number of days, the secretary of agriculture publishes a final decision; the order can go into effect immediately, or it can be submitted for a vote by the affected producers, depending on the terms of the enabling legislation. It is through this process of hearings and referendums that producer support is determined.

Some acts require approval of not less than a majority of the producers voting in the referendum who produced for commercial sale some volume of the commodity during a representative time period. This is the case for the legislative authority for dairy, beef, and pork. The conditions for approval are much higher for some other commodities: the legislative authority for cotton, eggs, floral, honey, watermelons, and potatoes requires approval by a two-thirds vote of qualified producers.[30] The order also can become effective if the secretary of agriculture determines that the program is supported by a majority of the producers who vote, providing that those who vote affirmatively also handle or produce at least two-thirds of the volume marketed during a representative time period.

Refunds

Until the mid-1980s, refunds were authorized or required for most programs that operated under federal legislation as another way to determine producer support. Everyone affected under the order is required to pay the assessment; thus, the program is considered mandatory. Support for the program is considered weak if a substantial number of producers file for refunds. With a refund provision, requests for a refund are likely to escalate during hard times (that is, when prices are low because of heavy supplies), even though this might be the precise time when a good promotion program could provide the most benefits to the industry. Furthermore, after some portion of the producers has asked for a refund, others feel that they are carrying an unfair burden, so they also ask for a refund. After fourteen years of operation, for example, the refund level for the egg promotion program had escalated to 45 percent, and the refund level for the cotton program had grown to 35 percent after twenty-two years. In contrast, after seventeen years, the refund level for potatoes had grown to only 18 percent. The heavy refund requests provided the momentum for these groups to ask Congress to pass legislation to eliminate the refund provisions. The legislation was passed in 1990.

Program Termination

To ensure that promotion programs function in an orderly way if producer support has eroded, the enabling legislation and the orders contain procedures for termination. The U.S. Secretary of Agriculture or the state's commissioner of agriculture (or equivalent) usually has the authority to terminate a program if, in his or her opinion, the program is not in conformity with the declared policy or intent of the legislation. In most of the promotion programs, a certain percentage (usually 10 percent) of the producers of a commodity can petition the secretary or commissioner to hold a hearing and/or conduct a referendum to determine if the program is still favored by a majority of the producers. Usually, a majority negative vote is required to terminate a promotion order. We know of no instance where producers have asked for a recall of a stand-alone legislated commodity promotion program, although at the time of this writing, a number of dairy farmers were circulating a petition to call for a referendum on the national dairy promotion program. Some industry leaders indicated that they were close to having the required number of signatures.

Administration and Policy Decisions

A board of directors is established to set policy and to make sure that the programs are administered properly, according to law, and in the best interests of the participating producers. Under federal legislation, the Secretary of Agriculture has the authority to appoint the board from nominations made according to the order. Membership is made up mostly of those who are assessed. Some state programs and at least one federal program require representation from processors or handlers of the commodity; when imports are also assessed, importers are represented on the board. The California programs require that a consumer representative be appointed to all boards, as do some of the federal programs. Some states have legislation that establishes commissions, which usually are autonomous and operate with a modest amount of oversight from the state government. But the degree of autonomy of any promotion board is determined by law and the terms of the specific federal or state legislation establishing the commodity promotion program.

The composition of boards of directors varies dramatically among programs, and different ways to nominate are specified; evidence of this diversity is presented in Table 4–2. The board or commission will usually employ a staff to develop and administer the promotion program. The size and quality of the staff will depend on the size of the board's budget and the extent of the program effort. It is the board's responsibility to represent the affected producers. The board also is fiduciarily responsible for all assessments and all expenditures. It has the responsibility to invest the funds trusted to them in such a way that the objectives of the program will be realized. Literally translated, this means that they should enhance producer welfare to the maximum extent possible, utilizing the authority vested in them by the enabling legislation.

Provisions Authorized and Limitations on the Use of Funds

The kinds of programs that promotion organizations are authorized or required to conduct may be specified in the enabling legislation, the order, and the promulgated rules and regulations. The promotion program legisla-

Table 4-2
Federal Commodity Promotion Programs

Commodity	Name	Current Composition	How Appointed
Beef	Beef Promotion and Research Board	108 producers and 5 importers (3-year terms)[a]	By secretary from nominations by eligible organizations
Cotton	Cotton Board	20 producers and 1 consumer representative (3-year terms)[b]	By secretary from nominations by eligible organizations
Dairy	National Dairy Promotion and Research Board	36 producers (3-year terms)	By secretary from nominations by eligible organizations
Eggs	American Egg Board	18 producers (2-year terms)	By secretary from nominations by eligible organizations
Flowers and plants	Floraboard	Up to 75 producers[c] and importers	By secretary from nominations by eligible organizations
Fluid milk	National Processors Advertising and Promotion Board	1 representative (fluid milk processor) from each of 12–15 regions, plus 5 at-large members[c]	By secretary from nominations by eligible organizations
Honey	Honey Board	7 producers, 2 handlers, 2 importers, 1 cooperative, and 1 public member	By secretary from nominations by National Honey Nominations Committee
Limes	Lime Board	7 producers, 3 importers, and 1 public representative	By secretary from nominations by producers and importers; public representative nominated by board

Mushrooms	Mushroom Council	4–9 producers and importers[c]	By secretary from nominations by producers and importers
Pecans	Pecan Marketing Board	8 growers, 4 shellers, 1 handler, 1 importer, 1 public, 1 nonvoting	By secretary from nominations by growers and shellers; importer and public representative nominated by board
Pork	National Pork Board	14 producers and 1 importer (3-year terms)	By secretary from nominations by the secretary-appointed National Pork Producers delegate body
Potatoes	National Potato Promotion Board	91 producers (3-year terms)	By secretary from nominations by producers and importers
Soybeans	United Soybean Board	60 producers, representative of geography and volume	By secretary from nominations by each state unit
Watermelons	National Watermelon Promotion Board	14 producers, 14 handlers, and 1 public member (proposed)	By secretary from nominations by producers and handlers

Source: Agricultural Marketing Service, U.S. Department of Agriculture, April 1991.

Note: "Secretary" refers to U.S. secretary of agriculture.

[a]Executive committee (10 members from board, 10 elected by Federation of State Beef Councils) develops budgets and programs.

[b]Importer representation added in 1990.

[c]Authorized composition (no program in effect).

tion generally authorizes activities that will expand demand or strengthen the commodity's position in the marketplace and maintain and expand domestic and foreign market use of the commodity. The activities, as discussed in an earlier chapter, are generally referred to as being "generic." Such generic market or demand expansion activities can include expenditures for media advertising, education programs for consumers or processors, public relations, consumer or trade promotions, new product development, market development, and research.

The federal enabling legislation specifies that funds cannot be used for political purposes (that is, to influence governmental policy or action). Most state-legislated programs do not have this limitation. In fact, influencing federal policy is sometimes the most important function of some state checkoff programs. Some programs limit research to only that which is designed to expand demand; thus, expenditures on market research, product quality, and new product or process development, economic analysis of demand, nutrition research, and program evaluation are authorized.

Most programs restrict the use of funds to generic promotion activities and prohibit the use for brand advertising. This restriction is controversial. The reason for the restriction has to do with equity; the support of a particular brand might benefit one processor/distributor over another. This would be true if the brand advertisement expanded demand for one advertised brand at the expense of others. On the other hand, some argue that working hand in hand with private firms is an effective way to increase aggregate demand. As noted in Chapter 2, brand advertising can potentially expand total demand. If the brand advertisement increases aggregate or primary demand without redistribution of market shares, then the use of producer money to support brand advertising will enhance producer welfare without making other industry participants worse off. With this possibility in mind, the authors of the dairy promotion order wrote in a provision to authorize the support of brand advertising. The National Dairy Promotion Board can, at its discretion, determine whether brand advertising should be used. An advantage of a brand rebate program is that the talents of individual professionals in the private firms can be more easily used to help develop the generic effort. In addition, brand and generic advertising can be complementary; under some conditions, they can be symbiotic.

Evaluation

An ongoing evaluation should be and usually is conducted by the agency with oversight responsibility and the board and staff of the promotion organization. Because the programs are mandated by Congress, it is in the public interest to evaluate to ensure consistency with the policy of the legislation. It is also in the interest of those funding the program to ensure that their investment is obtaining the greatest possible benefits. The dairy promotion legislation requires an annual evaluation by a third party, which is included in the Secretary of Agriculture's report to Congress.[31] For other federal promotion programs and for all state-authorized programs, the responsibility for the establishment of an evaluation process is entirely in the hands of the commodity board.

The producers who fund the programs through their assessments are likely to insist that every program effort be evaluated for economic effectiveness, but this is not always the case.[32] In some organizations, there is an underlying fear that the results may be negative. Also, there exists some degree of skepticism about evaluation techniques, especially economic evaluation techniques. Two types of evaluation research are generally used: market research and economic research.

Market Research. Market research involves the analysis of market size and potential, measurement of consumer awareness to the promotion program and consumer beliefs and attitude about the commodity, and consumer reaction to the products being promoted or to the advertising or promotion effort itself. Market research can be used to establish benchmark measures of existing market conditions; later studies can be used to determine how effective the promotion programs have been in achieving specified goals.

Questions can be designed to measure knowledge about facts or to derive opinions. Market research thus can be informative or diagnostic. It can solve measurements of consumer attitude toward the product or various attributes of the product (for example, milk is good for your health: do you agree or disagree? Beef contains 30 percent fat: do you agree or disagree?). Market research can also involve the determination, through unaided and aided recall questions, of how many individuals saw a particular advertisement on TV. Both consumer attitude studies and awareness studies are accomplished often through tracking studies; that is, consumers are surveyed periodically or continuously over time to measure changes in attitude and in awareness. This is done to determine if there is any linkage between the generic advertising and promotion activity and consumer behavior.

The results of market research are useful in designing advertising campaigns, determining viewer reaction, diagnosing effectiveness in getting a desired message to a target audience, and measuring impact on consumer attitudes toward the advertised product. But market research usually does not provide a measure of the economic benefits of the advertising or promotion effort. Rather, it shows the potential response for new products and acceptance after the product is put in place.

Economic Research. Economic research involves the determination of the economic benefits of the various activities of the promotion organization. These economic benefits may be measured in terms of increases in price or sales volume, gross income to the commodity group, farmer profit, or return on the advertising or promotion investment. An attempt is made to determine the net effect of the advertising or promotion investment; the term *net effect* refers to the measurement of the direct relationship between the amount of advertising or promotion effort put forth and the resultant change in economic benefits, independent of all other factors that might also influence these benefits.

The economic research can be conducted in several ways. One approach involves the study of actual market behavior associated with the advertising effort, without any direct control on the part of the researcher over either the advertising program or the market conditions. Data or information are obtained concerning the amount of the advertising effort and conditions in the market, such as product price, consumer income levels, and the price of competing goods. Statistical techniques are then used to determine the relationship among all of the factors that are determined to be important, as well as the relationship between the advertising effort and the expected economic benefit. Some form of econometric analysis is usually developed to make these measurements.

Another approach involves controlled market experimentation. In this case, the researcher exercises some degree of control over the manner in which the advertising or promotion effort is implemented. This might include the establishment of control markets alongside test market areas where different kinds or levels of activities are carried out.

Market research and economic research are both necessary to make sure that the producer promotion funds are being used in the most effective manner possible. Economic research is useful—in fact, necessary—for the board and staff to arrive at the most appropriate assessment rate and the most appropriate way to allocate funds across program activities.

Summary

Almost all of the funds to support domestic commodity promotion programs are collected under the authority of federal or state legislation. Commodity groups lobby the legislatures for authority to establish self-help programs through mandatory assessments on the entire volume of a commodity that is marketed. Once the legislation is in place, the Secretary of Agriculture (or the equivalent office in state government) puts out a call for proposals or suggestions for specific terms of a promotion order. Based on proposals, the Secretary publishes a proposed order, holds hearings, and asks for briefs from interested parties. After a prescribed period, official regulations are published in the *Federal Register*. The order specifies the procedures to follow in appointing a representative board of directors and defines the scope of authority in developing and implementing the program. A mandatory assessment rate or "promotion tax" is specified and the collecting person designated, along with the rules of enforcement. Export promotion programs are usually funded in part by federal appropriations, with matching funds from commodity organizations, trade organizations, cooperatives, or private firms.

Over the years, some commodity promotion legislation has grown out of crisis. Farmers turned to advertising during the depression days of the 1930s and got Congress to pass the Agricultural Marketing Agreement Act of 1937. One of the provisions authorized was promotion. Congress and state governments have passed stand-alone legislation to support promotion programs of many commodity groups, in part to help solve farm income problems caused by oversupply, low prices, or weak economic conditions. In legislation to support agriculture, promotion is just one of the tools provided to commodity groups to influence the market or demand for their products.

To ensure strong support of a particular mandated promotion program, due process is observed by holding public hearings and asking for comments. The affected producers or suppliers are asked to vote in a referendum to guarantee that a majority are in favor either before assessments are begun or at some specified time afterward. A provision is also provided for termination if the Secretary of Agriculture concludes that the program is operating in a way inconsistent with the policy and intent of the act. In all orders, a provision is made for the affected producers to petition for termination.

A designated government agency has oversight responsibility for each legislatively mandated promotion program. In federal programs for agricultural commodities, the U.S. Department of Agriculture is responsible. In the dairy promotion program, the legislation requires that an annual report to Congress include an impact evaluation by a third party. Although other programs conduct impact evaluation studies, such a requirement is not generally written into the law. In the next chapter, we will provide more detail relating to several important programs.

5

A Description of Commodity Promotion Programs

In this chapter, we provide a description of the commodity advertising and promotion programs operating in the United States in the early 1990s. The importance of assessment rates, coverage, joint ventures, program longevity, and program effort and orientation are noted. The major federal programs are detailed, along with an overview of programs operating under the Agricultural Marketing Agreement Act of 1937. Finally, state programs are described, with a more in-depth description given for those for Florida citrus, California raisins, and Washington apples.

An Overview

In 1989, we contacted all the known commodity promotion organizations and state departments of agriculture in the United States. The survey provided information about the basis of support for promotion programs, budget and budget allocations, organizational arrangement, and program activities, as tabulated in Table 5–1. Fifty-five commodities collectively received and invested almost $700 million in promotion program activities. The total budget includes money from all sources: producer checkoff programs, voluntary contributions from producers or handlers, and direct appropriations from state or federal governments.[33] More than 90 percent was collected under the authority of federal or state legislation.

Ten of the commodity groups operated under federal legislation as of 1989. All except seafood and wine were funded by the producers of the commodity under legislated checkoff programs. Public funds were used almost entirely for seafood promotion effort; an excise tax against wine sales supported the wine promotion effort in several states. A large number of commodities also received public funds for export promotion activities. Funds for 13 commodities were collected under the authority of the Agricultural Marketing Agreement Act of 1937. Forty-two of the 55 commodity groups had some form of state legislation that provided authority for checkoff funds. Twenty-two involve one or more trade associations.

More than one-half of the commodities received public funds to support export promotion programs. Two federal programs, the Cooperator Program under PL 480 and the Target Export Assistance Program, accounted for $111.5 million.[34] Only two commodities, seafood and wine, receive direct appropriations for domestic promotion programs. The Fish and Seafood Promotion Act of 1986 provided federal funding, $6.5 million through 1991, for domestic promotion and market development. Several states, and specifically New York, have established promotion and market development programs for the wine/grape industries of their states that use public funds. Other states have levied excise taxes. For example, Ohio has an excise tax on wine, with the revenues being used to promote the Ohio wine industry.

A later survey indicated total expenditures of about $751 million from 116 commodity promotion organizations (see Table 5–2) representing 52 commodities (Lenz, Forker, and Hurst, 1991). These organizations employed a staff of 2,017. This latter survey did not provide as complete a coverage of all promotion organizations, and therefore the number of organizations counted is smaller. Also, because the survey was completed at a later date and more programs have become mandatory, the total amount of money involved should be larger. The money involved in both cases is probably an underestimate of the total dollar investment for all commodity promotion programs nationwide.

Checkoff Rates

The legislative authority specifies a checkoff assessment rate or places a limit in absolute or percentage terms. For example, the dairy promotion act specifies that fifteen cents per hundredweight be collected by the first handler; the assessment must be paid on all milk marketed by all dairy farmers. Five cents of the fifteen must be forwarded to the National Dairy Promotion and Research Board (NDB). Milk producers can specify that a local or regional promotion organization is to receive all or a portion of the remaining ten cents. The legislation for the pork program specifies an initial assessment rate at 0.25 percent of market value, but then the board is authorized to increase the rate by 0.10 percentage points annually up to a maximum of 0.50 percent of market value. The actual rate in 1992 was 0.35 percent. Assessment rates and the coverage for the stand-alone federally legislated programs are given in Table 5–3.

What is the proper level of assessment, and how is it determined? The rate must be politically acceptable to the farmers involved. It must be small enough so that it does not have a profound or disastrous impact on produc-

Table 5–1
Commodities with Promotion Programs

Commodity	Budget (thousand $)	Federal Legislation	AMAA of 1937	State Legislation	Trade Association	Public Funds[a]
Dairy	$209,100	X		X	X	
Citrus	93,436		X	X		E
Beef	72,540	X		X	X	E
Pork	32,996	X		X	X	
Raisins	30,487			X		E
Cotton	25,340	X		X	X	E
Apples	18,036			X		E
Foods[b]	15,714				X	E
Potatoes	15,471	X		X	X	E
Soybeans	15,373			X		E
Prunes	13,590			X		E
Wine	12,147			X		D/E
Walnuts	10,428		X	X		E
Peaches	9,427		X	X		E
Grapes	9,079			X	X	E
Eggs	9,004	X		X	X	
Avocados	8,783		X	X		
Corn	8,745			X	X	E
Seafood	8,500	X		X	X	D/E
Rice	7,706			X	X	E
Wool	7,433	X			X	
Almonds	7,414		X		X	E
Wheat	6,656			X		E
Beans	5,193			X	X	E
Strawberries	4,715			X		
Poultry	4,670			X	X	E
Pears	3,595		X	X	X	E
Kiwi fruit	3,098			X		E
Pistachio	3,043			X		
Peanuts	2,905			X	X	E
Lettuce	2,704			X		
Chocolate	2,500				X	E
Honey	2,308	X		X		
Plums	1,709		X			
Cherries	1,668			X	X	E
Olives	1,632		X			
Leather	1,500				X	E

Table 5–1 continued

Commodity	Budget (thousand $)	Federal Legislation	AMAA of 1937	State Legislation	Trade Association	Public Funds^a
			Basis of Support			
Tomatoes	1,268		X	X		
Wood	1,200				X	E
Catfish	1,000			X		
Onions	857		X			
Milo	552			X	X	
Watermelons^c	500	X				
Turkey	496			X		
Figs	478			X		
Carrots	401			X		
Apricots	390			X		
Artichokes	351			X		
Ginseng	250			X		
Hops	205			X		
Melons	172		X			
Asparagus	159			X		
Dates	135		X			
Papayas	127		X			
Cranberries	93			X		
Total	$697,279	10	13	42	22	27

Source: Survey by authors.

Note: Budgets are for the most recent fiscal year prior to January 1990. Amount includes all sources, including public funds.

^a E = public funds for export promotion; D = public funds for domestic promotion.

^b Canned and processed foods.

^c Anticipated amount.

tion profits; yet it must be large enough to support an effective promotion and research effort. Except for a few high-value fruits and nuts, the rate is less than 1 percent of the farm value of the commodity. An exact percentage figure is elusive because the price of a commodity can vary dramatically from year to year. For example, the beef assessment, which is on a per-head basis, varies greatly in percentage terms. Some animals are sold at $400 per head or less, while others are sold at more than $1,000 per head. The milk assessment of fifteen cents per hundredweight is slightly in excess of 1 percent of what most dairymen receive, but it may be less than 1 percent of the value received by dairymen in higher-priced areas such as Florida or in areas where a high percentage of the milk is utilized as fluid milk.

The level of assessment ideally should be large enough to maximize economic returns from the investment. At the margin, the last dollar of

Table 5–2
Number of Commodity Promotion Organizations, Total Staff, and Total Budgets, United States, 1990

Commodity Category	Number of Respondents	Total Staff	Total Budget (thousand)
Grains and oilseeds	14	262	$48,047
Dairy	39	603	208,856
Fruits and nuts	30	410	217,903
Meat, poultry, seafood, and eggs	12	254	193,854
Vegetables	11	71	23,867
Fibers	4	316	56,379
Other	6	101	3,070
Total	116	2,017	$751,976

Source: Lenz, Forker, and Hurst (1991).

investment should yield one dollar of additional returns to the producer group providing the funding. For a fixed budget, the last dollar invested in each program activity should have the same return as the last dollar invested in every other program activity. Of course, this probably never occurs in reality.

Coverage

The coverage is complete for most commodities only if assessments are mandatory, national, and nonrefundable. Coverage depends on the existence of a refund provision and, of course, the percentage of producers that ask for a refund. Prior to 1990 (when the refund provision was eliminated) less than 55 percent of egg volume was covered, because 45 percent of the funds collected were refunded. Less than 65 percent of the cotton production was covered, because 35 percent of the funds were refunded. Some mandated programs exempt small producers (Table 5–3); although the number exempted might be large, the percentage of volume exempted will likely be small.

State-mandated programs cover only the volume produced within the boundaries of the state. Some state programs also assess imported volumes. For those commodities that are grown almost entirely within the state (for example, kiwi fruit, almonds, olives, prunes, and raisins produced or grown only in California), the coverage can be complete. For other commodities (such as corn, soybeans, and apples) that are grown in many states, the coverage is complete only to the extent that every state in which production occurs has a checkoff program.

How imports are assessed is also important. If imports are not assessed, then foreign producers and importers are getting a free ride on the domestic producers' promotion efforts. Imports are assessed under the national programs for beef, pork, cotton, and honey, where import volume is significant.

Table 5–3
Federal Commodity Promotion Programs: Assessment Rate and Coverage

Commodity	Authorized Rate	Coverage[a]
Beef	$1 per head	All cattle producers and importers
Cotton	$1 per bale plus up to 1% of bale value	Producers and importers
Dairy	15¢ cwt.	Dairy farmers
Eggs	Up to 10¢ per 30-dozen case (current rate is 5¢)	Producers with 30,000 or more laying hens
Fluid milk[b]	20¢ per 100 pounds of all fluid milk products marketed	Processors who market consumer-type packages
Honey	$0.01 per lb.	Producers and importers of more than 6,000 lbs. per year; all 50 states, Puerto Rico, and District of Columbia
Limes[b]	$.01 per lb.	Producers, producer-handlers, importers of more than 35,000 lbs. yearly; all 50 states, Puerto Rico, and District of Columbia
Mushrooms[b]	1st year, up to ¼¢ per lb; 2nd year, up to ⅓¢; 3rd year, up to ½¢; subsequent years, up to 1¢	Producers, importers, of more than 500,000 lbs. yearly; all 50 states, Puerto Rico, and District of Columbia
Pecans[b]	Prior to referendum, ½¢ per lb. for in-shell; afterward, up to 2¢ per lb.; twice the rate for shelled	Growers, grower-shellers, importers; all 50 states, Puerto Rico, and District of Columbia
Pork[c]	0.25% of market value; may increase by 0.1 annually, not to exceed 0.50%	All producers of porcine animals and importers
Potatoes	$.02 per cwt. or up to .5 of 1% of 10-year average price	Producers growing 5 or more acres; importers, Irish potatoes; all 50 states
Soybeans	½ of 1% of net market value of soybeans sold	Producers
Watermelons	Fixed by secretary of agriculture; not to exceed 2¢ per cwt. for producers and handlers	Handlers and producers growing 5 or more acres

Source: Agricultural Marketing Service, U.S. Department of Agriculture, April 1991.
[a] All producers in the 48 contiguous United States unless otherwise noted.
[b] Programs not implemented as of early 1992.
[c] Rate in 1992 is 0.35 percent.

105

It is difficult, however, to enforce assessment of imports under state legislation. The Florida law for citrus places an assessment on foreign-country imports of orange juice entering Florida ports, but Florida does not have authority to assess imports entering ports in other states. An increasing portion of imported orange juice is imported into ports in states other than Florida (Ward and Kilmer, 1989, p. 134). Avoidance of the promotion assessment is one incentive for importing through non-Florida ports, but, of course, other economic incentives also exist. Coverage is important because it influences the amount of money available and the manner in which costs are shared in relation to the benefits.

Joint Ventures

Some generic promotion programs are joint ventures between a promotion organization and an agricultural marketing cooperative or a proprietary food-processing company. These entities might share costs or match funds through an advertising rebate program. Until 1990, the Florida Citrus Commission had an advertising rebate program in which citrus marketing firms were reimbursed for part of their brand advertising as long as the advertisement contained a Florida citrus identification and other requirements.

A joint venture can be between two different commodity promotion organizations: the dairy board and the beef board jointly fund advertisements for cheeseburgers. Or, a joint venture can be with brand advertisements for cookies and milk with Nabisco. The economic advantage of joint ventures can come from the sharing of costs for a particular campaign. To be appropriate, the joint promotion effort must benefit each participant more than if the same amount of money was invested independently.

Most export promotion programs are joint ventures between the federal or state government, commodity promotion organizations, and commodity trade organizations. Some programs, however, encourage the federal government to enter into joint venture arrangements with proprietary firms. This latter arrangement is used to encourage private firms to invest in market development in countries where they might not otherwise do so.

Program Longevity

Some generic commodity promotion programs have been in existence for several decades. The older programs are generally more complex, with firmly entrenched boards and perhaps more complex management structures, higher overhead, and more complex and sophisticated programs. They are also the ones that have likely been the best managed by the farmer boards and the hired management and at least perceived as being successful by the producers of the commodity.

Program Effort and Orientation

The intensity of the program is likely to be related to the size of the budget. The types of program activities or program orientation are related to the size of the budget but could also be influenced by the type of commodity, the focus of the promotion effort, the extent to which the commodity is processed, and the nature of the market for the commodity. The appropriateness of a particular orientation is likely to be debated, but an orientation toward heavy media advertising is more likely for a commodity that maintains its identity at the consumer level. A commodity with a technical story to tell will likely focus on print advertising. Orientation for a commodity that is substantially changed in form is more likely to be directed toward technical research, new product and process development, and trade promotion and education efforts.

National Programs Operating under Federal Legislation

Several commodity groups now operate promotion programs established under commodity-specific federal legislation. The commodities with active national programs in early 1992 were dairy, beef, soybeans, pork, cotton, potatoes, eggs, sheep, honey, and watermelons (Table 5–4).[35] Programs for fresh mushrooms, pecans, and limes were in the process of being developed in 1992. The national organization budgets for these active federal programs totaled about $240 million. This accounts for about one-half of the total assessment dollars for these commodities when one also includes the money spent by state and regional organizations promoting the same commodities.

Each commodity promotion program has unique history and a unique promotion program. The legislative authority for each evolved out of a different set of economic circumstances and a different political stance by the commodity group. In the remainder of this section, we will describe how each program is organized and operated at the national level and how they relate to the state and regional organizations.

The National Dairy Promotion Program

Organization and Funding. The national dairy promotion program is based on a national assessment of fifteen cents per hundredweight levied against all milk marketed. In 1991, the assessment levied against 181,570 dairy production units provided $219 million (Figure 5–1). The National Dairy Promotion and Research Board (NDB) received $76.9 million, the Wisconsin Milk Marketing Board (WMMB) received $21.3 million, and the California Milk Producers Advisory Board received $20.9 million. What was left went

Table 5–4 National Promotion Programs Operating under Stand-Alone Federal Legislation, 1992

National Board	Year Implemented	National Assessment Income (thousand $)	1990 Refunds (thousand $)	Latest vote[b] Year	% Approval
National Dairy Research and Promotion Board	1984	$76,670		1985	90
Cattleman's Beef Promotion and Research Board	1986	43,149[c]		1988	79
United Soybean Board	1991	40,000[d]	—		—[e]
Cotton Board	1966–67	31,780	$10,659[f]	1991	
National Pork Board	1986	24,762[c]		1988	78
National Egg Board	1976	7,348			
National Board Promotion Board	1972	6,073	1,116[g]	1991	81
Honey Board	1987	2,663[c]	345[h]	1991	91
National Watermelon Promotion Board	1989	954	101	1989	52[i]

[a] Only the income received or retained by the national board. Source is AMS, USDA.
[b] Latest referendum.
[c] Includes assessments on imports.
[d] Estimated annual income, assessments began September 1, 1991.
[e] Referendum to be conducted in 1993–94.
[f] Refund provision terminated in 1991.
[g] Plan was amended in August 1991 to assess imports and terminate refunds.
[h] Producers and importers voted (72 percent) in August 1991 to terminate assessment refund provision.
[i] 72 percent of volume.

to a number of regional and state promotion organizations, most of whom are affiliated with the United Dairy Industry Association (UDIA). Each organization qualified to receive funds has its own producer board of directors, and most have their own staff. Some operate under the authority of state legislation (for example, the New York Milk Promotion Advisory Board operates as a quasi state agency and provides most of the funds of the American Dairy Association and Dairy Council, Inc.[36], whereas others operate independently (for example, Dairy Farmers, Inc., was organized by Florida dairy farmers through their cooperatives).

UDIA serves as a support and service organization for a number of local organizations.[37] Each affiliated unit elects representatives to a delegate body and to a board of directors. The directors set policy and hire a staff to administer their program. In total, the UDIA units account for 45 percent of the milk promotion dollars; each affiliated unit makes payments to UDIA to

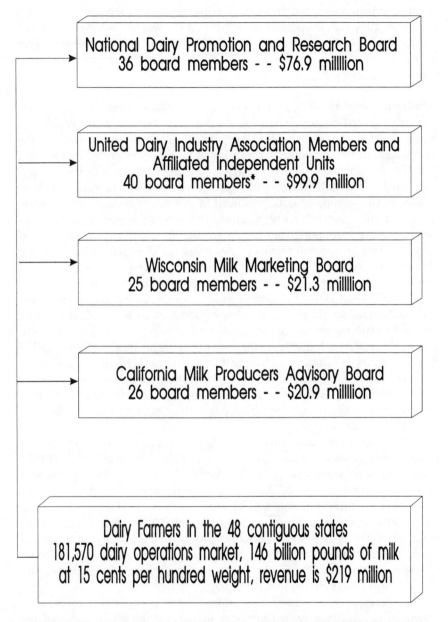

National Dairy Promotion and Research Board
36 board members - - $76.9 millllion

United Dairy Industry Association Members and
Affiliated Independent Units
40 board members* - - $99.9 million

Wisconsin Milk Marketing Board
25 board members - - $21.3 millllion

California Milk Producers Advisory Board
26 board members - - $20.9 millllion

Dairy Farmers in the 48 contiguous states
181,570 dairy operations market, 146 billion pounds of milk
at 15 cents per hundred weight, revenue is $219 million

* UDIA has 40 board members and a delegate of 145. Each affiliated unit also has an elected or appointed Board of Directors. Total number of producers involved easily exceeds 600. The independent units include units in Oregon, Washington, Louisiana, and Pennsylvania.

Figure 5–1. Organizational Structure of the National Dairy Promotion
          Program, 1991

cover operating costs and services. Two large state organizations operate independently, the Wisconsin Milk Marketing Board (WMMB) and the California Milk Producers Advisory Board (CMAB). Both operate under state legislative authority. They account for almost 20 percent of the milk promotion dollars.[38]

Administration. All of the milk promotion organizations, through their boards of directors, are responsible to the dairy farmers that provide the funds. Boards of state-legislated programs are usually appointed by the state's secretary of agriculture from a list of nominees provided by specified dairy farmer organizations. The thirty-six-member National Dairy Board is appointed by the U.S. Secretary of Agriculture, with representation proportionate to the volume of milk produced in thirteen regions of the country. Boards of milk promotion organizations that operate under voluntary support or contract support from legislated organizations are usually elected directly by the constituent members. Because each qualified milk promotion organization has a farmer board of directors, there is a great deal of grass-roots farmer involvement in the operation of the programs.

The National Dairy Promotion and Research Board has an employee staff authorized at thirty-one persons in 1992, with a president as chief operating officer and vice presidents for advertising, evaluation, research, and public relations. It also has a director of export promotion. The board of directors elects its officers—a chairman, vice chairman, treasurer, and secretary. The board has four standing committees (with nine members each) to cover advertising, evaluation, research, and public relations. A finance committee is made up of the officers and the chairs of each of the four standing committees.

One of the important functions of the NDB is to see to it that all dairy farmer assessments are collected and forwarded to either itself or a qualified dairy promotion organization. During the fiscal year 1984–85, the first year of the operation of the NDB, the combined expenditure for all dairy promotion organizations was $209.1 million (Table 5–5). Of this amount, 43 percent represented program activity of the NDB, and the other 57 percent covered program activities of eighty qualified promotion organizations. Ninety-one percent of the NDB program money was invested in advertising, whereas 68 percent of the funds of the qualified promotion organizations was invested in advertising.

Six years later, the combined expenditures were $224.2 million, of which 34 percent represented program activity of the NDB. More of the producers were directing their ten cents to one of the local organizations, now sixty-eight in number. The proportion of the NDB effort devoted to advertising dropped slightly (to 75 percent) as it invested a larger proportion in nutrition research and education and in new product development. Qualified promotion organizations with more money increased their invest-

Table 5–5
Expenditures of the Nationwide Dairy Promotion Program,
1984–85 and 1990–91

| | | 1984–85 | | | 1990–91 | |
| | | *Qualified* | *Combined* | | *Qualified* | *Combined* |
Program Area	*NDPRB*	*Programs*	*Programs*	*NDPRB*	*Programs*	*Programs*
Advertising						
Fluid milk	$20.9	$50.8	$71.7	$15.9	$51.1	$67.0
Cheese	31.1	18.2	49.3	20.5	31.8	52.3
Butter	7.4	4.1	11.5	7.9	3.5	11.4
Calcium	18.3	1.9	20.2	4.8	—	4.8
Other	4.5	6.3	10.8	8.6	11.1	19.7
Total	$82.2	$81.3	$163.5	$57.7	$97.5	$155.2
Nutrition and product research and education	$3.8	$25.3	$29.1	$10.9	$34.5	$45.4
Evaluation	1.5	1.0	2.5	2.3	2.0	4.3
Other	2.5	11.5	14.0	6.3	13.0	19.3
Total expenditures	$90.0	$119.1	$209.1	$77.2	$147.0	224.2

Source: Tauer and Forker (1987), p. 217; National Dairy Board annual reports; USDA reports to Congress.
Note: Expenditures in millions of dollars.

ments in cheese advertising by 75 percent and in research and education by 36 percent. Their investment in evaluation was doubled.

Program Activities. Most of the NDB advertising budget is directed to television, radio, and print media advertising (Table 5–6). Expenditures declined between 1986 and 1991 for two reasons. NDB accumulated funds the first year while getting organized, and so it had a large carryover going into its first year of operation. Also, more dairymen have asked that 10 cents of their assessment be forwarded to a local or regional qualified promotion organization; of the 15-cent assessment, the national board received a net of 5.28 cents in fiscal year 1991.

The United Dairy Industry Association develops program material for its member units. For a basic fee, it conducts marketing and economic research, develops educational material, and develops commercials and promotion material (Table 5–7). In addition, it provides services for members that include buying advertising time, distributing education material, and conducting research. This provision of services accounts for more than 80 percent of its annual budget.

The Wisconsin Milk Marketing Board conducts an independent program with funds from Wisconsin dairy farmers. Its annual program and administration budget is over $20 million (Table 5–8). Because most of the milk produced in Wisconsin is used in the manufacture of cheese, the

Table 5–6
Revenue and Expenditures of the National Dairy Board, 1986, 1990, and 1991

Category	FY 1986	FY 1990	FY 1991
Revenue			
Assessments	$83.7	$75.1	$76.9
Interest income	1.3	2.1	1.9
Total revenue	$85.0	$77.2	$78.8
Expenses			
Advertising			
Fluid milk	$13.5	$15.0	$15.9
Cheese	21.3	20.4	20.5
Butter	3.8	11.3	7.9
Calcium	18.2	5.3	4.8
Ice cream	4.3	5.9	6.7
Other	—	2.2	1.9
Subtotal	$61.1	$60.3	$57.7
Nutrition and product research	$10.4	$9.8	$10.9
Evaluation	1.4	2.5	2.3
Industry communication and public relations	0.5	2.9	3.6
Administration	2.4	2.3	2.4
Uncommitted/other	9.1	—	.3
Total expenditures	$84.9	$77.8	$77.2

Source: National Dairy Board and USDA annual reports (fiscal years ending April 30).
Note: Columns may not add due to rounding. Amounts shown in millions of dollars.

WMMB focuses on cheese promotion and on the differentiation of Wisconsin cheese from cheese produced elsewhere. The California Milk Producers Advisory Board conducts its own program, as do the states of Oregon and Washington; the three state organizations cooperate informally. CMPAB has an annual budget of over $20 million (Table 5–9).

A concept that has been traditional in the dairy promotion industry is that the promotion dollars should follow the milk to market: Money collected from producers whose milk is used in cheese should be used in cheese advertising, money collected from producers whose milk is used for fluid milk in the Boston market should be used to promote fluid milk in the Boston market, and money collected from dairymen whose milk is used for fluid purposes and sold in New York City should support fluid milk advertising and promotion in New York City. For example, the New York arrangement provides that checkoff funds collected from New York producers who ship milk to processors in the Boston area go directly to the promotion organization that handles the generic milk advertising for the Boston market. Similarly, money from California producers is used to promote the products that are made from California milk in the markets in which they are sold. This

Table 5–7
Revenues and Expenditures of the United Dairy Industry Association, 1986, 1990, and 1991.

Category	1986	1990	1991
Revenues:			
Basic program support:			
Member fees and due	$8.6	$4.1	$4.5
Sale of material	2.3	2.7	2.4
Other income	0.7	1.2	1.1
Restricted program funds[a]	51.0	28.6	27.0
Total revenue	$62.6	$36.5	35.1
Expenses:			
Basic programs:			
Advertising and market services	$2.5	$0.6	$0.6
Education and research	8.0	4.1	3.2
Marketing and economic research	0.8	0.5	0.5
Communications	0.7	0.6	0.6
Operations	1.1	2.4	3.2
Loss on restructuring[b]	—	0.2	—
Restricted programs:			
National advertising pools[a]	23.6	13.0	11.6
User pay programs	4.4	1.8	1.9
Market intensification	21.1	13.9	13.5
Total expenses	$62.3	$37.2	$35.1

Source: UDIA annual reports and financial statements.

Note: Columns may not add due to rounding. Amounts shown in millions of dollars.

[a] The amount for 1986 technically was not restricted, but represents comparable program activity in 1990 and 1991.

[b] Loss on disposal of obsolete material and sale of property.

policy generally holds for local and regional units. NDB, representing all U.S. producers, operates a national program and tries to allocate dollars to obtain the greatest benefit to all U.S. dairy farmers.

This manner of allocation is reflected in the budgets of the promotion organizations. The organizations develop specific advertising programs for each product group: fluid milk, cheese, butter, and ice cream. But they also develop more general programs for dairy products as a whole. Most prominent in the years 1985–88 was a special campaign to educate consumers on the value of dairy products as a source of dietary calcium.

Television, radio, and print media advertising account for a large portion of the expenditures (See Table 5–5). Different themes are used for the different products. "Milk, It Does a Body Good," has been used by the NDB, UDIA, and CMPAB as the central theme in fluid milk advertisements. "Milk, Nature's Health Kick" is also used for fluid milk advertisements targeted to children and teenagers. "Don't Forget the Cheese" and "Give 'Em a Little Pat of Butter" are themes for cheese and butter, respectively, that have been used. Ice cream has been promoted with the phrase "Ice Cream, the Treat That

Table 5–8
Expenditures of the Wisconsin Milk Marketing Board, 1986, 1990, and 1991

Category	1986	1990	1991
Administration	$0.8	$0.9	$0.9
Program services			
Education	2.1	2.2	2.1
Consumer and trade relations	—	2.2	2.7
Producer and industry relations	1.1	0.9	1.0
Research	3.1	2.0	1.8
Market development	14.6	11.9	14.9
Planning	—	0.8	0.8
Total	$21.7	$20.9	$24.2

Source: WMMB annual reports.
Note: Expenditures in millions of dollars.

Treats You Good." The calcium advertisements have featured fluid milk, cheese, ice cream, and other dairy products and focus on a theme of "Dairy Calcium, Calcium the Way Nature Intended."

The above themes were developed by the creative talents of advertising agencies in cooperation with the staffs of the promotion organizations. Market research was used to help identify the theme and target audience for each product. Because teens consume large quantities of fluids and tend to be heavy milk drinkers, but also are subject to a barrage of other beverage advertising, youths between the ages of six and sixteen are targeted for part of the fluid milk promotion. The purpose is to tell them that milk is good for their bodies and their health; the ads show how a young child that drinks milk will grow up strong and attractive. Adults, however, consume a lot less fluid milk than teens. To try to prevent his lessening of milk consumption as individuals age, the NDB also targeted young adults between the ages of eighteen and thirty-four drawing heavily on television and radio.

Because of the more local nature of the fluid milk market, a large portion of fluid milk advertising is funded by the local qualified promotion organizations. This is either done through UDIA or through independent contracts with local ad agencies. The promotion organizations that operate in the Baltimore-Philadelphia-Washington (D.C.) area and in the states of Washington, Oregon, and California each develop and carry out a different approach designed to appeal to the unique ethnic, socioeconomic, and life-style groups in the respective markets.

From the nutrition research funded by the dairy promotion organizations, a linkage between lack of calcium and osteoporosis was further shown, and dairy calcium was proven to be beneficial in prevention. Because this is especially a problem with women and becomes more serious in older women, the calcium advertisements targeted women between the ages of twenty-five

Table 5–9
Budgeted Expenditures of the California Milk Advisory Boards, 1989, 1990, and 1991

Category	FY 1989	FY 1990	FY 1991
Advertising and promotion			
Fluid milk	$11.0	$11.5	$12.5
Manufactured products	5.7	6.3	6.7
Subtotal	$16.7	$17.8	$19.2
Research and product development	$1.1	$1.1	$1.2
Administration and operations	0.9	0.9	0.9
Communication services	0.6	0.6	0.7
Marketing services	0.4	0.4	0.4
Total	$19.7	$20.8	$22.4

Source: California Department of Food and Agriculture, combined budgets of the California Milk Producers Advisory Board and California Manufactured Milk Advisory Board.
Note: Expenditures in millions of dollars.

and fifty-four. Calcium advertisements use print media because the message is too complex to be conveyed on a fifteen- or thirty-second television or radio commercial.

The cheese campaign of the NDB and UDIA focuses on trying to convince women to buy an extra package of cheese the next time they shop. They target light and medium users of cheese because research indicates that this group offers the greatest opportunity for market enhancement. Television ads are supplemented with print ads to suggest easy and simple ways to use more cheese. Wisconsin and California have both developed separate cheese campaigns designed to differentiate their cheeses from those produced in other states. Thus, Wisconsin producers promote the large variety of cheeses produced in the state and state that "Wisconsin Cheeses are Winners." Since Wisconsin cheese is marketed throughout the United States, the Wisconsin program is nationwide. Concurrent with media advertising, WMMB employees work closely with food retailers to encourage them to offer special promotions for Wisconsin cheese. To this end, they will share the cost of a food retailer's cheese advertising if the retailer's ads promote generic Wisconsin cheese. Although a large share of the milk promotion dollars is invested in media advertising, each organization's program has many other components. Each organization defines its program quite differently, so one cannot easily develop a budget for each component. The same general terminology in the budgets does not translate into identical program activities. It is possible, however, to describe the total dairy promotion program in meaningful ways.

Media advertising is used to communicate directly to consumers the positive attributes of dairy products. It is hoped that this strategy will pull more milk through the commercial distribution system. Market research is conducted to determine target audiences, appropriate themes, and consumer awareness. Ad agencies are employed to create the messages to be conveyed and the manner of conveying it. The promotion organizations support new product and process development, primarily through subregional dairy food research centers located at the University of California at Davis, California Polytechnic State University, the University of Minnesota, South Dakota University, Cornell University, the University of Vermont, North Carolina State University, Mississippi State University, Brigham Young University, Oregon State University, Utah State University, and the University of Wisconsin. The centers' activities are funded approximately one-third by NDB, one-third by local promotion organizations, and one-third by industry contributions.

Nutrition research is supported in an attempt to identify the attributes of dairy products that are beneficial to health. The results are conveyed through education programs, seminars and conferences, and print directly to medical, health, and diet professionals who advise consumers on what to eat or who prepare food for institutional feeding. To the extent possible, the results are conveyed to consumers through the media. NDB has established an NDB Institute for Nutrition and Cardiovascular Research at Oregon Health Sciences University, a Genetics and Nutrition Institution at the University of California at Berkeley, and a Dietary Lipids Institute at Columbia University.

Concurrent with the support of nutrition research, the dairy farmers organized and supported a network of local dairy councils. These councils are staffed and organized to communicate professional nutritional information directly to teachers in local schools, doctors and nurses in local hospitals, dieticians in institutional feeding establishments, the local press, and consumer groups.

Summary. In summary, in terms of the program elements of concern, the dairy promotion program is strongly supported by the nation's dairy farmers and the political process.[39] The coverage is complete because assessments are mandatory and nonrefundable; imports are not significant. Organizational arrangements are complex because of the concurrent operating nature of a national organization (which accounts for about one-third of the funds and program activity) and several state and regional organizations (which account for the other two-thirds). This complex organization has some advantages in terms of the large number of dairy farmers involved on the various boards, as well as the competition between staff for funds and program excellence. It also makes sense because of the manner in which returns are pooled through the federal milk marketing orders. Different order areas have different portions of the milk supply utilized as fluid, the highest-priced usage. Different areas can allocate funds to the product categories that will yield the greatest increase in the value of the pooled funds. The disadvantages include problems of coordination, fragmented program activities, and the time and resource commitment of the dairy farmers who serve on the national, state, and regional boards.

The National Beef Promotion Program

Organization and Funding. The nationwide beef promotion program began in 1986. It is administered by an 11-member executive committee of the 113-member Beef Promotion and Research Board. Of the board's membership, 108 represent the domestic beef industry, and 5 represent beef and beef product importers. The assessments are remitted to a qualified state beef council or to the board. About one-half of the assessment money is retained by the councils, and the other half is forwarded to the board.

Program implementation is accomplished under contract by the National Livestock and Meat Board. The meat board has represented interests of red meat producers and allied organizations since the early 1920s. In the early 1960s, the meat board organized three special groups: the Beef Industry Council, the Pork Industry Group, and the Lamb Committee. The Beef Industry Council was organized to promote the welfare of the beef industry.

A one-dollar checkoff, which was mandated to begin in 1986, is collected every time a live bovine animal is sold. This includes baby calves, dairy cattle, and all ages of beef cattle. Money is forwarded to local state beef producer promotion councils. At least fifty cents are mandated to go to the Beef Promotion and Research Board. The state beef producer promotion councils have discretion over the money that is retained; they can forward additional money to be Beef Promotion and Research Board, send it directly to the Beef Industry Council, or develop their own local advertising and promotion programs. The Beef Promotion and Research Board retains funds for administrative costs and program activities that include communications, industry and consumer information, and research, but most of the funds are forwarded to the Beef Industry Council for program implementation (Figure 5–2). Under the order, an operating committee decides program expenditure amounts. The operating committee is comprised of 10 members of the beef board and 10 members elected by the Beef Industry Council. The mission of the National Livestock and Meat Board, as stated in their 1987–88 annual report, is to "protect and increase demand for beef, veal, pork, lamb, and processed meats through consumer marketing programs, thereby enhancing profit opportunities for the livestock and meat industry."

The Beef Promotion and Research Order, which effectuated the enabling legislation, strongly implies in its wording that the beef board should utilize the resources (organizations)already in existence for program implementation. At the time of the establishment of the order, there were several state beef councils in existence, as well as the Beef Industry Council of the National Livestock and Meat Board.

Of the $43.5 million received by the Beef Promotion and Research Board in fiscal year, $37.9 million was forwarded to the National Livestock and Meat Board for program functions (Table 5–10). In addition, the National Livestock and Meat Board received $17.8 million from the qualified state

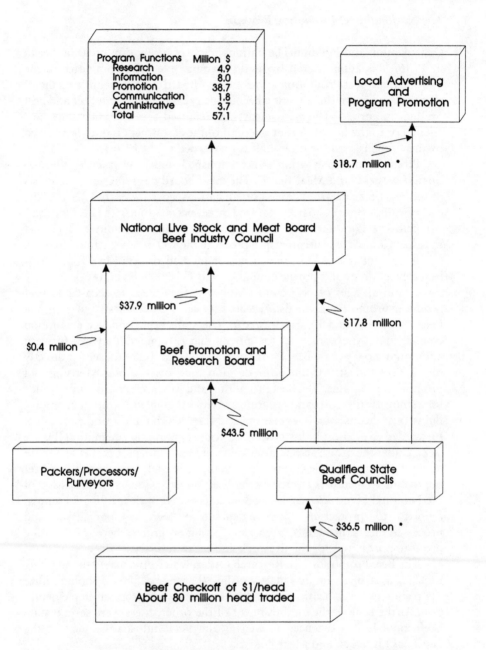

Program Functions	Million $
Research	4.9
Information	8.0
Promotion	38.7
Communication	1.8
Administrative	3.7
Total	57.1

Local Advertising
and
Program Promotion

$18.7 million *

National Live Stock and Meat Board
Beef Industry Council

$37.9 million

$0.4 million

$17.8 million

Beef Promotion and
Research Board

$43.5 million

Packers/Processors/
Purveyors

Qualified State
Beef Councils

$36.5 million *

Beef Checkoff of $1/head
About 80 million head traded

**Figure 5–2. Organizational Structure of the National Beef Promotion
Programs, 1990–91**

Source: Annual Reports of Beef Board and Beef Councils.
*Estimated

beef councils (Table 5–11). Those funds, along with $0.4 million received from processors, packers, and purveyors in the form of voluntary contributions and dues, along with money received for services and interest on funds, provide the National Beef Industry Council with $57.0 million to invest in beef promotion and research activities. Of this total, 67 percent was invested in promotion, 17 percent in consumer and producer information, and 8.5 percent in research.

Program Activities. The Beef Industry Council identifies in its annual reports a multidimensional promotion effort that includes research, advertising, consumer information, education, industry feedback, and food service and retail promotion. Research involves projects on diet and health issues, new product development, and marketing. Research has been used to help prove that beef is leaner and lower in calories and cholesterol than many consumers believe. This research has also been used to help identify new markets and products for beef producers so that the industry can respond positively to the health-conscious consumer.

Advertising is heavy on television but also includes radio and print. Television personalities have been used in "Real Food for Real People" campaigns to position beef as a great-tasting, convenient, nutritious food that fits into today's life-styles. Print ads and recognizable personalities on radio have been used to convince infrequent beef users that beef is good for

Table 5–10
Revenue and Expenditures of the Beef Promotion and Research Board, 1988, 1990, and 1991

Category	FY 1988	FY 1990	FY 1991
Revenue			
Assessments	$45.1	$43.5	$43.1
Interest	1.7	1.7	2.2
Other	—	0.1	—
Total revenue	$46.9	$45.2	$45.4
Expenses			
Promotion	$28.1	$29.1	$30.3
Research	0.7	4.7	2.6
Consumer information	1.8	6.4	4.1
Industry information	0.5	4.3	3.4
Producer communications	3.4	1.2	1.4
Foreign marketing	—	1.1	3.2
Program development	—	0.3	0.3
Program evaluation	—	0.1	—
Total program expenses	$34.6	$47.1	$45.3
Administration	1.7	1.7	1.8
Total expenses	$36.3	$48.8	$47.1

Source: Beef Promotion and Research Board annual reports.
Note: Columns may not add due to rounding. Amounts shown in millions of dollars.

Table 5–11
Revenue Source and Program Expenditures of the National Live Stock
and Meat Board on Beef/Veal Promotion, 1986, 1990, and 1991

Item	FY 1986	FY 1990	FY 1991[9]
Revenue Source			
Beef Promotion Board	$0.0	$47.7	$37.9
State check-off	12.5	25.2	17.8
Processors	0.7	0.6	0.4
Services/Interest	1.0	0.9	0.9
Total	$14.2	$74.4	$57.0
Program expenditures			
Research	$1.8	$5.4	$4.9
Information	2.0	12.7	8.0
Promotion	10.2	52.7	38.7
Industry communication	—	—	1.8
Administration	0.8	1.7	3.7
Total	$14.8	$72.5	$57.1

Source: National Live Stock and Meat Board annual reports.
Note: Amounts shown in millions of dollars.
[9] Year ending September 30.

them and fits their life-styles. The Beef Industry Council also supported research that led to the development of a "lean" hamburger that in 1992 was sold nationwide by a major fast-food company.

A "Beef is Back" public relations campaign was used to enhance the national advertising effort. Top chefs, athletes, nutrition experts, and a "National Beef Cook-Off" were used to gain positive media coverage. As a result, positive articles appeared in *Newsweek* and the *New York Times*. Positive television coverage occurred on the "CBS Evening News," CNN, and "The Wall Street Journal Report." This consumer information effort provides the industry positive exposure to millions of individuals at a modest cost.

Under the title of education, the council brochures (*Exploring Meat and Health*), diet kits (*A Change of Plate*) and booklets for physicians (*A Good Start* and *A Food Guide for the First Five Years*). This information is used to encourage professionals in the science and medical communities to put beef in a positive light when they counsel consumers. The information must be technically accurate and based on valid research to be creditable. Also, a newspaper is used to keep producers informed of current views. A monthly magazine is published for the meat processing industry, and a radio news line is distributed to farm broadcasters. Broadcasters can also call a toll-free number for prerecorded radio stories.

In addition, the Beef Industry Council conducts promotion efforts to encourage the food service industry to add new beef dishes to their menu. "Meat merchandising kits" and fact sheets are provided to retail food stores to encourage them to promote the sale of beef. In a joint effort with the American Dairy Association, "gourmet cheeseburgers" were merchandised in retail stores and food service establishments. The market research conducted by the council indicates that consumers are more aware of the positive attributes of beef than they were prior to the industries enhanced promotion campaign. There is some indication that the industry is serving customers a greater variety of beef cuts in a size and style more consistent with current attitudes.

Summary. The national beef promotion program is supported by all producers of beef because of the nationally mandated nonrefundable assessment on all bovine animals sold for beef. This coverage of the industry is complete. The continuing concern over health issues associated with beef consumption, the welfare of beef producers, and a periodically depressed price situation have provided the economic and political basis to support the mandatory checkoff.

The United Soybean Board

Collection of the assessment for the national soybean program is the responsibility of the sixty-three member United Soybean Board. Program activities are carried out under contract by the American Soybean Association, which lobbied for and sponsored the enabling legislation. This national program provides for uniform assessments for all producers in the United States and helps coordinate promotion programs for many of the state organizations already in existence. Twenty-nine qualified state soybean boards collect the assessments, which began September 1, 1991, at 0.5 percent of net market value, yielding about $40 million. A referendum was set for eighteen or thirty-six months from July 9, 1990; ten percent of the funds collected prior to the referendum were to be set aside for refunds. After the referendum, a refund provision will probably continue but be limited to 10 percent of the board's income. Of the $40 million to be collected, about one-half will be retained by the state boards. The national board in 1992 allocated 34 percent of the remainder to international promotion, 28 percent to research, 16 percent to promotions and consumer information, and 11 percent each to producer communications and industry information.[40]

Soybeans are a major export crop, with a large portion going into industrial uses. The commodity is not visible to consumers; as a result, most of the promotion dollars are invested in export promotion, process and product research, and industry promotion activities. Very little is invested in direct consumer advertising. Program activities and focus will likely change, however, as the board gains experience and a better understanding of what can and cannot be done with promotion activities and with newly developing soybean products.

The Cotton Board

The cotton program, created by Cotton,Inc., in 1965, is the oldest stand-alone federal program, after those for wool and mohair. The federal program was first authorized in 1966; it began as part of a federal grant program to deal with the low price and income problem of cotton growers. A promotion and research program to expand demand was coupled with the price support program. For the years 1972 through 1977, Congress authorized the deduction of up to $10 million annually from the price support payments to cotton growers, to be used for promotion and market development. Since 1977, however, all the funds have come from producer checkoffs. The funding level of $25 million prior to 1990 was what remained after 35 percent of the assessment had been refunded. In 1990, the refund authority was terminated, and authority was granted for assessment on imports; as a result, the funding level has increased to $38 million. The Cotton Board collects the assessment and retains about $1.5 million for administration, producer relations and research. The balance is forwarded to Cotton, Inc., which conducts, under contract, both domestic and foreign advertising and promotion activities (Table 5–12). About one-half of the funds are used for technical research and technical support to the industries that use cotton. More of the balance is used to advertise and promote cotton at the consumer level.

To many, this producer-funded research and promotion program represents a great success story. In 1970, double knits dominated the apparel industry, and cotton was considered to have a limited future. In 1975, cotton's retail share of the apparel and home fabric market was only 34 percent. By 1988, though, cotton's share had increased to 51 percent and continued to grow. Many feel that the ability to compete is a result of new technology stemming from research in fabric production that has been funded in part by the cotton growers' research and promotion program.

The National Pork Promotion Program

Organization and Funding. The National Pork Promotion Program is administered by the National Pork Board, which is made up of fifteen producers or importers who serve a three-year term. The producers must represent at least twelve states. The assessment rate was initially 0.25 percent of market value, but this was increased to 0.35 percent of market value effective December 1, 1991. The board is authorized to increase the amount by 0.10 percentage points annually to a maximum of 0.50 percent. The current rate of 0.35 percent generates a producer checkoff income of about $40 million annually.

Initial legislation, as in the beef program, required cooperation with existing local and national organizations. Different from the beef industry program, however, the funds are forwarded directly by the collecting person

Table 5–12
Cotton Incorporated Budgets, 1988, 1990, and 1991

Item	1988	1990	1991
Agricultural research			
Farm-to-mill	$392	$444	$361
Crop improvement	729	832	938
Fiber quality research			
Fiber quality	892	881	1,120
Textile research and implementation			
Fabric development	1,093	1,066	1,040
Technical services	1,128	1,571	1,949
Product and process research	677	435	453
Textile research implementation	—	—	230
Nonwovens/floor coverings	—	657	723
Fiber processing/data research	821	821	1,087
International marketing			
Technical services	184	309	446
New products	689	537	341
Fiber quality	222	284	344
Meetings/presentations	258	176	274
Foreign services	97	160	636
Targeted export assistance	—	1,000	1,000
U.S. marketing	2,153	891	880
Market development	768	600	548
Marketing services			
Advertising and public relations	8,930	12,093	12,226
Retail merchandising	210	853	790
Fashion marketing	1,043	987	1,125
Administrative services	1,855	1,953	2,042
Total	$22,141	$26,550	$28,553

Source: Cotton Incorporated annual reports.
Note: Amounts shown in thousands of dollars.

to the National Pork Board. It is mandatory that the pork board distributes some of these funds to state associations. The amount to be distributed is determined by the national pork producers' delegate body, but it cannot be less than 16.5 percent of the revenue generated from that state's marketings. The delegate body, appointed by the U. S. Secretary of Agriculture is currently composed of approximately 170 pork producers nominated from each state, as well as importer representatives. The delegate body meets once a year to set the national checkoff rate, determine the percentage of checkoff funds to be returned to each state, and nominate producers and/or importers to serve on the National Pork Board. Of the total distribution of funds in 1991, about 18 percent was distributed to the state associations. The board invested 78 percent in promotion, research, and consumer information activities, and about 4 percent was used to cover the cost of operations (Table 5–13).

Table 5–13
Revenue and Expenditures of National Pork Board, 1989,
1990, and 1991

Item	1989	1990	1991
Revenue			
Producer checkoff income	$26.7	$31.3	$29.9
Interest income	0.4	0.5	0.4
Other income	—	—	0.2
Total revenue	$27.1	$31.8	$30.5
Mandatory expenses			
Mandatory distribution to state			
associations	$5.7	$6.6	$6.3
National Park Producers Council	5.5	—	—
Total mandatory expenses	$11.2	$6.6	$6.3
Program funding			
Promotion	$12.0	$14.1	$18.6
Research	1.8	3.5	4.2
Consumer information	1.7	2.8	3.6
Total program	$15.5	$20.4	$26.4
Operations			
Administration	$.3	$.3	$.3
Resource management	0.4	0.4	0.4
Policy development	0.2	0.2	0.2
Communication	0.5	0.5	0.5
Total operations	$1.4	$1.4	$1.4
Total expenses	$28.1	$28.4	$34.0

Source: National Pork Board annual reports.
Note: Columns may not add due to rounding. Amounts shown in millions of dollars.

Program Activities. The pork board contracts with several existing industry organizations to carry out its programs. The National Pork Producers' Council, which also sponsored the legislation for the national program, is the primary contractor, conducting checkoff-funded programs in the areas of consumer advertising and promotion, retail merchandising, product improvement and production technology, food service, consumer affairs, and foreign market development. The National Pork Producers' Council then further contracts with the U.S. Meat Export Federation to do specific foreign promotions. Another primary contractor is the National Live Stock and Meat Board's Pork Industry Group. This group conducts checkoff programs in the area of consumer information, nutrition and new product research, and education. These contract arrangements are, according to the 1991 annual report of the National Pork Board, "in accordance with producers' wishes not to create additional levels of bureaucracy or duplication of effort, thus more efficiently and effectively utilizing producer checkoff funds." (p. 4).

Early in the development of the National Pork Promotion Program, the advertising agency working with the board created the message, "Pork, the Other White Meat." This registered phrase is used in order to challenge the misconceptions that consumers have that pork is high in fat, calories, and cholesterol. The message positions pork alongside traditional white meats such as poultry, turkey, and fish as a nutritious, healthful food item. The promotion program is heavily weighted toward media advertising, with 45 percent of the program funds being used for that purpose. When one adds other nonmedia forms of promotion, the total allocation is about 63 percent; the balance of the program funds is used for research (17 percent) and consumer information (20 percent).

In their advertisements, the pork board targets women between twenty-five and fifty-four years of age. The board's research indicates 82 percent of consumers polled in selected targeted markets now have total recall of the white-meat message. The "Pork, the Other White Meat" message has been used in television commercials (initially in the major metropolitan markets) and in consumer magazines; in 1991, television advertising was expanded to national networks and cable. The board also is heavily involved in retail merchandising through five regional merchandisers who make personal contacts with retail meat directors across the nation. To entice local retailers to participate in pork promotion programs, the board offers cooperative advertising funding, posters, recipes, product labels, and other point-of-purchase materials. It also has been heavily involved in tie-in promotion campaigns with other food manufacturers.

The pork board has worked very hard to get retailers heavily involved in promoting pork. Direct contacts and retail training seminars are used to show retailers how to increase pork sales and provide tips on how to talk to consumers. Meat-cutting demonstrations and packaging tips are also offered. Consumer information programs aimed at informing doctors, dietitians, and other health care professionals about pork's positive nutritional profile are conducted. In its 1991 report, the pork board indicated that 48,000 dieticians and 108,000 physicians had been exposed to its promotion material.

The board also has an information bureau that in 1991 answered 5,000 calls on topics ranging from cooking tips to historical data, recipes, food safety, and nutrition information. Through its public relation activities, it develops key pork messages and recipes that appear in newspapers and magazines throughout America. Its educational program is an attempt to reach out to home economics teachers throughout the country with information about pork. It has developed videos, teacher guides, student activity sheets, a wall chart of pork cuts, and an evaluation form to help gauge the program's effectiveness.

As with the national Beef Promotion and Research Board, the National Pork Board has funded new product development projects to design low-fat products for use in fast-food outlets. Just as the beef industry has a "lean" hamburger, the pork industry now has a "lean" sausage. The pork board works closely with such fast-food retailers as McDonald's and Burger King to encourage them to increase the number and variety of offerings using pork meat. Noncommercial food service outlets (such as corporate cafeterias, schools, and hospitals) are also targeted with pork menus and recipes.

To improve the quality of the product that goes to the consumer, the board has established a "pork quality assurance program." In its 1991 report, it shows that producers representing nearly one-half of the nation's hog production enrolled in the program. This program is designed to encourage producers and processors to deliver the type and quality of meat that consumers really prefer. Considered very important by the pork board is its introduction of trademarked bonus pork cuts. Through 1991, it had developed three: "Chef's Prime," "Chef's Prime Fillet," and "American Cut."

Along with this quality assurance program, the board has developed a foreign market development program to increase export volume; prior to 1991, it had targeted Japan and Mexico. According to the 1991 annual report, it had been quite successful through its emphasis on the pork quality assurance program, the use of point-of-sale material, and direct contact with importers. From the annual report, it also appears that the board is embarking on a very aggressive export promotion campaign in cooperation with pork exporters and other meat-exporting organizations.

The American Egg Board

The egg program was one of the two smallest at the national level in the mid-1980s, with a budget of about $2.5 million. The national budget was much larger in 1974, however, when the United Egg Producers originally had lobbied successfully for the legislation. Until 1990, the egg promotion order required that assessments be refunded on request. Initially, a small number requested refunds, so that the national budget was near $5 million. In 1988, 45 percent of the assessment was refunded. But in 1990, the refund provision was terminated, and assessment income exceeded $7 million in 1990 and 1991. This is an example of the free-rider problem associated with a refund provision.

The American Egg Board is responsible for the national program. In addition to the national program, several states have assessments and programs of their own. Eggs represent a commodity that has been subjected to a tremendous amount of adverse publicity; high in cholesterol content, their consumption is believed to be linked to heart disease. Brown and Schrader (1990) provided quantifiable evidence that the presence of cholesterol information decreased the demand for eggs. Eggs have also been connected with illness and death caused by salmonella poisoning. The egg promotion programs thus has focused on trying to create a more positive image by focusing on the nutrient value and the many uses of eggs in cooking and meal preparations. The egg board also began a research effort in 1991 to determine more specifically the effect ("if any") of eating eggs on blood cholesterol level. Because of the adverse publicity, some of the board's effort have been defensive, and every attempt is made to focus on the positive attributes of eggs as a healthy food.

With the increase in available funds (Table 5–14), more dollars have been devoted to advertising. Until 1990, most of the funds were used for nutrition research and education program and publicity. The $3 million now allocated, however, is still a small amount for a national program; because of this, the egg board (with the advice of an advertising agency) has decided to target a small segment of the population. All TV advertisements are on syndicated cartoon programs for children. This is a long-term strategy: if children can be informed of the positive attributes of eggs, it is hoped that they will consume more as children and continue to do so as adults. As with all commodity groups, the egg board needs to be cognizant of the political risks of advertising directly and specifically to children's market.

The National Potato Promotion Program

Only about one-third of the national $15 million potato program budget comes from federally legislated assessments; all varieties of Irish potatoes are

Table 5–14
Revenue and Expenditures of the American Egg Board,
1989, 1990, and 1991

Category	1989	1990	1991
Revenue			
Net assessments	$4,303	$7,845[a]	$7, 641
Interest income	88	190	239
Total	$4,391	$8,035	$7,880
Expenses			
Advertising	$384	$3,558	$3,675
Food service	295	301	468
Nutrition	1,285	1,189	1,374
Product/machine development	32	36	12
Consumer education[b]	438	455	540
State support	151	204	306
Materials distribution	80	52	66
Industry relations	200	236	220
Long-range planning	—	—	12
Administration/compliance	443	473	512
Total	$3,308	$6,504	$7,184

Source: American Egg Board annual reports.

Note: Columns may not add due to rounding. Amounts shown in thousands of dollars.

[a] Includes funds released from escrow.

[b] Includes National Egg Cooking Contest.

assessed under the Potato Research and Promotion Act. The balance is collected under the authority of state legislation, with Idaho accounting for another one-third of the total. At the national level, about 18 percent of the assessment was refunded in 1988 (with cotton, the refund authority was terminated in 1990). The National Potato Council was responsible for the initial legislation and was also influential in getting the refund provision eliminated. The National Potato Promotion Board administers the national program, and the state boards coordinate their activities with each other through the potato board.

The 1991 annual report of the National Potato Promotion Board lists the following accomplishments to date: dramatically changed attitudes regarding potato nutrients and calories, rearranged methods of displaying and promoting potatoes in retail supermarkets, overseas markets developed for U.S. potatoes and potato products, partnership with the Snack Food Association in active promotion of potato chips, and creation of a more contemporary image of potatoes among consumers, food media and restaurant chefs. New accomplishments in 1991 included uniting the industry and preparing to respond to food safety issues, developing a CBS radio campaign touting the convenience aspects of potatoes, renewing interest in traditional eastern European potato dishes via an innovative promotional theme, expanding retail merchandising promotions into the summer with a patriotic theme, beginning promotional work with in-store delicatessens, and linking potato growers with positive family values through a contest that recognized outstanding teens. To accomplish this, the board has used radio and print advertising, prepared material for food editors, held special events, had the month of February designated as "Potato Lovers Month," designed promotional material for overseas markets, and developed and distributed nutritional material to schools.

Honey Promotion

The honey promotion program under federal authority started in 1988. The annual promotion budget is just over $2 million. Seven producers, two handlers, two importers, and one honey cooperative representative make up the Honey Board, which is responsible for the collection and disbursement of funds. The American Bee Keepers Association joined honey processors to lobby for the federal honey promotion program legislation. Radio and print media are used to influence consumers directly. Print media are also used to influence the use of honey by bakeries and restaurants. The board has established a honey hotline to respond to food formulation questions and to increase the introduction of new food products with honey as an ingredient.

Governmental support for the honey program extends far beyond concern for honey demand. Government honey stocks have grown over time, at a heavy cost to the public. Even so, probably the most important reason to assure a strong honey market can be made when recognizing the economic value of pollination by the honey bee. One could possibly argue that this commodity is a candidate for direct government promotional support because of the economic benefit that bee pollination has on agriculture. We are not advocating this policy; we simply recognize the uniqueness of the honey industry. It is also this uniqueness and multidimensional value that will likely make it difficult for the industry segments to agree on program strategy.

The Watermelon Promotion Program

The watermelon promotion program was approved by producers in 1989. Leadership for getting this legislation passed is credited to the National Watermelon Association. Program administration is the responsibility of the National Watermelon Promotion Board, which is composed of fourteen producers, fourteen handlers, and one public member. No breakdown of the approximate $1 million budget was available at the time of this writing, but the 1991 program and the 1992 marketing plan included a wide range of promotion activities, including the development of recipes and information about the watermelon and the watermelon industry. This information is distributed to newspaper and magazine food editors, retail food stores, food service operators, and produce associations. The distribution of this information is designed to increase demand by institutional users and to increase consumer awareness of the value and many uses of watermelon as a food. Material distributed in 1992 was used on TV and radio network shows and in newspapers, magazines, and trade journals.

Seafood

Generic promotion in the seafood industry at the national level is almost entirely supported by public funds. The act that established and funded the national program was for a set peroid; of $8.5 million in total promotion funds, 76 percent was from a congressional appropriation to the National Fish and Seafood Promotion Council for domestic promotion. Public funds have been provided for this commodity because of the small nature of the fishing units. In many areas, seafood is a struggling industry, even though the demand for the product is strong. Targeted Export Assistance programs funds account for the balance of the seafood promotion dollars and go to state organizations, Alaska receiving the most money. The TEA funds are used to help develop export markets.

The National Fish and Seafood Council and the Marine and Fisheries Services of the Department of Interior are responsible for program development. In addition to the national program, several states have their own state-funded promotion programs. The Catfish Institute also operates a promotion program that is supported by voluntary checkoffs from feed manufacturers supplying the catfish industry, especially in Alabama and Mississippi. If a catfish feed manufacturer or supplier agrees to participate, it must provide the checkoff against all tonnage sold.

Federal Marketing Order Programs

Promotion programs for fourteen different commodities were operating in 1989 under the authority of the Agricultural Marketing Agreement Act of 1937 (Tables 5–1 and 5–15). California producers supported programs for nuts (almonds and walnuts), fresh fruits (nectarines, peaches, pears, and plums), and dates. Florida producers supported programs for avocados, limes and fresh tomatoes. Producers in Texas supported promotion programs for citrus and melons. Texas producers joined producers in Idaho to support a promotion program for onions. Hawaii papaya producers sup-

Table 5–15
Federal Marketing Orders with Advertising Programs, 1989

Commodity	States	Order Number	Year Started	Total Budget	Promotion Budget
Almonds	CA	981	1950	$914	$744
Avocados	FL	915	1954	59	6
Celery	FL	967	1965	—	50
Cherries (sweet)	WA	923	1957	—	—
Citrus	TX	906	1960	461	461
Dates	CA	987	1955	135	135
Grapes (Tokay)	CA	926	1940	—	26
Limes	FL	911	1955	—	25
Melons	TX	979	1979	172	121
Nectarines	CA	916	1958	1,689	1,580
Olives	CA	932	1965	1,632	1,773
Onions	ID, TX, OR	958	1957	857	736
Papayas	HI	928	1971	127	119
Peaches, fresh	CA	917	1939	1,217	1,179
Pears	CA	917	1939	739	713
Pears, winter	OR, WA, CA	927	1939	2,356	2,246
Plums	CA	917	1939	1,709	1,650
Prunes, dried	CA	993	1949	—	30
Tomatoes, fresh	FL	966	1955	499	391
Walnuts	CA	984	1948	893	639
Totals				$13,459	$12,624

Source: Agricultural Marketing Service, U. S. Department of Agriculture.
Note: Amounts shown in thousands of dollars.

ported a federal marketing order for promotion. Pear producers in the northwestern states also had their own federal marketing order promotion program.

Note that only fruits, vegetables, and nuts have promotion programs under the federal marketing order legislation. With few exceptions, the legislation is restricted to fresh fruits and vegetables. It should also be noted, as mentioned in the preceding chapter, that the primary purpose of federal marketing orders is not promotion; it is the imposition of uniform quality and packaging standards and the regulation of the flow of the commodity to market (Jesse and Johnson, 1981). Producers of milk and eggs could establish promotion programs under this legislation as amended, but they have elected for separate legislation. The promotion activities operating under the federal order program are modest and involve mostly public relations activities, educational programs, research, and some print and radio advertising.

New Programs in the Making

As of April 1992, fresh mushroom, pecan and lime promotion orders were in the rule-making process within the U.S. Department of Agriculture. The pecan and lime orders were further along; assessments on pecans will generate about $6 million for research and promotion, and the lime program will yield about $2 million annually. The fresh mushroom program requires an up-front referendum before assessments can begin. Lime and pecan growers will be asked to approve their programs twenty-four months after they begin.

The fluid milk processor assessment, authorized in 1990, would provide funds to substantially increase the investment in fluid milk advertising. As of early 1992, various proposals were being discussed, with the Milk Industry Foundation taking the lead in getting the fluid milk processing industry to consider the alternatives authorized in the legislation. If the industry can agree on the terms for a proposed program, then the Secretary of Agriculture will follow due process as specified in the legislation. A referendum is required prior to implementation.

In a few instances, several commodity groups have joined together. The fresh vegetable industry as of this writing was in the process of trying to obtain legislative authority for a national promotion program. Fresh vegetables have many characteristics in common, including freshness, healthfulness, low calorie content, crispness, nutrition, and attractiveness. This is an example of collective action by a larger group to increase the scope of coverage and to focus on the common attributes of a mix of commodities. It is also a way to accumulate a large enough pool of funds to achieve economic efficiency in the management and implementation of a promotion effort. If the various segments of the vegetable industry can agree on terms of a program, the diversity of interests and marketing conditions under which they operate will provide a major challenge in program planning and implementation.

Some observations about the Federal Promotion Programs

The federal promotion programs have several things in common. First, each is administered by a complex organizational arrangement. Each has a national governing board; each has a national administrative staff, and each contracts with other organizations for delivery of services and programs. The organizational structure is political, and the programs are fragmented. The cotton promotion program is perhaps the least fragmented because it is conducted by one national organization, which receives all of its funds from the national cotton promotion board. The dairy, beef, and pork programs involve not only national boards for each but also several state or regional promotion organizations. These local and regional organizations also have boards of directors and a management staff.

Second, the federal programs consist of a mix of media advertising, trade promotion, consumer and trade education, public relations, and research. Television advertising is important and dominates in groups with large budgets.

Third, each commodity has gone through periods, sometimes extended, of low prices brought on by production increases greater than the market could accommodate at reasonable prices, by contracting demand, or by a combination of the two. But almost all commodities go through price cycles, and price is normally considered (especially by economists) to be the primary adjustment factor to balance demand against available supplies. The ever-changing market environment has provided the motivation and justification for the establishment and continued existence of most of the national commodity promotion programs.

A Changing Market Environment

Competition from Man-Made Fibers. The two commodities with early legislative authority, wool and cotton, faced a rapidly declining market because of the introduction of man-made or synthetic fibers (such as rayon), following World War II. These two commodities faced very favorable market conditions through the 1940s because of the strong demand generated by World War II. Production had expanded dramatically because of the favorable prices. The rayon fibers, also a by-product of the war effort, were less expensive to produce and had some characteristics preferred by the textile industry and consumers; in addition, the prices of wool and cotton were supported by the federal government. Faced with increasing program costs, Congress passed separate acts to authorize research and promotion efforts to increase the demand for these natural fibers. In addition, it authorized the Department of Agriculture to divert a portion of the support payment of each producer to the research and promotion effort. Initially, a large part of the effort was invested in technical and new product research; as new ways to handle the fibers were developed, the money was used for promotion, education, and technical assistance. The cotton promotion and research effort is viewed as having been very successful. The wool promotion and research effort also is considered successful by many interested observers.

Health Fears, Changing Life-Styles, and Declining Markets. The potato and egg industries have very dissimilar markets, but per capita consumption for both had been declining for several years by the 1970s, due in part to health concerns. Potatoes were considered fattening. Eggs were shunned because of their high cholesterol content and fear that consumption was linked to risk of heart disease. Although overexpansion of production was a major cause of cyclically low prices, there was also a perception in the industry that part of the problem was in the marketplace. Neither industry was known for creative marketing, so there was an idea that the problem could be solved, at least partially, by more aggressive promotion. The promotion programs were intended to counter the negative images and to develop new products or ways to use eggs and potatoes. The market for potatoes has expanded dramatically, at least in part because of the use of potatoes in the growing fast-food market. Demand for eggs has continued to weaken, at least in part because of the continuing concern about cholesterol. Price stability has not been realized in either case, because price is primarily a supply adjustment problem.

The demand for beef, and pork products also suffered as well because of the perception that the fat content of the products was high, contained cholesterol, and was linked to heart diseases. The dairy industry has also been negatively affected by health concerns. Chang and Kinnucan (1991b) provide empirical evidence that the "measured consumer awareness of the health effects of blood cholesterol has contributed to the secular decline in butter consumption in Canada (p. 1195)." The study further indicates that despite unfavorable information the industry advertising campaign was shown to have a positive effect on butter demand.

Burdensome Government Stocks. The dairy industry has had a well-developed and organized promotion and research effort funded by dairy farmers for many years. Dairy industry leaders had been trying for several years to obtain mandatory nonrefundable assessment authority (that is, require all producers to share in the cost of market expansion activities). A large portion of the nation's milk supply was already being assessed under state legislation prior to 1983; California, New York, and Wisconsin had passed nonrefundable assessment legislation in the 1970s. Although the momentum was already there, the primary force behind the passage of the legislation in 1983 was the high cost to the government of the dairy price support program, which had reached almost $3 billion annually by the early 1980s. Dairy promotion programs, one of four provisions of the Dairy and Tobacco Adjustment Act of 1983, required all dairy farmers to pay for a program that would expand the demand for milk and thus help reduce the quantity purchased by the government support prices. The promotion part was one of four provisions designed simultaneously to reduce milk supplies and to strengthen the demand for dairy products.[41]

As with the dairy industry, Congress had gotten itself into a high-cost support program for the honey industry by the early 1980s. By 1985, the stocks of honey in storage amounted to about 72 percent of annual domestic production. The high support price encouraged excess production and large import volumes.

Depressed Farm Prices. Prices for beef at the farm are cyclical, and at times the prices are depressed to below the cost of production for many producers. This cyclical behavior runs counter to the production cycle. In addition, red meat has received a great deal of negative press because of the perceived relation of animal fat intake and cholesterol to the incidence of heart disease. Per capita consumption of beef hit its peak level in 1976 at 94.4 pounds. By 1985 per capita consumption was 79.1 pounds, and the 1989 forecast was 69.9 pounds, less than per capita poultry consumption for the first time in history. The desire to obtain better prices and to counter the negative images, as well as the increased competition from poultry and fish, provided the motivation for a beef promotion program.

The beef promotion program enacted in 1985 followed about ten years of lobbying. The industry leaders perceived the sometimes low prices as being the result of health concerns about their product and shrinking demand. Enabling legislation for a beef promotion program was first passed in 1976; it authorized a program only if the producers approved in advance. The 1985 amendment to the earlier legislation specified a mandatory assessment and a program in advance of any referendum. When asked to vote eighteen months later, 79 percent voted for continuation.

Low producer prices and weakening demand, brought on in part by the negative attitude toward red meat, were also among the motivations for the enactment of a national pork promotion program. Like the beef producers, the pork producers approved a national promotion program only after they had been required to contribute for a period of time and after a program had been put in place. When they did vote, 78 percent approved continuation.

Positive Public Attitudes Toward Checkoff Programs

In 1992, most commodity groups and federal and state legislators seemed to have a positive view about commodity checkoff programs to fund generic promotion efforts. It is almost certain that, with the passage of time, more commodity groups will ask for and obtain legislative authority for checkoffs to support promotion efforts. Those that have had authority but with refund provisions have been able to get the provisions eliminated. The perception in 1992 is that generic promotion and research can provide positive benefits to a commodity group, and that a mandatory nonrefundable assessment is desirable because it is the only way to ensure that every producer shares in the cost of the effort in relation to the benefit realized.

A Complex Set of Promotion Programs Activities

Most groups utilize almost all of the program activities available, in one form or another. Those with the largest budgets are able to develop a comprehensive approach and use all of the options. Thus, the dairy, beef, pork, and cotton organizations have program activities that cover almost the complete range of possibilities. They spend a large portion of their budget on media, primarily television. The dairy, beef, and pork groups invest sizable sums in nutrition-and-health-related research. The cotton group focuses more on new product and process research and technical assistance to the textile industry.

The potato group has focused on print advertising rather than TV and radio, with the justification that they have a complex nutritional message to deliver to consumers. Major emphasis is placed also on in-store promotion, consumer education, and publicity for domestic promotions. For the export market, they have focused on a small number of countries (with Japan getting the most attention) and utilize consumer education, in-store promotion, and food service promotion.

The egg group, because of its small budget at the national level, focuses on public relations, nutrition and health research, and consumer education. State program activities operate independent of the national program. The California program, because of a larger budget and a smaller market area to cover, involves heavy media advertising and retail promotion activities in California and the adjoining states where their eggs are marketed.

The wool group promotes wool and lamb through technical research and direct promotion to the textile industry. Consumer advertising is mostly in the form of print media designed to explain the advantages of wool as a natural fiber. Because wool is an ingredient in the textile industry, the group funds technical support to the clothing, carpet, and furniture industries. It also works with the textile design industry to influence the selection of wool as a basic material.

Creative Advertising Themes

The commodity promotion groups identify commodity or product attributes on which to focus their advertising and promotion campaigns. They develop themes, slogans, or messages around these attributes and direct them to target audiences that they hope will be most receptive and/or responsive. For food products, the generic message often focuses on nutrition and health attributes, but sometimes the focus is on other attributes or product characteristics such as taste, satisfaction or prestige. Because health is and has been an issue for dairy products, beef, and pork, the organizations for each have identified positive product characteristics to promote. They have supported research either to counter the negative image directly or to identify attributes that will offset the negative attribute. Clearly, dairy, beef, and pork products contain attributes perceived by many as negative, yet they also contain beneficial and essential nutrients.

The dairy group uses "Milk, It Does a Body Good" as a theme for fluid milk and uses youth, excitement, and healthy bodies in its TV commercials. It has also identified calcium as an important nutrient component of dairy products and has supplied consumers, health professionals, food editors, and schoolteachers with technical information about the beneficial value of dairy products in the diet. The calcium message requires the transfer of more information than can be carried in a fifteen- or thirty-second TV or radio commercial, so print media are used. Themes for the other dairy products include "Don't forget the cheese" (with the commercials directed toward light and medium users of all ages), "Give 'em a little pat of butter," and "Only 36 calories, the same as margarine." Ice cream promotion was first focused on television advertisements directed toward consumers; later the focus was on restaurants and retail stores, with the theme of "Scoop Up Profits with Ice Cream."

The beef promotion organizations do not confront the heart disease issue directly. Instead, they try to move the industry toward delivering leaner meat to the consumer, at which point they can promote the protein content of meat, the benefits of beef in the diet, its taste, the prestige factor, and the idea that beef can be served and enjoyed in small portions. Their themes include "Beef, the Real Food" and "Today's Trimmer Beef." The strategy is to encourage consumers to consume smaller, leaner portions more often. "Think Beef" is used to encourage food service operators to include beef in menu planning. In 1992, the industry changed the advertising theme to "Beef: It's What's for Dinner."

The pork promotion organizations have developed a strategy to reposition pork as a white meat rather than a red meat. Their theme is "Pork, the Other White Meat." As a red meat, pork has had the negative image of being associated with other red meats that have negative health images. Positioning pork as a new product alongside chicken and fish associates pork with meat products that in the 1980s, had positive health and nutrition images. The National Pork Producers Council has developed a trademark term, "American Cut," for a particular lean cut of pork for the restaurant or home menu.

The cotton group has established the "Seal of Cotton," to be used in all commercials and on textiles containing all cotton, as well as the term "Natural Blend" to mean 100 percent cotton. An important target audience for cotton is the textile and textile design industry. To help firms in the use of cotton, they have established the Cottonworks Fabric Library, with locations in New York City, Dallas, and Los Angeles.

The potato group first supported research to document the nutrient value of potatoes. They then developed an educational and advertising campaign to position potatoes as high in nutritional value and low in calorie count. When the promotion program began, potatoes were considered low in nutrients and fattening. The promotion group feels that the strategy has changed the image substantially, and it decided in 1988 that it was time to change strategy (Mercer, 1988) to stress the convenience of potatoes in response to the perceived changes in the current life-style of the U.S. consumer. Annual per capita consumption of potatoes, which is as much a function of available supplies as of demand, has averaged between 110 pounds and 120 pounds during the past fifteen years.

The honey group uses a symbol (the "Honeybear") to portray "a forgivable greediness for a fabulous taste—and more." The service mark can be used on manufactured food products when honey is the primary sweetener. Because the group's budget is small, most of the promotion is directed to food manufactures, food service establishments, and food editors, with a modest portion of the budget for print and radio advertisements. They have joined with food manufacturers in offering coupons; one coupon provides a mail-in offer for a "Honey, I Love You" Honeybear with proof of purchase. The campaign focuses on the diversity of uses and value as a sweetener.

Other Reasons

Perhaps one of the most important reasons for the increase in commodity promotion activities is the development of media and media technology. The availability of television provides instant access to the homes of many more people and provides an opportunity for more creative ways to provide information directly to consumers.

With the improvement in communication and transportation technology, more emphasis has been placed on international trade, and international trade has become very competitive. The collective action of commodity groups provides a mechanism for individual producers to have a say in the competitive international market.

Promotion Programs under State Legislation

Forty-three states have some form of legislation that permits producers of commodities to assess themselves to support market development and promotion activities (Table 5–16).[42] In total, these states have 261 commodity promotion programs, almost all funded by producer checkoffs. The legislative basis and the different kind of arrangements are discussed in some detail in the previous chapter; in 1989, the 261 programs represented 55 commodities (Table 5–17). Some of these programs operate quite independent of any national affiliation (for example, the citrus program in Florida and the raisin program in California). Others serve as a means of collecting money that is forwarded to a national organization.

Many of the state-legislated programs that now exist were put in place initially in the period from 1961 to 1980; however more than 70 were put in place between 1980 and 1986 (Spatz, 1989, p. 5). The total amount of money involved is a little hard to identify, but by 1989 the amount easily exceeded $250 million—not including some part of the $200 million dairy promotion program, where state legislation directs about $120 million to local organizations. The number of dollars involved has grown substantially during the last thirty years. Spatz estimated that the combined budgets for all state-legislated programs, excluding dairy, amounted to over $200 million in 1986.[43] Morrison (1984) estimated an amount slightly over $100 million in 1979, including dairy promotions.

The states with the largest number of commodities involved are California, Oregon, and Washington (Table 5–17); the state with the largest combined budgets are California and Florida. California has a large total program because of the large number of commodities involved and because some of them have large budgets. In 1989, California commodity groups had 23 state-legislated promotion programs involving significant promotion. The largest were dairy products ($20 million), raisins ($20 million), avocadoes and prunes ($8 million each), and table grapes ($7 million). The Florida program is large because of the budget of the Florida Citrus Commission, which in 1989 was over $70 million. State programs for dairy products, beef, and pork that were already in place in many states were forerunners for the national legislation for those commodities that became part of the farm bills of 1983, 1985, and 1990. Many of the commodity groups that now have programs in several states will likely obtain federally legislated programs during the last decade of the twentieth century.

The Evolution of State Programs

The evolutionary process for major commodities that are produced in several states is as follows. One or more states where the commodity is important economically will enact legislation for a state program. After some time, an attempt will be made to make the assessment rate uniform across all states. A movement to enact federal legislation with a no-refund clause then will begin to make sure that every producer in the United States shares equally in the costs of the program. The last such major commodity group to obtain federal legislation that had gone through a long evolutionary process was soybeans, in 1990.

The commodity groups that have state-legislated programs in several states but do not yet have federally legislated programs are corn, wheat, apples, peaches, peanuts, rice, and wine. A national program for wheat was in place, but refunds were possible and the assessment was against end-product manufacturers and not producers. This national program was terminated in 1989. The state programs assess producers.

The California egg promotion program has a budget of over $5 million, while the American Egg Board's budget in 1988 was about $2.6 million. The National Potato Promotion Board's budget was slightly under $5 million, while Idaho's budget was almost $6 million. With the larger budget and a smaller market area to cover, the California egg promotion program involved paid media advertising; the national program did not. With the removal of the refund provision for eggs and potatoes, the program mix at the national level will change.

States with Concentrations of Production

Most of the other state-legislated programs are for commodities that are produced in a small number of states (such as hops in Washington and ginseng roots in Wisconsin), or where production is concentrated in a small number of geographically separated states (such as oranges in California and Florida). Unless the budget of a commodity promotion group exceeds $5 million (in 1989 dollars), it is not likely that its promotion program will involve television advertising. Most of the programs with small budgets will involve public relations, representation at trade shows, and producer and processor education on how best to use, merchandise, or market the commodity and its products. As budgets increase in size, it is likely that the promotion activities will involve, in order, consumer education; market, product, and process research; and then print and radio advertising. Also, as the advertising budget increases in size, the media advertising effort will expand from local or regional advertising to national and network advertising. The nature of the program will, of course, depend on the nature of the commodity, the nature of the product at the consumer level, and the geographical, actual, or potential spread of the market.

Three of the largest state-legislated programs are Florida citrus, California raisins, and Washington apples. They utilize a wide range of promotion strategies. The first two spend substantial sums on media advertising, espe-

Table 5–16
States with Legislated Commodity Promotion Programs, 1989

State	Number	Commodity
Alabama	5	Beef; cotton; dairy; peanuts; soybeans
Alaska	1	Marine products
Arizona	2	Beef; wheat
Arkansas	2	Beef cattle; soybeans
California	23	Apricots; fresh artichokes; avocados; dry beans; beef and veal; carrots; eggs and egg products; figs; table grapes; honey; kiwi fruit; iceberg lettuce; cling peaches; pistachios; prunes; raisins; rice; fresh and frozen strawberries; fresh tomatoes; turkey; walnuts; wheat; wine; and wine grapes
Colorado	5	Apples; peaches; potatoes; Irish potatoes; wheat
Connecticut	1	Apples
Delaware	0	
Florida	4	Citrus; peanuts; soybeans; tobacco
Georgia	9	Apples; cotton; dairy; eggs; peaches; peanuts; sweet potatoes; soybeans; tobacco
Hawaii	0	
Idaho	8	Alfalfa seed; apples; edible dry beans; dairy; dry peas, lentils, chickpeas; potatoes; sheep; wheat
Illinois	7	Apples; beef; corn; eggs; peaches; soybeans; wool
Indiana	2	Beef cattle; turkey
Iowa	7	Beef; corn; eggs; pork; sheep and wool; soybeans; turkey
Kansas	6	Beef; corn; grain sorghum; pork; soybeans; wheat
Kentucky	5	Beef; dairy; pork; soybeans; burley tobacco
Louisiana	4	Crawfish; dairy; rice; soybeans; wheat; corn; milo
Maine	3	Apples; dairy; wild blueberries
Maryland	2	Apples; soybeans
Massachusetts	0	
Michigan	10	Asparagus; dry beans; beef and veal; carrots; tart and sweet cherries; dairy; onions; plums; potatoes; soybeans
Minnesota	8	Dry beans; beef; dairy; eggs; wild rice; soybeans; turkey; wheat
Mississippi	2	Eggs; soybeans
Missouri	10	Apples; beef; corn; dairy; eggs; lamb and wool; peaches; rice; soybeans; turkey
Montana	3	Beef; pork; wheat and barley
Nebraska	7	Beef; corn; eggs and turkeys; grain sorghum; potatoes; soybeans; wheat
Nevada	0	
New Hampshire	1	Dairy
New Jersey	7	Apples; asparagus; dairy; eggs and turkeys; sweet potatoes; white potatoes; soybeans
New Mexico	0	
New York	4	Apples; sour cherries; dairy; wine

Table 5–16 continued

State	Number	Commodity
North Carolina	10	Beef; corn; cotton; eggs; peaches; peanuts; potatoes; soybeans and soybean products; tobacco; fresh tomatoes
North Dakota	9	Barley; dry beans; beef; dairy; potatoes; soybeans; sunflowers; turkey; wheat
Ohio	5	Apples; beef; eggs; grapes and wine; turkey
Oklahoma	5	Beef; peanuts; pecans; pork; wheat
Oregon	23	Beef; highland bentgrass; blueberries; sweet cherries; chewings and creeping red; dungeness crab; cranberries; tall fescue seed; fryers; wine grapes; hazelnuts; hops; onions; orchardgrass seed; bartlett pears; plum and prune (processed); potatoes; rye grass; salmon (troll-caught); seafood (trawl-caught); strawberries; wheat; wool
Pennsylvania	1	Dairy
Rhode Island	0	
South Carolina	6	Beef; dairy; eggs; peaches; pork; soybeans
South Dakota	3	Soybeans; sunflowers; wheat
Tennessee	2	Dairy; soybeans
Texas	7	Corn; milo; peanuts; pork; rice; soybeans; wheat
Utah	5	Apples; beef; sweet cherries; tart cherries; turkey
Vermont	2	Apples; dairy
Virginia	11	Apples; beef; corn; dairy; eggs; marine products; peanuts; pork; sweet potatoes; soybeans; tobacco
Washington	15	Apples; barley; beef; blueberries; cherries; dairy; eggs; hops; dry peas; lentils; chickpeas; potatoes; seed potatoes; poultry (fryers); red raspberries; wheat; wine
West Virginia	0	
Wisconsin	7	Cherries (tart); corn; cranberries; dairy; ginseng root and seed; mint oil; soybeans
Wyoming	2	Beef; wheat
Total (43 states)	261	

Source: Survey files of Karen Spatz, Agricultural Cooperative Service, U.S. Department of Agriculture, and survey by authors.

cially television. Much effort is invested in differentiating the Washington-produced varieties of apples from varieties produced in other states or countries. The Florida citrus program focuses on Florida orange juice. Florida orange juice advertisements did not differentiate Florida juice from juice produced elsewhere until large volumes began to be imported into the United States in the early 1980s (Ward and Kilmer, 1989). Since then, various attempts have been made to position the Florida-produced orange juice as a different and superior product.

U.S. raisins are produced only in California. Therefore, it is not necessary to identify the raisin as distinctively produced in California for the

Table 5–17
Commodities with State-Legislated Promotion Programs, 1989

Commodity	Number	State
Livestock and poultry products	(86)	
Beef	24	Alabama, Arizona, Arkansas, California, Illinois, Indiana, Iowa, Kansas, Kentucky, Michigan, Minnesota, Missouri, Montana, Nebraska, North Carolina, North Dakota, Ohio, Oklahoma, Oregon, South Carolina, Utah, Virginia, Washington, Wyoming
Dairy	20	Alabama, Georgia, Idaho, Kentucky, Louisiana, Maine, Michigan, Minnesota, Missouri, New Hampshire, New Jersey, New York, North Dakota, Pennsylvania, South Carolina, Tennessee, Vermont, Virginia, Washington, Wisconsin
Eggs	14	California, Georgia, Illinois, Iowa, Minnesota, Mississippi, Missouri, Nebraska, New Jersey, North Carolina, Ohio, South Carolina, Virginia, Washington
Pork	11	Alabama, Iowa, Kansas, Kentucky, Louisiana, Montana, North Carolina, Oklahoma, South Carolina, Texas, Virginia
Poultry	2	Oregon, Washington
Sheep and wool	5	Idaho, Illinois, Iowa, Missouri, Oregon
Turkey	10	California, Indiana, Iowa, Minnesota, Missouri, Nebraska, New Jersey, North Dakota, Ohio, Utah
Grains	(41)	
Barley	3	Montana, North Dakota, Washington
Corn	10	Illinois, Iowa, Kansas, Louisiana, Missouri, Nebraska, North Carolina, Texas, Virginia, Wisconsin
Milo	4	Kansas, Louisiana, Nebraska, Texas
Rice	5	California, Louisiana, Minnesota, Missouri, Texas
Seeds	3	Idaho, Oregon, Washington
Wheat	16	Arizona, California, Colorado, Idaho, Kansas, Louisiana, Minnesota, Montana, Nebraska, North Dakota, Oklahoma, Oregon, South Dakota, Texas, Washington, Wyoming
Oilseed crops	(33)	
Peanuts	7	Alabama, Florida, Georgia, North Carolina, Oklahoma, Texas, Virginia
Soybeans	24	Alabama, Arkansas, Florida, Georgia, Illinois, Iowa, Kansas, Kentucky, Louisiana, Maryland, Michigan, Minnesota, Mississippi, Missouri, Nebraska, New Jersey, North Carolina, North Dakota, South Carolina, South Dakota, Tennessee, Texas, Virginia, Wisconsin
Sunflowers	2	North Dakota, South Dakota
Vine and tree fruits	(50)	
Apples	15	Colorado, Connecticut, Georgia, Idaho, Illinois, Maine, Maryland, Missouri, New Jersey, New York, Ohio, Utah, Vermont, Virginia, Washington
Apricots	1	California
Avocados	1	California
Cherries	6	Michigan, New York, Oregon, Utah, Washington, Wisconsin
Citrus	1	Florida
Figs	1	California
Grapes	3	California, Ohio, Oregon

Table 5–17 continued

Commodity	Number	State
Hazelnuts	1	Oregon
Kiwi fruit	1	California
Peaches	7	California, Colorado, Georgia, Illinois, Missouri, North Carolina, South Carolina
Pears	1	Oregon
Pecans	1	Oklahoma
Pistachios	1	California
Plums	2	Michigan, Oregon
Prunes	2	California, Oregon
Raisins	1	California
Walnuts	1	California
Wine	4	California, New York, Ohio, Washington
Vegetables and small fruits	(16)	
Artichokes	1	California
Asparagus	2	Michigan, New Jersey
Blueberries	3	Maine, Oregon, Washington
Carrots	2	California, Michigan
Cranberries	2	Oregon, Wisconsin
Lettuce, iceberg	1	California
Raspberries	1	Washington
Strawberries	2	California, Oregon
Tomatoes	2	California, North Carolina
Bulb and tuber crops	(14)	
Onions	2	Michigan, Oregon
Potatoes	9	Colorado, Idaho, Michigan, Nebraska, New Jersey, North Carolina, North Dakota, Oregon, Washington
Sweet potatoes	3	Georgia, New Jersey, Virginia
Fibers	(3)	
Cotton	3	Alabama, Georgia, North Carolina
Marine products	4	Louisiana, Oregon, Virginia, Alaska
Other	(17)	
Beans, dry	5	California, Idaho, Michigan, Minnesota, North Dakota
Ginseng	1	Wisconsin
Honey	1	California
Hops	2	Oregon, Washington
Lentils, etc.	2	Idaho, Washington
Mint oil	1	Wisconsin
Tobacco	5	Florida, Georgia, Kentucky, North Carolina, Virginia
Total (55 commodities)	264	

Source: Survey files of Karen Spatz, Agricultural Cooperative Service, U.S. Department of Agriculture, and survey of authors.

domestic market. In foreign markets, however, the California raisin group has attempted to identify quite clearly the differences between the California raisin and the sultana raisin produced in other parts of the world. More information is presented here for these three commodities to provide the reader with more insight into how state-legislated programs function.

Florida Citrus

Organization and Funding. The Florida Citrus Commission was established by a special act of the state legislature in 1935. Program policy is the responsibility of a 12-member commission (made up of 7 growers, 3 processors, and 2 fresh fruit shippers) appointed by the governor. A staff of 150 administers the comprehensive program, which includes economic analysis and outlook, scientific research, the collection of statistical data, domestic media advertising, merchandising, and public relations as well as export promotion in Europe and the Far East. A budget of $68.4 million in 1988–89 and $61.2 million in 1991–92 makes the Florida citrus program the largest of any state-legislated promotion program (Table 5–18). Heavy emphasis on media advertising began in the 1960s and in 1991–92 accounted for 53 percent of the total budget. International market development accounts for 16 percent; merchandising, food service, and other marketing programs account for another 12 percent. The balance of the budget (26 percent) is invested in research and administration.

The revenue to support this program is collected in the form of an excise tax on citrus production and on imports, with a separate rate set for oranges, grapefruit, and specialty citrus fruit. Within each type, a separate rate is set

Table 5–18
Program Expenditures of the Florida Department of Citrus,
1988–89 to 1991–92

Category	1988–89	1989–90	1990–91	1991–92 Budget
Advertising				
Processed products	$24,054	$22,352	$27,488	$25,920
Fresh fruit	5,777	2,404	6,304	6,617
Rebate program	9,704	4,430	1,857	0
International marketing	12,159	8,488	12,557	9,943
Merchandising	4,720	4,408	4,782	5,138
Food service	563	563	565	639
Other marketing programs	1,641	1,756	2,068	1,607
Research				
Market	1,164	1,065	1,330	1,599
Economic	377	389	413	442
Scientific	1,793	1,824	2,390	2,337
Public/industry relations	2,249	1,403	1,915	2,461
Administration	4,163	3,977	5,058	4,489
Total	$68,363	$53,060	$66,725	$61,193

Source: Florida Department of Citrus.
Note: Columns do not add due to rounding. Amounts shown in thousands of dollars.

for fresh and processed fruit. The tax rates for 1985–86 and 1988–89 (in parentheses) were as follows per 1⅗ bushel equivalent box: oranges, $0.18 ($0.24) for fresh and $0.145 ($0.217) for processed; grapefruit, $0.25 ($0.31) for fresh and $0.05 ($0.28) for processed; specialty, $0.155 ($0.28) for fresh and $0.145 ($0.155) for processed. Foreign imports into Florida are taxed at the same rate as domestic production.[44] Assessment rates for 1988–89 generated revenues in the amount of $57 million. In addition, the commission received $10.33 million from the Targeted Export Assistance program. Investment and other earnings brought the total for the year to $69.3 million.

Because of freeze damage, Florida citrus production trended downward from 1978–79 to 1984–85, but it is now trending upward. Concurrent with the reduction in domestic production, imports increased dramatically. With increases in domestic supplies, the import volume since has declined. At its low point, Florida orange juice consumed in the United States represented less than 50 percent of the total. By 1998–99, Florida source supply will represent 82 percent, a market share enjoyed in 1980.

Program Activities. The program for Florida citrus focuses heavily on the promotion of processed products and on processed oranges (55 percent in dollar amounts). The balance is used to promote processed grapefruit (16 percent) and fresh oranges, grapefruits and specialty citrus (27 percent). Although the volume of orange juice sales have been relatively steady during the last decade, the market share has declined dramatically because of substantial increases in the consumption of soft drinks, water, and other pure juices, especially apple juice. Market research indicates that the positive image of orange juice has slipped relative to soft drinks.

The strategy of the Florida Citrus Commission is to persuade consumers to choose Florida orange juice over other juices and to position 100% pure orange juice as a refreshment beverage that delivers a unique good-for-you, good-tasting package of benefits. Themes used have included "There's nothing like it in the world" and "It makes you feel so good." This latter theme uses a creative strategy that 100% pure Florida orange juice has a combination of attributes ranging from great taste to great nutritive values that other juices and juice drinks do not have. Network television, spot television, radio, and print ads are all used to convey the message directly to consumers; perhaps the greatest achievement of the commission was the repositioning of orange juice as juice that could be enjoyed and consumed on any occasion and not just for breakfast. In addition, a field staff works directly with supermarkets and food service establishments to encourage them to feature orange juice. A trade incentive program is used to reimburse these retailers for documented promotional activities. The focus of the national promotion programs with the trade is on the healthy profit that can be made by featuring orange juice.

Brand Advertising Rebate Program. To encourage processors to invest in promotion, the commission established a six-year brand advertising rebate program in the 1982–83 crop year. Total expenditures for the program will be $44.4 million. The program is considered successful by some because brand advertising has increased dramatically since the program's inception. Whether this program should continue, however, has been debated. One study suggested that citrus juice brand advertising merely increases market shares of the leading brands without increasing aggregate demand. Other studies indicate complimentarity between the brand and generic advertising in increasing aggregate demand. In 1991 the rebate program was terminated primarily because the rebate had grown too large and was cutting into other program support. Research results that address this issue are discussed in Chapter 7.

Export Promotion. An international marketing effort is an important part of the Florida Citrus Commission's promotion effort. Fresh grapefruit and processed products are promoted in Europe, and fresh grapefruit, fresh oranges, and processed grapefruit are promoted in the Far East. The total value of Florida fresh and processed citrus exports in 1987–88 was $290 million, an all-time high and a 78 percent increase in two years. Almost 60 percent of this was from the export of fresh citrus, mostly grapefruit; the balance was about two-thirds processed orange products and one-third processed grapefruit. The promotion efforts focus heavily on fresh grapefruit in Europe and on fresh citrus in Japan.

The strategy for Europe is to persuade consumers to choose Florida grapefruit over other varieties by positioning it as the sweetest, juiciest, most enjoyable grapefruit available. This strategy is used to justify the price premium that exists. In addition, the commission uses education programs to emphasize the unique characteristics of Florida grapefruit and to inform customer of the best way to select a good grapefruit. In the Far East, the strategy is similar, with more emphasis on expanding distribution and improving the consumer's knowledge about the seasonality and unique attributes of Florida grapefruit and oranges. A combination of media with messages direct to consumers and a field staff working directly with distributors and on public relations is used in all target countries. The combination is tailored to fit the unique situation in each country.

California Raisins

Organization and Funding. The promotion program of the California Raisin Advisory Board has three unique characteristics when compared to other commodity promotion programs. Both the producers and the packers pay an assessment; in 1989, each contributed twenty-eight dollars per ton of free tonnage. The amount of assessment is set each year by the advisory board. There is a limit of 6.5 percent of the anticipated price, with half coming from the packer and half from the grower. There is an advertising rebate program for brand advertising up to 50 percent of actual advertising expenses. If the firms' assessments are not rebated, the money is used for generic promotion. About 30 percent of the packer assessment is rebated each year. The promotion programs operate in conjunction with a federal order set-aside program. The set-aside tonnage is not assessed at the same rate, and the actual assessment depends on the final disposition of that tonnage. This means the advertising and promotion programs can be coordinated with the supply of raisins available in the marketplace. This is accomplished by having the same person as the executive officer for both programs and by having an overlap in board membership. It also means that the assessment rate can be coordinated with program needs.

Because the packers also pay into the promotion program, the board of directors is made up of the same number of packers as growers (seven each). In addition to the fourteen growers and packers, the board has one public member, one representative from the Federal Order Raisin Advisory Board and one from the raisin-producer bargaining association. Board members are nominated by marketing cooperatives and appointed by the California Director of Food and Agriculture.

Program Activities. The program is implemented by a general manager. Three professionals manage the export promotion program, and three the domestic promotion program. According to the general manager, the raisin promotion program was established out of frustration following the end of World War II. During the war, there had been a tremendously strong demand for raisins. The production had expanded sharply, but after World War II the market weakened dramatically. The first attempt to improve conditions was the establishment of a supply management program with a very small amount of money for promotion. But over the years, the growers and packers developed a view that substantial benefits could be realized from an advertising and promotion program. Thus, by 1988–89 the promotion program had a total budget of $23 million. Over half ($15.0 million) was invested in consumer advertising and promotion (Table 5–19), $3.6 million was invested in export promotion activities, and $1.6 was invested in consumer publicity. The balance was invested in industry promotion and publicity, research and special activities, and administration. The budget has declined since the 1988–89 level because of less royalty income from their trademark dancing raisin characters. With a decline in revenue, less money has been allocated to advertising and more to publicity.

During the 1970s, the central focus of the raisin advertising campaign was on the natural characteristics of the product. The board promoted

Table 5–19
Budgeted Expenditures of the California Raisin Advisory Board,
1988–89 to 1990–91

Category	1988–89	1989–90	1990–91
Consumer advertising and promotion	$15,000	$13,400	$8,900
Export promotion	3,600	4,600	3,800
Consumer publicity	1,600	1,500	1,250
Industry promotion and publicity	450	700	1,700
Research	250	340	275
Special activities	400	500	200
Administration	1,800	1,160	1,663
Raisin Bowl	0	200	200
Total	$23,100	$22,400	$17,988

Source: California Raisin Advisory Board.
Note: Amounts shown in thousands of dollars.

raisins as a natural snack for children, with a target audience of mothers. By the end of the decade, this program seemed to have run out of steam. Health and natural were no longer news items; everyone was in the "natural" business. So, during the early 1980s, the board did more research and concluded that there were three perceptions about raisins that were useful: raisins were for snacks, they were valuable for use in the bakery, and they were consumed spontaneously. The board also learned that there was a small but growing market for raisins as food additive. In the early 1980s the board promoted this latter idea, but the impact was modest. In 1985, after more research, it concluded that everybody already knew all there was to know about the rationality of consuming raisins and that the emotional reaction to raisin consumption was very negative.

Probably the most creative advertising campaign among commodity groups came out of the desire to improve the image of raisins in the minds of consumers. The "claymation" animated-raisin commercials have won many advertising awards and are in strong demand. Licensing the use of the animated-raisin trademark to others earned the California Raisin Advisory Board about $3 million in 1988. Packers used the animated raisin for brand advertising; it was also licensed for T-shirts, erasers, and other paraphernalia. But by 1991, revenues from this source had practically vanished. The board's management feels that its program has successfully improved the image of the raisin, but that it is now time to develop a subtle but more aggressive hard-sell approach. It is searching for a solid claim on nutrition.

In addition to the $4.3 million of grower and packer money invested in export promotion, the board obtains Targeted Export Assistance programs funds for foreign market development. The amount of these funds varied from $4 million to $12.5 million annually during the 1980s. Because of differences in culture, tradition, and government regulations, it is necessary to develop a different strategy for each country. The raisin board developed separate strategies for nine European countries and nine Asiatic countries in 1988, but the theme is uniform. The raisin is positioned as a nutritious and natural food. The campaigns stress the value of the raisin in the diet for fitness and as a snack.

Washington Apples

Organization and Funding. The purpose of the Washington Apple Commission is to "create growing worldwide demand for Washington fresh apples by building favorable product awareness and positive industry image; providing consumer trade and grower education; and offering industry leadership, vision, and marketing support in order to provide the best possible return to the grower."[45] This commission was established by state legislation. The thirteen-member board is elected by producers to represent districts of the state; they meet monthly to conduct the required business and to provide direction to the staff. Revenue for the 1990–91 fiscal year was $22.0 million, based on an assessment rate of $0.435 per hundredweight of fresh apples (Table 5–20). In addition, the commission received $3.5 million under the export enhancement programs from the U.S. Department of Agriculture to support apple export promotion.

Table 5–20
Revenues and Expenses of the Washington State Apple Commission, 1987–88 to 1990–91

Category	1987–88	1988–89	1989–90	1990–91
Advertising assessments	$13,425	$14,280	$18,102	$18,096
FAS reimbursements	1,445	1,899	2,637	3,558
Other revenues	169	170	164	376
Total revenue	$15,039	$16,349	$20,903	$22,030
Operating expenses				
Advertising	$6,048	$6,302	$7,331	$7,677
Marketing	3,709	3,684	4,559	4,715
Export	2,112	2,770	3,575	4,618
Food service	558	367	612	963
Communications	850	2,343	1,174	1,443
New markets	261	433	473	527
Administration	795	751	797	1,209
Industry organizations	323	524	540	638
Total operating expenses	$14,656	$17,174	$19,061	$21,790
Net revenue over expenses	$383	($825)	$1,842	$241

Source: Washington State Apple Commission annual reports.
Note: Columns may not add due to rounding. Amounts shown in thousands of dollars.

Revenue increased from 1987–88 to 1989–90 because of larger apple crops. This year-to-year variation in income for commodity promotion programs is typical. Revenue based on assessments per hundredweight or physical unit of measure is higher in heavy crop years and lower in small crop years. This provides more money in the heavy crop years to provide additional revenue to expand the demand for the larger crop. Assessments based on the value of a commodity sometimes work countercyclical to the need for funds, but for apples this is not true.[46] The revenue increase from 1989–90 to 1990–91 resulted primarily from increased government funding for export promotion.

Program Activities. Expenditures for the 1990–91 fiscal year totaled $21.8 million. The types of promotion activities in which the commission is involved include advertising, merchandising and promotion, international promotion, consumer relations, food service, and public relations. The commission also conducts research to determine the most effective program mix. In 1987–88 it invested 47 percent of its budget in media advertising in the largest consumer ad campaign ever for Washington apples. The slogan, shown over a picture of apples, "*A* is for Washington, apples at their very best." Eighty-nine percent of this advertising expenditure was on television or radio media, with the campaign taking place in forty-four markets in the country. This category also included advertising to the retail trade through industry magazines.

Because of the bumper crop in 1987–88, the commission increased its emphasis on merchandising and promotion to get a quick sales response. It stressed apple varietal information and provided incentive programs to the retailers. For example, retailers had a chance to win a "Washington Apple Bumper Crop Sweepstakes" that included a bumper of their choice—attached to a 1988 Jeep Comanche. The commission also prepared point-of-purchase materials, some was focused on sight appeal and others on diet. For example, one merchandising piece used a picture of apples and the slogan, "*A* is for diet." In international promotion, the commission developed material for the Scandinavian countries of Finland, Norway, and Sweden; the Asiatic countries of Taiwan, Singapore, Hong Kong, Malaysia, and Thailand; and the Middle Eastern countries of Saudi Arabia, the United Arab Emirates, Kuwait, Bahrain, Qatar, and Oman.

The consumer relations program targeted food editors of major magazines and newspapers and consumer advisers of major grocery store chains. It also promoted specific health and nutrition attributes of apples to diet and fitness editors to try to "influence the influencer." In the food service area, the commission teamed up with several large food service corporations to feature apples; it provided an "America's choice menu promotion kit" that restaurants could use to put together their own apple promotion program. The public relations activity is designed to keep the industry and the national and international produce trade informed of the activities of the commission. In addition, the commission provides scholarships to a small number of students.

The commission also attempts to develop new market niches; three of these were mentioned in the 1987–88 annual report. Research has indicated that Hispanics eat more fresh apples than Anglos, but that they have little knowledge of varieties for specific uses. The commission therefore established Hispanic promotion programs to include bilingual radio and billboard advertising retail promotions, bilingual point-of-sale materials, handling information, and copies of a video-tape explaining the apple industry. It also set up demonstration booths at several Hispanic festivals. A second market niche was the development of a program to support and provide materials for nonprofit or civic organizations for fund-raising activities using apples. For the third, the commission teamed up with one of the major convenience-store chains to place apple display racks in several thousand stores.

The Washington Apple Commission program is a multidimensional program that tries to exploit the positive image and the nutrient value of their state's unique apples. This campaign is coupled with a rigorous quality control program so that the apples will have uniform quality characteristics and attributes when purchased by consumers. The president of the commission discussed plans for the future in the 1990–91 annual report:

> In my view, achievements that have notable promise for the future are market entry to Mexico, curriculum development for healthy eating among school-aged children, a distinctive and award-winning advertising campaign featuring the "crunch" of Washington apples, promotion of new varieties, expansion of our representation in foreign countries, specification for Washington apples among military commissaries and food service distributors/operators, a strong industry relations program, a value-added philosophy to trade promotions, and (most importantly) attracting a professional staff that can make it happen.

The program of the Washington Apple Commission provides a way for all Washington apple producers to share in the cost and benefits of extending useful information to consumers about the value of Washington apples.

Promotion Programs Funded with Public Funds

Although most agricultural commodity generic promotion programs are funded by producers, some are supported from public funds. Two types of programs are common. One involves the use of public funds by federal and state governments for export promotion programs; the other involves state government programs designed to differentiate state-produced commodities from those grown in other states. The objective is to increase the demand for the commodities being promoted and thus to strengthen the states' agricultural sector. Both types of programs are justified in the cause of economic development. The legislation is usually not commodity specific, but the programs will often be developed around individual commodities or groups of commodities. In addition, several states have programs designed specifically to strengthen the demand for marine products and wine grapes.

Export Promotion

Both state and federal governments invest public funds in export promotion activities. Both invest with the idea that the activity will increase demand and thus increase prices and revenue flows for the commodity in question. Almost every major agricultural state has some form of export promotion program, but we do not have statistics to describe the nature or magnitude of them. The legislative basis for the federal export promotion programs is presented in Chapter 4. During the period 1987–89, fifty organizations received federal funds to support export promotion activities. Targeted Export Assistance (TEA) program funds are used primarily to support the development of foreign markets for fruits and vegetables (including potatoes, nuts, and vineyard products, Table 5–21).

Organizations that receive federal funds include trade organizations that have broad nationwide membership, marketing cooperatives, and state-legislated promotion organizations. Some examples of trade organizations are the American Soybean Association, the U.S. Meat Export Federation, and the Catfish Farmers of America. Some examples of state-legislated organizations include the California Raisin Advisory Board and the Florida

Table 5–21
Publicly Funded Export Promotion Programs, 1987–89

Commodity Group	Number	FY 1987	FY 1988	FY 1989
Targeted Export Assistance				
Livestock and poultry	5	$13,500	$8,750	$28,000
Grains and oil seeds	8	19,400	23,200	38,050
Fruits and vegetables	18	45,590	47,250	62,450
Fibers	1	6,800	1,450	15,000
Marine products	2	1,500	2,000	6,150
Other	12	7,030	8,150	26,100
Subtotal	46	$93,820	$90,800	$175,750
Export Incentive Program	4	$16,180	$19,200	$24,250
Total	50	$110,000	$110,000	$200,000

Source: Foreign Agricultural Service, U.S. Department of Agriculture report dated December 16, 1988.

Note: Amounts shown in thousands of dollars.

Department of Citrus. One federally legislated program, the National Potato Promotion Board, also receives TEA funds. Others, including the National Dairy Board and the Beef Industry Council of the National Livestock and Meat Board, are in the process of requesting funds. In 1991, the TEA program was replaced by the Market Promotion Program (MPP). Funding levels have continued at near $200 million per year; however, the amount is negotiated each year, and a somewhat smaller amount develops from a compromise appropriations process.

Export Incentive Program (EIP) funds can be used for brand advertising by cooperatives or private firms. One large recipient is Blue Diamond Growers, a California marketing cooperative that exports almonds and other nuts under the Blue Diamond label. The export promotion programs are multifaced, multidimensional, and as varied as the number of countries in which the activity takes place. Promotion organizations develop a specific plan for foreign market development; the plan needs to be viewed as possible and potentially effective before it will be funded by the U.S. Department of Agriculture. Because each foreign country has a different culture and because the consumers have different tastes and preferences, it is essential to develop a specific program for each target country

In 1988, 59 percent of the TEA funds were used for consumer media advertising and point-of-sale promotion, 35 percent was used to provide technical and other trade services, and 6 percent was used for trade advertising. Of all the money spent on export promotion where TEA funds were involved, 40 percent was provided by the participating firm, promotion organization, or a foreign third party.[47] The largest shares of the funds were invested in Japan (41 percent), other Pacific Rim countries (22 percent), and western European countries (32 percent).

There are many success stories concerning the use of public funds to help promote agricultural commodities abroad. A description of the program of the National Potato Promotion Board in cooperation with exporting firms and other regional trade organizations will provide some insight. French fries were first introduced into the Japanese market via the fast-food industry. The National Potato Promotion Board, along with other promotion organizations and potato distributors, advertise the french fry as a product that can be consumed at home. To penetrate the home market, however, the industry realized that it had to prefry the product so that it could be cooked in a toaster oven (french fries are prepared to be cooked in a microwave or a deep-fat fryer in other countries). It also realized that it had to package the potatoes in smaller packs. The National Potato Promotion Board advertised french-fried potatoes as "light, fluffy, and crunchy," using the trademark "Hokkari." Japanese television, newspapers, and magazines were used to communicate to consumers. The promoters also hung posters in all the subways of Hong Kong for a month, using the theme "When only the best is good enough" over pictures of mouth-watering American fries.

The introduction of some products into foreign markets requires changing consumers' perceptions of traditional food items. For example, in Spain, lentils had traditionally been considered filling, fattening, and hard to prepare. The campaign of the U.S. lentil industry included print and television advertising, in-store promotions, and a contest to develop Spanish recipes using U.S. lentils to change that attitude. It focused on the nutritional benefits of lentils, as well as the fact that U.S. lentils cook in about half the time required for lentils from other countries.

In the United Kingdom, the California Prune Board is trying to convince the British, through in-store advertising, that "California prunes are sweet nuggets of nutritional goodness on their morning cereal, in their lunchtime yogurt, and with the evening salad." The board is also touting "prunes for snacking." To appeal to the current health view, it uses such slogans as "prunes—the high-fiber fruit."

Public funds are also used to help introduce new products into the market, such as french fries (discussed above), crawfish, and wood products. Some of the public promotion money is used to provide technical assistance to food processors in foreign industries. These efforts focus on ways to improve processing efficiency and to help develop new products and new ways of merchandising the commodity.

"State-Grown" Programs

Many states use public funds to promote the agricultural industry of their state. Sometimes funds are used to match private-source funds to encourage the private sector to conduct quality control and promotion campaigns. The value of "state-grown" programs is even more highly debated than that of commodity programs. A commodity can be clearly differentiated from other commodities; however, it is more difficult to differentiate the quality of a commodity grown in one state from that grown in another.

The messages are designed to appeal to the parochial interests of the residents of the state. Some states have a rigorous quality control program associated with the use of the state's label and require that producers affix the label to their produce and adhere to rigorous quality standards. Other states, though, merely affix the "state-grown" label on local products. Users of the labels pay some modest fee for the use of the state logo. The money received, usually a modest amount, is co-mingled with public funds and then used to cover program costs and to mount advertising campaigns to encourage consumers to buy the state-grown product. Examples of the state logos are presented in Table 5–22.

States that use public funds for such promotion activities argue that it is in the public interest to maintain and create a strong demand for the state's products. The increased demand will help provide more jobs for the citizens of the state. Some analysts argue that "state-grown" programs provide few

Table 5.22
State Logos Used to Promote State Grown Commodities, 1990

State	Logo
Alaska	Alaska Grown
Delaware	First Rate from the First State; Delaware Grown
Colorado	Always Buy Colorado; I Grew Up in Colorado
Connecticut	Connecticut Grown
Georgia	Georgia, Always in Good Taste
Illinois	Illinois Product
Kansas	From the Land of Kansas
Maryland	Maryland with Pride; From Shore to Shore
Michigan	Yes, Michigan; Michigan Naturally; Michigan Premium
Missouri	Agri Missouri
New Jersey	Jersey Fresh from the Garden State; Jersey Fresh Quality
New York	New York "Seal of Quality"
North Carolina	Goodness Grows in North Carolina; Flavors of Carolina
North Dakota	Pride of Dakota
Texas	Taste of Texas
Vermont	Vermont Seal of Quality
Virginia	From Shore to Shore; Virginia's Finest
Wisconsin	Something Special from Wisconsin

benefits in view of the costs and improbability of extracting a premium in the market. Only if the state logo is identified with a specific commodity of differentiable high quality (such as Washington Apples) will the benefits be measurable. In an article devoted to this question, Holleran and Martin (1989) summarize as follows:

> Even if one concludes that such programs are generally not justifiable in an economic cost-benefit framework, they may well have significant social-political payoffs. At a time when agriculture is suffering through a period of painful adjustment, state programs send a message of concern and commitment. In a number of cases, there is a perception that the economic gap between farmers and their urban neighbors is widening. Agricultural promotion represents a "market-oriented" approach a state can take to close this gulf. The attempt may be meaningful to their farmers (pp. 74–75).

Their analysis supports the argument that single-commodity multistate programs will probably provide a more significant payoff.

Several states use public funds to promote the products of the marine product industry (that is, seafood) and the wine grape industry. Justification for public support is that these are new sectors of the economy; as new industries, they need public support to make sure of economic growth. Four states (Louisiana, Oregon, Virginia, and Alaska) use public funds to promote marine products, and four states (California, New York, Ohio, and Washington) use public funds to promote the wine industry. In some states, specifically Ohio, a wholesale-level excise tax on wine is used to reimburse the state for these expenditures. Therefore, in Ohio, the wine producers pay directly for the promotion activity, rather than the grape growers or the government. Most of this, of course, is passed on to the consumers of wine.

Summary

Almost every agricultural commodity produced in the United States has some form of a producer-funded advertising and promotion program. For many major commodities, the collection of money from the producer is accomplished under the authority of federal or state legislation and is mandatory. Every producer shares in the cost of the promotion effort. The rationale that everyone benefits from a generic commodity promotion program; therefore, everyone should pay. The assessments are levied in proportion to volume marketed, as a percentage of sales value or number of units (pounds or number of heads) sold.

State promotion checkoff programs were first to evolve. After some attempts at voluntary collection of funds to promote generic promotion activities, a commodity group would lobby for and obtain state enabling legislation for a mandatory checkoff to collect from every producer of the commodity. For commodities produced in more than one state and where more than one state had checkoff programs, there would be a movement to make assessments uniform across all states. Also, there would be a movement to coordinate program activities. Later, a movement to enact federal legislation would occur to make sure that every producer in the United States shared equally in the cost.

The number of commodities covered and the amount of money involved increased dramatically during the 1980s. Conventional wisdom now seems to be that commodity checkoff programs provide farmers with some control over their own destiny. By acting jointly, rather than as individuals, they can have some impact on the demand for their product and can fund activities that will add value to their product in the marketplace, through market development to include advertising, merchandising, public relations, education, and new product and process development. The preamble to the legislation states that such authority is in the public interest.

Public policy during the past decade has become supportive of commodity groups asking for mandatory legislation. Public policy has also shifted to favor no refund clauses in the enabling legislation; earlier national legislation required that farmer assessments be refunded if requested. So as public policy has become more supportive, the number of farmers involved in supporting, some involuntarily, generic promotion programs has increased dramatically.

Generally, the commodity promotion programs are managed by a staff that is hired by and directed by a farmer (sometimes processors and a consumer are added) board of directors appointed by the director of the state or federal agricultural department that is assigned oversight responsibility. In many programs, actual implementation is accomplished by other firms under contract. Market research firms are used to conduct surveys and advertising agencies are hired to create advertisements and place the ads with the media. For large programs, e.g., dairy, beef, pork, and soybeans, several regional and state promotion organizations are involved and the coordination of the program effort is a major undertaking.

Commodity groups with large budgets relay heavily on media advertising to educate consumers of the commodities' beneficial attributes. All of the groups use public relations efforts to develop a positive image through press and professional groups. Almost all of them use various forms of education programming. Some invest heavily in basic research to increase knowledge about the benefits and potential uses the commodity.

Every commodity has some unique set of attributes. Some of those attributes are obvious to consumers, others are not. Some commodities are easily identified by consumers, others are used primarily as ingredients and thus lose identity. Legislated promotion programs are most common and largest for those commodities that maintain their identity through the distribution system. Commodities that do maintain their identity rely heavily on media advertising to convey information directly to consumers.

Most foods have some unique set of nutrients. But the nutrient content is not visible and many consumers are not knowledgeable of the exact nature of the health benefits (or risks) of all commodities. Therefore, commodity groups invest in research to identify nutrient content and determine the benefits or risks associated with consumption. This information is used in advertisements and other information programs.

The objective of all the commodity promotion organizations is to increase the aggregate demand for the commodity. This means a market, larger over time than it would be without the advertising and promotion effort. The greater aggregate demand can be realized in the form of a larger volume being sold for higher value uses, higher prices for a given supply, and higher total revenues for all producers involved. Ideally, the assessment rate and expenditure level should be set so that net returns to those funding the program be maximized. But it is difficult to know, a priori, which program will work the best and thus how much should be invested in each. In the next two chapters we will develop concepts and ideas about how to measure the impact of the program effort and discuss the concepts of an optimal assessment and investment level and the optimal allocation of funds.

6

Evaluating Commodity Advertising and Promotion Programs

I n the previous chapters, we identified the breadth of commodity advertising and promotional programs found within the U.S. agricultural
system. Although there is considerable diversity in the programming and
implementation of activities, there are many management issues that are
common across commodities. One such issue is the need to have some
indication of the performance of the programs; that is, there needs to be an
assessment of the efforts. In this chapter, our intent is to review the efforts for
evaluation, highlighting the range of methods used to draw statistical inferences about the programs. We will deal with several mathematical and
empirical issues and methods. The chapter is not intended, however, to be a
treatise on empirical methods. Our purpose is to give the reader a perspective
on the types of evaluation techniques available and to indicate their use
across commodity programs. In the next chapter, several case studies are
presented that draw on these various methods.

Before going into the details, an overview of commodity evaluation can
be illustrated with the use of Figure 6–1. Evaluation efforts should first be
viewed in terms of the approach versus methods of analysis. The approach
sets the scope of the problem under consideration, whereas the method
defines the tools and measurement procedures appropriate to the particular
problem. Four components to the approach are shown in the figure. First,
given a specific commodity program or plans for an advertising campaign,
evaluation must be made with clearly defined objectives and performance
criteria. As initially illustrated in Figure 1–1 (in Chapter 1) and as discussed
in Chapter 3, the objectives and criteria for performance will differ depending on who is judging the programs. Performance to a firm may be measured
with improved market shares, while performance to the consumer is based
on reducing search costs. Measures of performance can be quite elusive at
times and not independent of political pressures. Nevertheless, if empirical
methods are to be adopted to draw statistical inferences, a set of criteria for

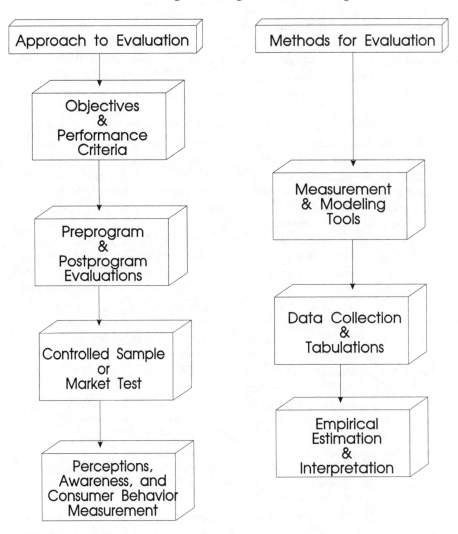

Figure 6–1. Evaluating Commodity Advertising and Promotion Programs

judging performance must be agreed upon. For commodity industries, such criteria often include growth in market size, increases in per capita consumption, positive rates of return from the advertising, increased product exposure, and improved consumer awareness.

The approach also depends on the history of program activities. In the planning stages, evaluation entails preprogram types of testing. Such tests are used to assist in the final program design. In contrast, postprogram evaluation looks back to ask the following questions; did the programs meet expectations? Did they have an impact on consumption of the product?

What were the strengths and weaknesses of selected programming efforts? As a rule, most economists involved in evaluation analyses have dealt with postprogram evaluation, whereas market researchers usually deal more with preprogram analyses. Postprogram evaluation assists in creating knowledge about past programs that can be useful in making decisions about future programs.

Once the performance and program periods are defined, then the approach must be considered within the context of the desired behavior of the target audience. Evaluations can be based on a controlled sample (such as an ongoing consumer panel) or drawn from market tests using actual consumer experiences in a noncontrolled environment. Both definitions of the audience or sources of data have their advantages and disadvantages, and these will be identified later in the chapter.

Finally, the approach defines what is to be collected. At one extreme, data on consumer or user awareness of commercials or new products may suffice, as awareness may provide an index of potential consumption. At the other extreme is actual consumption behavior. Consumers' intentions may not translate into actual purchases; thus, the signals from awareness and intentions can be misleading, since they may or may not lead to increases in the use of the advertised product. This is always a problem that must be recognized at the outset when designing evaluation efforts. The costs of sampling consumer intentions may be less than those of monitoring actual consumption behavior, yet the signals from the intentions may not provide positive proof that the programs are working. There is always a potential gap between intentions (where no expenditures occur) and consumption (where actual financial commitments are made). One probably cannot generalize about awareness leading, or not leading, to consumption; the results are most likely commodity specific. In Chapter 7, we show two cases where consumer awareness of advertising and promotion has translated into changes in consumption behavior.

The right side of Figure 6–1 shows the parallel boxes relating to the methods for evaluation. Although the methods are dependent on the approach for evaluation, without exception the methods include three phases. First, there must be a defined way to measure the program intensity and some way to model this intensity. Second, statistically correct procedures for collecting these data must be used. Data tabulation for analysis becomes an important part of the design and should be put in place early on during program planning. Third, appropriate empirical and statistical tools must be adopted. These tools include mathematics, statistics, economic theory, and computer programming. The purpose of using these tools is to provide an empirical linkage between the advertising efforts and consumption behavior. "Econometric" procedures are frequently used to provide the empirical estimates of this linkage; to be useful, however, these estimates must be interpreted. Part of this chapter is devoted to dealing with specific econometric tools for evaluating commodity programs.

Figure 6-1 includes many areas that are beyond the scope of our discussion. For example, we will not deal with sampling, survey design, behavior psychology, and a range of other issues implicit in the left-hand column. Our purpose in this chapter is to address those evaluation efforts most directly related to commodity advertising programs. Thus, our emphases will be on methods of analysis and unique problems that are often observed. We will first concentrate on postprogram evaluations and then deal with issues relating to preprogram testing.

Postprogram Evaluation

From Figure 6–1 it is assumed that the criteria for performance are defined and that the measurement of consumer action is selected. Performance criteria are used to determine if the demand for the promoted product has changed, and data have been collected on actual consumption, whether from controlled panels, test markets, or the actual markets. Furthermore, the appropriate measures of the advertising and promotion are known and recorded consistently. Clearly, we have skirted over many important issues with these assumptions; these will be addressed in the data section of this chapter.

In the most simplistic terms, are generic advertising and promotion and the market demand linked for the commodity being evaluated? To address empirically this issue of linking advertising with demand, the following steps must be accomplished:

- There must be a theoretical linkage between the advertising and demand, as initially set forth in Chapters 2 and 3. This linkage incorporates specific modeling efforts, including mathematical functions that meet a priori restrictions.

- Once a logical model is designed that is representative of the problem, the model must be empirically measurable through the use of appropriate statistical tools.

- Meaningful interpretations of the results must be given to relate the statistical findings back to the initial problem.

Concept of Evaluation Modeling

Modeling is an abstract representation of actual events. Through modeling, we hypothesize that advertising and promotion (which we will call A) leads to changes in the demand (D) for the selected commodity. Although D has not yet been explicitly defined, the argument is that advertising (A) produces changes in D; increases in advertising will likely increase D, and if advertising is decreased, D will also decline. Thus, D is a function of A: $D = f(z, A)$, letting all other variables influencing D be represented with z. Much of the empirical postprogram evaluation efforts relate to establishing this function and estimating the coefficients linking demand with advertising and promotion. Two important areas of interest relate to the specification of $f(z, A)$ and the specification of the function for bringing advertising into the $f(z, A)$ model. We will deal first with issues relating to the form of A and then with the conceptual issues relating to the function $f(z, A)$.

Functional Form. Three aspects of the implicit function for $f(z, A)$ must be addressed with every evaluation effort: the functional form must be specified, the analysis period defined, and the appropriate data and empirical tools used. The functional form must be determined at the first step. In short, what should be the theoretical linkage between consumer behavior (that is, consumption) and advertising? As one views the problem, there are several theoretical dimensions to the functional form that should hold (Ward, 1992a):

- Demand should continue at some positive level even where there is no advertising or promotion of the commodity. Demand for most products do not go to zero when programs stop. The extent of the demand adjustment, however, will differ with each product.

- Demand is likely to approach some upward limit in direct response to the advertising and promotional expenditures. This is true because consumers can only consume so much of a given product within a specific time. Likewise, consumers can only absorb so much information within a given time span.

- The rate of response to the checkoff effort can differ. Consumers may respond quickly to new information after only limited exposure. Alternatively, a major effort in expenditures may be needed to achieve a meaningful response. The introduction of a new product with highly publishable attributes may produce a quick response, whereas other products that consumers already know about may require considerably more investment to produce the desired response. In some situations it may not be possible to generate significant gains, because consumers already have high consumption levels and know the product attributes.

- Even with significant expenditures, there may be some delay between the advertising or information exposure and the response. As noted in Chapter 1, this is typically called the advertising carryover effect. The delay will differ from commodity to commodity.

- Over time, effectiveness of the same program may change because of consumer perception levels and changes in product knowledge. When establishing the linkage between expenditures and demand, this potential for change in the linkage must be considered.

Many of the historical models used to evaluate commodity programs have not satisfied one or more of the above preconditions primarily because of the implicit functions used. Developments in model specification, however, have contributed to conceptual models that satisfy the above conditions (Ward, 1992a). Below we will develop a specific function that satisfies the above criteria and then later show how it can be used in dealing with other issues associated with program evaluation.

A New Advertising Model Specification. Because commodity advertising and promotional programs are usually funded under a regional or national checkoff, expenditures on advertising and promotion are defined as CK, the checkoff expenditures, instead of A. Demand is then a function of CK: $D = f(z, CK)$. For a wide range of models and without much loss in generality, the function $D = f(z, CK)$ can also be written as $D = \eta \, \theta$ where η is the function representing the demand variables z and θ is the function for the checkoff expenditures. Also, the function is multiplicative; that is, $\log (D) = \log (\eta) + \log (\theta)$. It is the form of θ that is of interest at this juncture, because θ shows the adjustment in demand associated with changes in advertising and promotional expenditures.

Equation 6–1 provides one specification of θ that satisfies the theoretical modeling conditions noted above:

$$\theta = \left(1 + \exp\left(-\frac{\Gamma}{CK_t}\right)\right)^{\delta} \tag{6.1}$$

where $\Gamma \geq 0$ and $0 \leq \delta \leq 1.0$. Both Γ and δ are coefficients that must be estimated to determine the economic impact of the advertising expenditures or the checkoff efforts. Understanding the properties of equation 6–1 is fundamental to the evaluation model; that is, what happens as CK is changed? First, as CK approaches zero (such as where there is no advertising and promotional program), it is easily shown that $\lim \theta_{(CK \to 0)} = 1.0$. This limit shows that when there are no advertising or promotional activities, the demand function is $D = \eta$, since θ is now equal to one. Demand continues to exist even with no programming efforts and is only a function of η or $f(z)$. This is very realistic, because we know that consumption will generally exist in the absence of advertising and promotion. The issue is how much lower demand is when $\theta = 1.0$. Secondly, if advertising and promotion expenditures approached a large number (in other words, infinity), the limit of the equation reaches an upper value. That is, $\lim \theta_{(CK \to \infty)} = 2.0^{\delta}$, with 2.0^{δ} being the upper limit to the program gains for the period under consideration.

Thus, the limits to the impact of the checkoff expenditures lie between 1.0 and 2.0^δ, with the limit being dependent on the estimate for δ.

Whereas δ sets the upper limit to the advertising response, Γ determines the speed or rate of gain associated with different program expenditure levels. When Γ is small (less than 1.0), the initial program gains are substantial but then level off as expenditures continue to increase. When $\Gamma > 1.0$, however, the initial gains are low but will eventually increase with larger program expenditures. If either Γ or δ equal zero, the programs are ineffective in changing demand.

The full range of equation 6–1 can be illustrated with Figure 6–2. When advertising and promotion are set to zero, demand is still positive, as noted by the lower point on the demand axis of the figure. If checkoff efforts had no impact on demand, then $\theta = 1.0$, and again the level of demand remains fixed at some positive level. If δ is positive and significant, however, gains in demand occur as illustrated, with the upper limits drawn with the two curves. The upward curve exists over the lower one because δ is estimated to be larger for the first case (upper curve) versus the second case or lower curve. Each case is shown to approach the upper limit at different rates. The top curve is drawn to illustrate an initial rapid response to the advertising and then a decreasing rate as expenditures increase. In contrast, the lower curve illustrates a much lower initial response to the expenditures. Eventually, the demand response increases and levels off as the upper limit is approached. The rate of response depends on the estimated value of Γ in equation 6–1.

For postprogram evaluation, a conceptual model has now been illustrated that can be used in most empirical analyses. The empirical analysis entails estimating the coefficients δ and Γ. For a wide range of advertising models, estimating these two coefficients is not too difficult to accomplish. For the example above, where demand was defined to be $D = \eta \, \theta$ and without concern for the other variables in the model at this point, the model can be transformed where

$$\log (D) = \log (\eta) + \delta \log \left(1 + \exp \left(-\tfrac{\Gamma}{CK_t}\right)\right). \tag{6.2}$$

Equation 6–2 is linear in all parameters except Γ; however, various search procedures are available for estimating Γ (Ward, 1992a.) Without going into further details, it suffices to note that meaningful estimates of this function can be derived and used to model advertising and promotional programs that conform to prior theoretical considerations. In later case studies, two applications of this approach are included with analyses of the beef and apple industries. Other case studies will illustrate alternative specifications for incorporating advertising into the models. The advantage of this model is that it places realistic upper and lower limits to the advertising effectiveness, whereas many other functional forms (including those previously used by us) do not satisfy the same modeling conditions. These upper

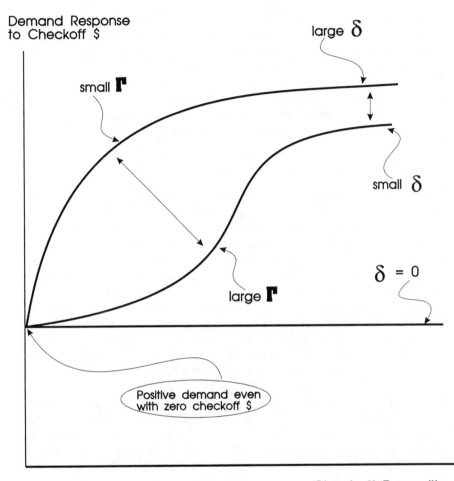

Figure 6–2. Theoretical Demand Response to Checkoff Expenditures

and lower limits to the model are particularly important when exploring different expenditure policy alternatives ranging from zero to high expenditure levels.

Advertising elasticities are often used as an index for discussing program effectiveness. The elasticity is simply the percentage change in demand associated with a percentage change in the checkoff effort. For equation 6–2, the checkoff elasticity is easily derived:

$$\varepsilon_{CK} = \frac{\delta\Gamma}{(1 + \exp^{(\Gamma/CK)}CK} \qquad (6.3)$$

This advertising elasticity is dependent on the expenditure level (CK) and the parameters δ and Γ. In equation 6–3, the elasticity always increases with δ, because larger values of δ always lead to higher upward limits to the program effectiveness. The elasticity may change in either direction with Γ, depending on its magnitude and the level of CK. The importance of knowing an elasticity is useful for simulations but also for general discussions of the overall effectiveness of a particular program. Also, the elasticities are comparable across commodities for reference purposes.

Concepts of Causality

In equation 6–2, consumer behavior was expressed as $D = f(z, CK)$ or $D = \eta\theta$. For the same period (for example, a month or quarter), the advertising causality always flows from the advertising effort (CK) to some recorded consumer response (D). If this linkage is weak, after an extended period CK is usually adjusted to correct for a poor response to the initial effort. Postprogram evaluations of commodity programs are usually concerned with the impact of the program expenditures on the demand for the commodity. Given unique aspects for agricultural commodities, what is included in D and z above become particularly important. The issues relating to causality in advertising models usually focus not on the advertising variable(s) but on the other variables entering the model. The causality issues can also be traced back to the types of data that are being used.

Using Panel Data. Suppose that consumption behavior data have been collected from a panel of consumers who report their periodic purchasing habits. They will typically report the amount purchased, the price paid, any purchasing rebates or deals, and possibly other purchases and prices. Also, consumer profiles are usually known. For this type of data, demand (D) can be represented with purchases of the commodity as the left-hand side variable in equation 6–2. Prices and other related variables are part of the z matrix of right-hand side variables. Consumption is some function of prices and other variables, and a function of the advertising effort ongoing during the reporting periods. Using this model and consumer panel data, establishing the linkage between consumption and advertising can be completed.

Using Market Clearing Data. Causality problems become difficult when evaluations are based on market-clearing data versus individual consumer responses. Market data are the composite totals of all consumers faced with changing supplies. The observed data represent neither the demand nor the supply but rather the coordinates where supply (the amount available at a point in time) and demand are equal. For most agricultural products, supplies are predetermined for any fixed period less than one year, such as a month or quarter. Agricultural production is such that it is difficult to

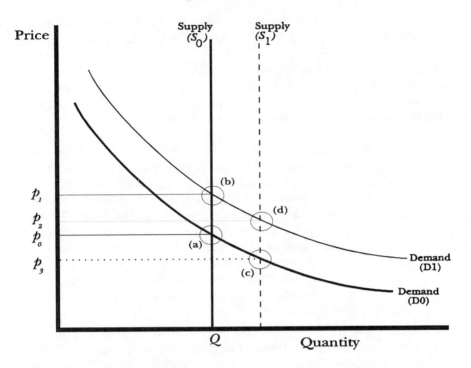

Figure 6–3. Price Changes in Response to Adjustments in Supply and Demand

increase supplies in response to favorable prices during the same period. For a fixed supply, the commodity price is determined by the available market supplies. Price is dependent on quantities of the good available or the market supplies. Causality runs from quantities to prices. Using market data for this example, the evaluation models should be specified with price as the left-hand side variable. D in equation 6–2 is price dependent, and z includes the quantity supplied, along with other demand factors. The empirical linkage with advertising is between the expenditures and the commodity price.

Figure 6–3 illustrates the typical case for many agricultural goods. For a specific period, supply is drawn as S_0 and is nonresponsive to current prices; that is, supplies are perfectly vertical for the same period. The market price occurs where D_0 crosses the supply line, as labeled with point (a). If consumers respond to the advertising, demand may shift from D_0 to D_1, giving a new equilibrium price at point (b) assuming supplies remain at S_0. If in a subsequent period supplies change from S_0 and S_1 and demand remains at the new level, the market clearing price drops to point (d), where $S_1 = D_1$. Market data are coordinates where supply and demand cross; thus, researchers only see those points denoted with (a), (b), (c), and (d), and not the lines drawn in Figure 6–3. Only through the empirical analysis of the distribution of observed data can the supply and demand lines be determined.

Theoretical Relationships. The theoretical relationships can be placed into three problem groups that have direct bearing on evaluating supply and demand modeling. In each of these groups, the model is based on reported market data and not individual consumer responses.

Case 1: Supplies are predetermined for a given period and are thus not responsive to price changing during that period. In Figure 6–3, the supply curves are perfectly vertical. Shifts in supplies are related to nonprice events for the same period; however, the shifts may be in response to previous period prices. This is frequently referred to as the "cobweb" model. For advertising evaluation purposes, the theoretical model is specified where p = f(q, z, CK), letting p = price, q = supplies, z = other variables, and CK = the advertising and promotional expenditures. Note that in this case, the form of CK can still enter the model as outlined earlier in this chapter.

Case 2: Prices are predetermined through controls, price supports, or other types of policies directly influencing the price level. The quantity of the product is at least partially storable. For this case, the model may be specified with q = f(p, z, CK), using the same definitions as in Case 1.

Case 3: Both supplies and demand are responsive to price changes in the same period. Demand will always change with prices. Supplies are also assumed to be sensitive to the price levels. It is with this type of problem that the modeling effort becomes crucial and more complicated. Two equations exist, one for supply and one for demand, with both being a function of current market prices. Demand is defined as q_d, letting q_d = f(p, z, CK), and supply, q_s, is set letting q_s = f(p, w), where w is variables that cause supplies to change (such as weather, productivity, or management). Assuming that storage is netted out of q_s, then the market is in equilibrium where $q_s = q_d$ or when f(p, z, CK) = f(p, w). Once the specific forms of both equations are known, a reduced-form equation can be specified where p = f(z, w, CK); that is, prices are dependent on both supply and demand factors as well as the checkoff. Estimation of this case requires the use of simultaneous equations and the discussion of the procedures are beyond the scope of this chapter. The procedures are well known and can be found in any introductory econometric texts (Greene, 1990; Gujarati, 1988).

Causality is both theoretical and empirical. To emphasize again, if the data collected are a direct measure of consumer behavior or purchasing, the models flow from price to consumption: $q = f(p, z, CK)$. Consumer data do not reflect all available supplies. They simply show how consumers behave when faced with prices and other factors influencing their decision making, including advertising. If market-clearing data are used, though, then both q and p reflect supply and demand conditions and the models must be specified according to one of the cases noted. In Chapter 7, case studies for beef and apples (compared with dairy and citrus) illustrate examples of these evaluation-modeling issues.

Advertising Carryover Effects

Recall from Chapter 2 that generic efforts are usually intended to precipitate and remind, with the purpose of keeping consumers informed about the product attributes and any changes. These efforts translate into a longer-term advertising effects that are referred to as the advertising carryover effect. In postprogram evaluations, such carryover effects must be part of the total analysis. From a modeling standpoint, the issue is how best to include previous program efforts in the current period analysis and model.

Again using the function where $D = f(z, CK)$, the carryover effect can be included by noting that D also depends on previous programming efforts. In other words, advertising and promotion from previous periods are likely to have an impact on decisions in the current period. Conceptually, the demand function can be rewritten to let $D = f(z, CK, CK_{-1}, CK_{-2}, CK_{-3}, CK_{-4}, \ldots)$, where now D depends on the current expenditures (denoted with CK) and previous period's expenditures (denoted with CK_{-i}, where i represents the previous periods. The coefficients associated with CK_{-i} provide the linkage between current demand and previous programming efforts.

For discussion purposes, assume the coefficients δ_0, δ_1, δ_2, δ_3, δ_4, . . . correspond to the current and lagged checkoff expenditures in the above equation. The δ's could represent those in equation 6–1 or another functional form. The relative magnitudes of the parameters completely reveal the advertising carryover effect. For most commodity checkoff programs, two types of patterns are generally seen. First, $\delta_0 > \delta_1 > \delta_2 > \delta_3 > \delta_4 > \ldots > 0$ implies that advertising in the current period has the greatest impact on demand; the previous advertising is next, followed by subsequent and continued declines in the parameter values as more distant advertising efforts are included. If after δ_0 (the immediate impact) the remaining δ's decline rapidly, the market is said to have a low advertising carryover effect, or a rapid advertising decay rate. If instead the remaining δ's show a slow decrease in value, the model points to a long-term advertising carryover effect or low advertising decay rate. The impact of previous efforts decays gradually and, thus, has an important impact on current consumption.

Another frequently observed carryover effect for commodity advertising programs occurs where $\delta_0 < \delta_1 < \ldots < \delta_k > \delta_{k+1} > \delta_{k+2} > \ldots$. The largest impact is seen after k periods, since δ_k is the largest parameter and $\delta_k > \delta_0$. The peak effect of the advertising is realized k periods after the effort, with the carryover effect initially rising and then falling after k lagged periods. A practical example of this is seen with fluid milk. The generic advertising affects current consumption of milk, but its greatest impact is after several months. Finally, after about twelve months, the lagged impact goes to zero. If all δ's = 0 beyond δ_0, then all program planning and strategies must simply be based on expenditures for the current period. When δ's > 0 beyond the first period, however, the programming strategies become considerably more complicated. Decisions for the current period programs create a stream of impacts beyond the current response.

Figure 6.4 illustrates the lagged effects as represented with the δ's. Curve (a) shows advertising programs in the current period having the greatest impact, followed with a continued decline from the remaining lagged periods. Curve (b), in contrast, shows the case where the current programs have a positive impact during the same period as the programs were started, but it takes some time before the maximum response to the programs is realized. With curve (b), the carryover effect rises after the first period and then reaches a peak. Eventually, the carryover effect starts to decline, as must be the case for every advertising and promotional program. The models denoted with the δ's above are simply providing a numerical way for estimating the relationships in Figure 6–4. As we will see in the case studies in Chapter 7, the conclusions about lagged advertising effects differ considerably across commodities, periods of analysis, and studies.

As part of the overall postprogram evaluations, it is imperative that the δ's be estimated. Although the actual estimation process is beyond the scope of our discussions, the general area of empirical analysis is called *distributive lags*. Techniques for dealing with distributive lags are used to estimate the δ's. Polynomial or Almon lag procedures are the methods used most often for estimating advertising carryover effects (Greene, 1990).

Polynomial lag procedures draw on the condition that lagged parameters follow some type of pattern over the lagged periods, as suggested above with the δ_k's. For example, one could represent the lagged structure for the δ_k's as follows:

$$\delta_k = \lambda_0 + \lambda_1(k) + \lambda_2(k^2) \qquad (6.4)$$

In this equation, the k's represent the lagged periods and the λ's the lag structure. The advantage of this equation over including all lags (δ's) in the demand model is that the complete lagged structure can be represented with the three λ parameters and not all of the δ's. Furthermore, additional restrictions can even be placed on the equation (such as $\delta_{k+m} = 0$, allowing the

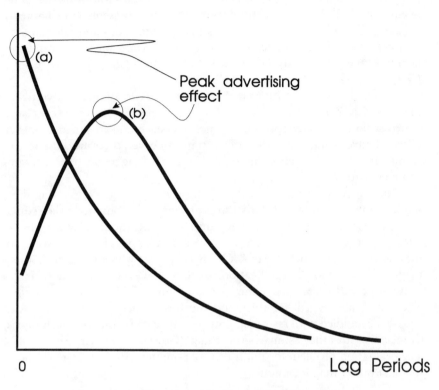

**Advertising
Effect (parameters)**

(a)

Peak advertising
effect

(b)

0   Lag Periods

Figure 6–4. Conceptual Lagged Advertising Effects

lagged structure to be estimated using only λ_1 and λ_2). This procedure is not unique to advertising problems but is readily applicable to them.

Modeling Multiple Programs

Many (if not most) generic programs have several dimensions to their demand-enhancing efforts that need to be analyzed as separate components to the analysis. For example, checkoff programs may include uniquely different media, such as radio versus television. The beef industry's programs use both types of advertising, as well as consumer and industry information programs that are considerably different in their content. The different approaches imply different target audiences; the industry would like to know the effectiveness of each type of program.

Conceptually, the demand models $D = f(z, CK)$ or $D = f(z, CK, CK_{-1}, CK_{-2}, CK_{-3}, CK_{-4}, \ldots)$ can accommodate a more detailed breakdown of the program expenditures. For convenience, assume that there are two types of programs, *CK1* and *CK2*, instead of just *CK*. Equation 6–2 thus could be shown as $D = f(z, CK1, CK2)$ or $D = \eta\theta_1\theta_2$, with the θ's following the model in equation 6–1. A graphic presentation of this was presented in Chapter 3. A case study of promotion for apples (using both radio and television) in Chapter 7 provides an application of this model. The same model can easily facilitate the lagged structure, with $D = f(z, CK1, CK1_{-1}, CK1_{-2}, CK1_{-3} \ldots CK2, CK2_{-1}, CK2_{-2}, CK2_{-3}. \ldots)$.

Although *CK1* and *CK2* were defined as two types of media advertising, the same disaggregation of *CK* could be according to other categories, such as promotion of different products, generic versus brand advertising, or even different advertising copy. Most of the time, however, there are a number of empirical issues that complicate one's ability to disaggregate the programs completely for analysis.

There is nothing inherit in the equation that prevents estimating these models; however, data and statistical problems often complicate the estimation process. For example, if *CK1* and *CK2* expenditures were always allocated in some fixed proportion, it would be impossible to separate out the effects of *CK1* from those of *CK2*. This is a data problem that has nothing to do with the model specification. Inclusion of several lagged variables decreases the degrees of freedom available for reliable model estimation. These multiple lagged variables and the loss of degrees of freedom can usually be handled with restricted polynomial lagged estimation techniques, as well as with other estimation methods (Greene, 1990; Gujarati, 1988). The evaluation problem for multiple programming efforts is usually one of the data rather than technique.

Advertising Modeling Stability

Again using the model where $D = f(z, CK)$, another interesting postprogram evaluation issue is to determine if the measured effectiveness of the programs is stable over time. That is, do the parameters linking *CK* and *D* remain constant, or do they change in some way over time? Three major conditions can contribute to parameter change over time:

1. There may be significant *programming improvements* in terms of copy, media selection, and messages. Thus, for the same expenditure levels, the effectiveness may improve (or deteriorate) depending on the underlying changes in the message and delivery. Even changes in advertising agencies could contribute to a change in effectiveness.

2. Consumers may simply become *saturated* and insensitive to repeated messages. Their knowledge base increases and their exposure to competing advertising messages likely increase over time. Thus, for the same

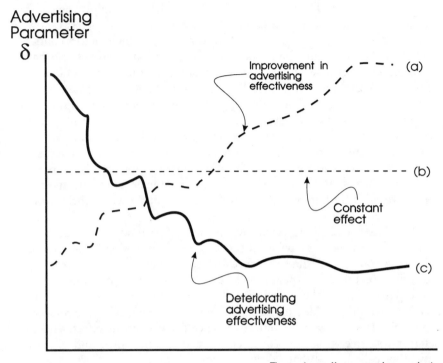

Figure 6–5. Changing Advertising Effectiveness Over Time

expenditure effort, the response may decline. By the very nature of consumer behavior, some randomness in consumer responses can be expected.

3. Finally, there may be underlying changes in the *characteristics* of the commodity and technology that lead to advertising and promotion having more (or less) effect on consumers. As an example, production technology has lead to more lean beef production. Consumers may become more receptive to advertising signals because of improvements in the product advertised.

Figure 6–5 can be used to illustrate the stability concept. Using the model $D = f(z, CK)$ with δ being the parameter relating to CK, then three situations are illustrated in the figure. First, if δ is estimated and shown to be constant through time, then there is evidence of stability in the advertising effectiveness. The only question is whether or not the coefficient is statistically significant and has the correct sign and magnitude. In this figure we have shown each case with a positive coefficient, thus implying some positive gain from the advertising. The positive sloping curve (a) denotes improvements in the advertising coefficient over time. While the program parameter is shown to increase, the same analysis may not show precisely which factors contributed to the improvement. The rising δ's only show that improvements have taken place. Of course, this is vital information to the overall evaluation efforts, even though one would like to know what contributed to the improvement. As a working example, gradual improvements in copy design may not bring about an overnight increase in advertising effectiveness. With continued emphasis on creative improvements, however, the same expenditures may began to show a larger gain. An upward path to the advertising coefficient in Figure 6–5 would not be unreasonable. Note in this figure that line (b) represents the case of complete stability in the program effectiveness. A positive value for b implies a positive program impact where the advertising coefficient is fixed.

The downward sloping curve (c) in Figure 6–5 points to a significant problem for an industry using advertising and promotion as a demand-enhancing tool. Over time the checkoff parameters have declined, thus indicating that the same expenditure levels in the latter periods are generating less response than for the earlier periods. Such a strong trend as portrayed in this figure would provide a major signal that something needs to be corrected if possible. The programs are effective (since $\delta > 0$), but the effectiveness is deteriorating over time. Improved copy, media, scheduling, and intensity may all be called for. Whatever the remedy, the evaluation effort assuredly points to the problem. In both the rising and falling parameter cases, less than smooth adjustments have been illustrated in order to depict the normal kinds of evolutions in advertising effectiveness that might be expected. The exact pattern of change is dependent on the specific case being analyzed.

This aspect of postprogram evaluations requires sophisticated empirical techniques that cannot be discussed in detail in this text. The procedures for testing the stability of the advertising parameters are based on the econometric literature dealing with time-varying parameters. Applications of the Cooley-Prescott model and Kalman filtering are the two most often used techniques for studying parameter stability. Both techniques provide measurement of the path of parameter adjustment through time and would specifically reveal if either pattern shown in Figure 6–5 exists for a specific commodity program. One example of the Cooley-Prescott technique applied to generic advertising is by Ward and Myers (1979).

Though we are not exploring the procedures in depth in this book, permanent and temporary variations in the parameter need to be noted, because they are relevant to advertising evaluation efforts. The *advertising coefficient* may change over time in a deterministic or permanent way, using model efforts that measure shifts with such discrete variables as time or seasonal adjustors. A study of fluid milk by Ward and Dixon (1989) tested for changes in milk advertising effectiveness over time by interacting the milk advertising with yearly increments in time. An alternative and more flexible form is to assume that the coefficient has both random (temporary) and permanent change components. In principle, most of the varying parameter models have a variation of the form where δ_{0t} is the advertising coefficient referenced earlier, but also now for just period t. If this parameter changes through time, the path may follow a Markovian process where $\delta_{0t} = H\delta_{0(t-1)} + v_t$; that is, the parameter today is a function of the previous period plus some random variation noted with v. The adjustment process captured with H is the most revealing part of this model, since it shows whether or not the parameter is moving in a particular direction over time. Both the Cooley-Prescott model and the Kalman filter are variations of this general specification (Harvey, 1989).

Varying parameter models dealing with advertising issues will likely become more important to our studies, because they provide a way to back into dealing with several data problems. In particular, issues pertaining to changing copy and media, as well as structural changes within the media industry, are nearly impossible to document empirically. Such profound adjustments would be expected to influence the overall program performance and hence the measured parameters (δ's) in the econometric models. At a minimum, the directional changes suggested with Figure 6–5 indicate to policymakers whether to continue as usual, stop the programs, enhance them, or revamp old strategies completely. Likewise, the procedure has importance to testing new programs after they have been in place for sometime. Time-varying parameter techniques can provide the researcher with insight into revising modeling specifications. For example, through time-varying parameters, one can see the significant downward shift in beef demand over the decade since 1979. The pattern of shifts can be remodeled with more specific variables that are likely to reflect the cause of the shifts (such as health concerns and beef consumption.)

Demand Systems Modeling

Another approach to evaluating advertising has been based on complete demand systems. In the model used above, demand was specified as $D = f(z, CK)$, where z included the direct price and cross-price effects and other variables. Theoretically, it can be shown that many functional forms for single equation models do not satisfy the assumptions of demand theory. Demand systems models have been developed in an effort to develop empirical models that come closer to satisfying the theoretical properties. The basic argument is that within a class of goods that includes substitutable products, any demand model must satisfy several well known demand properties (Deaton and Muellbauer, 1980; Pollak and Wales, 1992). Our intention in this discussion is not to develop the models, but to illustrate their role in advertising evaluation. The reader is referred to an overview of this topic in a paper by Brown and Lee (1992).

Most of the demand system models start with the premise that consumers have an expenditure system of selected substitutable goods that are some function of price, prices of other goods within the class, and some concept of consumer utility. After applying the appropriate optimization on this expenditure system, most of the models yield several budget-share equations for W_i, where w is the expenditure on good i over total expenditures on all goods within the product class. Expenditures on good i are related to the commodity's own price and prices of all substitutes within the class. Advertising has been included in the functional form where $w_i = W(p_i, p_j, A_i, A_j)$. If, for example, there were k commodities within the class, there would be $(k - 1)$ equations to estimate. The actual functional form for W depends on the expenditure model adopted.

As a rule, the inclusion of advertising in demand systems (either current or lagged) has lacked the conceptual properties denoted early in this chapter. Most of the demand systems models have concentrated primarily on the systems issues and only secondarily on the advertising issues. Also, most of the models have been estimated with market-clearing data without dealing with the causality issues discussed earlier. Although the models have limitations, they do give an alternative way to view demand problems and the role of advertising. Given acceptable estimates, the models show both the direct effects of advertising (say, A_i) on demand for good i and the potential cross-advertising effects on other goods included in the system. The complexity of demand systems has usually led to including advertising in simplistic and often less than desirable forms; on the other hand, more theoretically consistent demand functions are specified. Improvement in one aspect may be negated by weaknesses with the appropriate inclusion of advertising expenditures (Green, 1985; Green, Carmen, and McManus, 1991; Goddard and Amuah, 1989; Brown and Lee, 1992).

Marketing Margins and Symmetry

An important issue that is part of evaluation is whether or not those who pay the checkoff assessments are receiving the benefits. Checkoff programs are directed to consumers with the purpose of increasing demand. Producers pay the cost of these programs and, hence, must know if the gains in retail demand are passed back to them. The difference between the retail, wholesale, and shipping-point market levels is called the *marketing margin*. If retail demand increases and no gains are realized to the producers, clearly the marketing margin has increased. If benefits are not partially passed back to producers, the checkoff programs will ultimately fail. In Figure 6–3, we showed the example where demand increases from D_0 to D_1 and, with supplies fixed, the price increased from P to P_1. If these demands were at the retail level, then clearly part of the increase $(P_1 - P)$ must be evident at the producer level if producers are to benefit.

Though there is a considerable literature on measuring marketing margins, most of the studies deal with the issue in one of two ways. In one method, econometric models are specified for each market level and then tied together by accounting for distribution costs and profits. This approach is often complex because of the number of equations that are required to estimate the linkage between market levels. The other method is to have one demand equation (as in Figure 6–3) and then a second equation where prices at one level are expressed as a function of the prices at the other level. This type of equation shows how much of a retail change, for example, is reflected at the producer level or other appropriate levels: for example, $P_s = f(P_r)$, or shipping-point prices are some function of the retail price of the commodity of interest. For most models, the econometric procedures discussed in other sections of this chapter apply. In other words, there is nothing particularly unique about modeling margins versus other economic problems.

There is, however, one unique area worthy of note. Cases are often cited wherein price rises pass through the market system at a different rate from price declines. If the responses depend on the direction of change, then the models are said to exhibit *asymmetric* characteristics. If retail price declines are quickly reflected in wholesale and shipping-point prices while rising prices are not, then the asymmetry becomes of immediate concern to producers. The downsides of the market are not offset by the upside in this case.

Evaluation of advertising programs could also be addressed in terms of the potential asymmetric effects. Rising checkoff expenditures may generate a rise in demand, as was illustrated in Figure 6–3 with shifts from D_0 to D_1. If a decrease in checkoff expenditures of the same amount were to take place, would the shift be back to D_0, or something different?

The procedure most often used for dealing with asymmetric effects is an application of the Wolfram model. This model gives coefficient estimates, for example, γ_1 and γ_2. The value γ_1 corresponds to the direct linkage between prices or between demand and advertising, as initially developed with $D = f(z, CK)$. This is called the *rising effect* or the *mapping* between increases in advertising and the demand or increases in retail prices and shipping-point prices, whereas γ_2 is a test of the difference between the rising and falling effects. If $\gamma_2 = 0$, then no asymmetry exists. If γ_2 is not equal to zero, then asymmetry exists and the falling portion of the effect is $\gamma_1 + \gamma_2$. Complete details of using this model while including distributed lagged effects can be found in Ward (1982).

Secondary Attraction Models

Up to this point, our focus has been on measuring the influence of commodity advertising on total demand. Total demand may also be influenced by brand advertising as discussed in Chapter 2, depending on the unique characteristics of the commodity. In contrast, another evaluation test is to determine if generic advertising is brand neutral or if it is having an impact on selected sections within the commodity industry.

Attraction models are based on the premise that brand marketing will attract consumers to the brand. A firm's share of the market (MS) is proportional to its attraction relative to the sum of all firms' attraction (AT); that is, $MS_i = AT_i/\Sigma(AT_j)$ and $AT_i = \Pi_k[f(X_{ki})^{\beta_k}]$, letting X_{ki} represent the k variable for brand i that influences consumers' attraction to the specific brand (Cooper and Nakanishi, 1990). If generic efforts are ongoing, attraction models may need to be respecified to incorporate the effects of CK, the checkoff expenditures ($AT_i = \Pi_k [f(X_{ki})^{\beta_k}, f(CK)]$.) If the generic advertising is brand neutral, market shares should show no evidence of being influenced by the generic programs. If generic advertising leads to shifts in the nonadvertised labels (such as private labels), however, one may see a decline in selected brand shares.

Attraction or market share models have potentially the most importance with joint ventures between generic and brand advertising efforts. For example, the Florida citrus industry once funded a program where brand advertisers could apply for generic funds to supplement their brand efforts if specific promotional criteria were met. This was truly a joint venture between two separate promotional interests. Similarly, joint ventures between private firms and federal agencies to assist with international market development exist. For these examples, the attraction models can be used to test the impact of the joint funding on the participating firm's market share.

Attraction models are simply a way of dealing with firm responses in an environment where considerable generic advertising exists. Inclusion of both generic and brand funding in the attraction models provides a direct way for testing the brand neutrality of generic efforts and the success of brand efforts. Further, the models could be specified to determine if generic and brand advertising are complementary in influencing demand in total and for the individual firm. Estimation procedures for these models are generally straightforward. One could also use these models to study market shares of one industry against another. For example, the share models could address the beef market share of all consumer expenditures on meats.

Discrete Choice Models

Causal models, as we have specified with $D = f(z, CK)$, are defined with variables that by definition take on a range of values; otherwise, the problem would be trivial. A range of values can differ considerably, depending on the selected criteria for judging performance. Changes in consumer expenditure shares for specific product or changes in per capita consumption imply a continuum of observed values. Such range of measurement may not always be of major importance. Rather, the index for performance may simply be whether or not consumers become buyers of the product after some promotional effort. The amount of purchase may not be as important as whether the consumers simply were receptive to change. Did the advertising produce an experimentation with the new product? Did the advertising create a change in cooking or eating practices? Has the promotion changed the frequency of shopping or the concern for more natural foods? Clearly, there are many questions and issues that could be answered with a yes or no. The model may still be $D = F(z, CK)$, but the measurement of D is discrete in the recorded responses. Such models are called *discrete choice* models, since the responses lie within a well-defined set of discrete choices. The range does not have to be merely yes or no, but the choices are still within a few well-defined groups. Discrete choice models are usually grouped into binomial (yes or no) or multinomial models where a specific count of the responses can be made.

Estimating the effects of advertising and promotional programs within the context of discrete responses calls for an entirely different set of empirical techniques. Conventional regression procedures that would be applied to the models discussed earlier are no longer appropriate. These models for evaluation can best be illustrated using the function $F(z, CK)$ as developed below:

$$\text{Prob}[D = 1] = f(z, CK)$$
$$\text{Prob}[D = 0] = 1 - f(z, CK)$$
$$(6.5)$$

The function $f(z, CK)$ still includes the advertising and promotion effects, but its measured impact provides a different interpretation. Specifically, the results in equation 6–5 show the estimated probability of achieving a response given values of both z and CK. That is, as checkoff expenditures (or any other advertising and promotion activity, for that matter) increase, will the probability of responding increase? Thus, the primary purpose of these models is to determine if the promotional efforts stimulate change. They are generally less useful for designing strategies and allocating expenditures.

As with those in other sections, the details of these methods are beyond our purpose in this book (see Maddala, 1977). The two most used discrete choice models, however, should be mentioned. Probit and logit models are the two most frequently used methods for dealing with discrete binomial choice models. Both are based on normal distributions, and both offer the advantage of lying within the ranges consistent with the estimation of probabilities.

The appropriateness of models of multiple discrete choices can be found in data sets useful for evaluating advertising programs. For example, assume that a panel of consumers has been monitored over time and that the panel members responded to several questions using a five-point ranking (strongly favor, favor, indifferent, against, and strongly against). The evaluation question would be to determine if the scaling is in any way related to the advertising and promotional efforts. A multinomial logit model may be the appropriate tool for dealing with the problem. See chapter 20 in William Greene's book for a good interpretation of discrete choice models (Greene, 1990).

Another related area that on occasion has importance to advertising evaluations is when performance variable has limited values (that is, one has a limited dependent variable). Suppose that an advertising program for automobile accessories was based on a mailing list of owners of new Cadillac cars. What can be inferred from this sample to the whole population? The sample population is part of the total population, yet the sample is probably truncated by some income scale, since Cadillacs are most likely purchased by upper-income consumers. The estimation problem using this type of data is said to have a *truncated* distribution. In this example, the sample is most likely truncated at or below some high income level (Greene, 1990).

Another dimension to limited dependent variables occurs when the indicator of performance has been censored; that is, when the recorded data is collected, values are given a fixed level under certain criteria. Suppose that a new promotion is put in place, but the consumer is also told that purchases are limited to no more than five units. We can attempt to relate the purchases to the promotion programs, but the data do not reveal the true demand because of the imposed limits per purchase. Data thus are censored because of limits artificially imposed on the program. A common method for addressing the estimation of models with censored data is to use the Tobit model (Greene, 1990; Maddala, 1977).

Overview of Postprogram Methods

Before moving into the next section, it is worth repeating the more important aspects of postprogram evaluation. The model $D = f(z, CK)$ includes three basic elements that must always be defined: (1) the definition and functional form for CK; (2) the causality and the functional form for $f(z, CK)$; and (3) the definition and measurement of D, the performance criteria. Answers to these issues in turn will determine the appropriate estimation techniques and unique problems that will be encountered. Empirical methods and the computer power to deal with them have improved in the last few years, thus opening up many new avenues for analysis. Such methods and the desire to push our computers to the limits, however, should not be the driving force to evaluations; rather, they should be the tool after the problems and needs are clearly known and a scientific approach to the analysis is set in place.

The discussion in this section also concentrated on evaluation methods where empirical linkages between the criteria for performance and the advertising and promotion effort exist. We clearly have not dealt with a vast amount of statistical tools that give insight into the effectiveness of advertising, yet econometric methods hold a unique position in that one can use the measured response results to draw statistical inferences and simulate marginal responses. Thus, the avenue for allocation and optimization among program activities is open.

Preprogram Evaluations

The unique aspect of postprogram evaluation is in its very definition: the event has taken place, consumers have (or have not) responded, historical data can be analyzed, and the results can be interpreted to draw economic inferences and conclusions. Later we will discuss data problems that one must be prepared to deal with, but for now we will turn to the problem of evaluation before the programs are put in place.

Preprogram evaluations can usually be categorized according to how information is brought to bear on the plan. As a rule, three areas can be identified as the major sources of information for making prepromotional decisions: experience and literature review; controlled experiments for pretesting; and market experiments for pretesting. Obviously, the selection among these will be limited by the financial resources, staff expertise, and the time schedule necessary for implementing programs. Timing may be the critical area, since it may simply be impossible to pursue every question of interest before going with a program. Commercial placements have to be scheduled months in advance, creative copy has to be designed, and organizational structures have to be in place. The risk from missing media "windows" and "media buys" may far outweigh the risk from not fully testing the programs as designed. It is at this point where experienced staff members who are abreast of important issues need to be in place.

An obvious problem that many researchers (especially academic researchers) encounter is that much of the pretesting is not published and is not available for review. It is often proprietary and thus not released. Often one is amazed at how little information is available when major financial commitments to programs are in place.

Experience in Preprogram Evaluation

Just as habit persistence exists among consumers, there is also habit persistence in the process of carrying out programs. Such persistence is often based on experience through trial and error over time. Although experience and preprogram evaluation are essential, one must always be cognizant of different perspectives when drawing on individual experiences. For example, advertising agencies have more experience in deciding on creative copy, media coordination, and timing. The same staff, though, should not be expected to understand within a short period the economics of a commodity industry. Agency staff who do not have experience in the area of a commodity industry may draw conclusions not fully appropriate for the industry. Sometimes this is seen with commodity checkoff programs when new agencies are hired; agencies will assign one or more persons to an account and in within a few months expect them to have expertise in the economics of the specific agribusiness industry. It is equally important to note that researchers such as economists usually have limited understanding of the creative design process. This is precisely why checkoff programs must have their own staff who understand the industry problems and objectives, the political setting, and financial limits.

Commodity industries face many issues that can be easily brought to the forefront by small groups with certain political agendas. One of the best examples of this can be found in the beef industry and issues relating to animal rights. Animals are raised to be slaughtered to meet part of our food needs; animal rights groups often cite selected (and often isolated) cases of inhumane procedures to protest this process. Creative copy intended to reach consumers may fail to recognize problems as important as this. How a product is presented, the wording of the copy, and the underlying message must be carefully analyzed within the context of issues beyond just food nutrition. Staff with experience in recognizing and dealing with important political and emotional issues must be an integral part of the preprogramming process. This is particularly true with advertising and promotion, because signals are being sent to a population with a wide range of perspectives and social agendas. The message must be carefully designed to address the purpose and not (through mistakes) to create other problems. Drawing on experience is not a scientific process, yet it is as essential as any other input to the preprogramming effort.

Commodity checkoff programs have an interesting dimension not found within many other groups heavily involved in programming design and implementation. Most commodity programs in the United States have a staff, hired agencies, and a board of directors. Unlike boards of directors of major corporations, the directors are also among the producers who underwrite the programs. Also, they are either appointed or elected to represent certain constituencies within their region. In some ways they have a greater vested interest, since they pay assessments and are committed to represent those who put them in the position. In this sense, they often are most closely tied to the decision-making process than stockholders or the board of directors in a corporation. In recognizing the importance of the board members to various checkoff programs, one must also be careful that the experiences of powerful board members do not overpower the total preprogramming decision process. For many of the board members, their experiences are with the agribusiness industry and production rather than with the generic marketing of a commodity. Just like with agencies, balanced perspective in decision making must be achieved, recognizing the limits of one's experiences and expertise.

Controlled Experiment and Pretesting

Controlled experiments for evaluating new programs usually have three dimensions in which information is to be collected: understanding and reaction to product attributes; reaction to advertising and promotion copy; and knowledge of the profiles of those in the controlled experiment and how different individuals respond. By the very definition of the process, controlled samples are intended to gain information about events in an environment that is also controlled. The process is often costly and not without its problems, with the major one being in extrapolating the findings to a broader audience.

Reactions to specific product attributes can be of profound importance to designing advertising copy. An excellent working example would be Tropicana's development of its Pure Premium orange juice in gallon containers. This product has been highly successful because of its attributes and because of substantial investments in advertising and promotion. When the product was first being developed, several issues about the appropriate containers were raised. A controlled panel of consumers was given many different gallon container designs, and their physical, visual, and emotional reactions to the containers were recorded. This information was used to redesign the container and to tailor commercials to fit the new product design. Clearly, thousands of examples or case studies could be cited that have the common element of learning from a simulated environment. The process is referred to as the *inductive* approach, where one extrapolates from a sample to the whole population of potential consumers.

The creative ways of setting up controlled experiments are beyond the scope of both this text and our expertise. We emphasize the importance of the process, however it is designed. Some agricultural commodities lend themselves to this process better than others, and of course this has to be taken into consideration. For example, it is relatively easy to gain consumers' reaction to new slogans such as "Pork, the Other White Meat" or "Orange Juice, It's Not Just for Breakfast Anymore." Investments in such controlled experiments provide the essential ingredient to moving forward with a full programming effort, with the ingredient being the consumer's reaction.

Most often, data from controlled experiments or from a small sample are obtained without knowledge of the distribution properties of the population from which the sample is drawn. When we know or can assume something about the distribution properties of the population from which the sample is drawn, then various parametric tests can be performed to make statistical inferences. The Z, t, and F tests are the most frequently used parametric tests for drawing statistical inferences. With pretests such as gathering consumer opinions in a particular (or not so particular) setting, however, little to nothing can be assumed about the total population. Thus, none of the normal parametric tests are valid. There is a growing field of nonparametric tests that have particular importance to preprogram evaluations of potentially successful advertising and promotional programs. It should be emphasized that when both parametric and nonparametric tests are available, the parametric alternative should be selected (Hollander and Wolfe, 1973; Parket, 1974).

Briefly, in order to understand the importance of testing in evaluation research, it is useful to have some concept of measurement scales. There are four measurements of scale in which all experimental (controlled or uncontrolled) data can be classed. The most simplistic and weakest measurement exists when the *observations* are classified by name, symbol, or characteristic. For example, classing consumers by Social Security number, products by UPC code, sport fishermen by their fishing license number, or boaters by their registration number are all examples of classification using a scheme that has little numerical meaning.

Data can be classified but also scored such that the scoring reflects some *relative ranking* between items or observations. A test of several commercials in a controlled environment may ask the participants to rank each commercial as poor, fair, good, or exceptional. Responses could be with 1, 2, 3, or 4, with 4 being exceptional. Clearly, the ranking implies some ordinal scaling of attributes among the commercials being evaluated; the statistical question is to judge significant differences among the scalings. Given the unknown distribution properties of simple classifications and order scaling, many nonparametric tests have evolved to deal with drawing inferences.

Some types of scaling draw on ranking as described above but also allow for a defined interval between rankings. If the *interval scale* is constant across rankings, then one can make comparisons between rankings, since the unit adjustments are constant. With interval scaling, conclusions can be made about whether a shift from scale 1 to 2 is equal to a shift from 3 to 4, because the units are defined. A conclusion that 4 is twice 2 cannot be made, however, because the reference (or beginning) point is not established. Finally, if the measurement scale includes both a zero point and fixed units, a complete comparison can be made; this is usually called a *ratio scale*. The conclusion from the scale results can be compared because the measurement is independent of the unit of measurement.

Pretesting of potential programs requires the use of data in some form. If the data are coded as classifications or rankings, then nonparametric procedures must be adopted, whereas, if the interval scale and/or the ratio scale are used, various parametric tests can be used (Parket, 1974). We emphasize these classifications to point to the importance of using the appropriate scientific tools.

Market Experiments and Evaluations

Time permitting, programs, commercials, and new products can be studied as pilot programs in selected markets. The process entails taking a subset of the population and pretesting their response to new programs in the actual marketplace. Unlike the controlled experiments, the only control is in the markets or audiences selected for study. This process is probably one of the more costly ways of pretesting programs, yet it is one of the ways providing results closest to actual consumer responses in a real market environment.

As with other procedures, the process is too detailed for our discussion; however, a few examples are worth noting. During the early stages of the national dairy board programs, a pilot study using a split cable-system design was used in one selected city. Part of the viewing audience was scheduled to receive the advertising message, whereas the test area was not. Theoretically, one should have sample data on those who did and did not receive the messages, and from this, one could measure consumers' responses in terms of their milk consumption. The results of that particular study were quite unsatisfactory, especially given the substantial funds devoted to the effort (A.D. Little, Inc., 1985).

Many products are pretested through various means. Free samples are often used to obtain consumer responses through various types of follow-up requests for information or impressions about the product. The collection of data and the use of the information may be useful for different types of analytical procedures. Clearly, the process must be fully understood before detailed statistical conclusions are drawn.

Checkoff Data and Data Issues

We will now turn to what is often the most frustrating aspect of evaluating commodity promotional programs—data problems. Building meaningful data bases for analysis is usually the most time-consuming aspect of evaluation research. The problem, performance criteria, and methods used should dictate the data needs; yet, from a practical side, one must evaluate programs with available data. Different empirical techniques are frequently used because of the nature of the available data sets. The end research product and reports usually do not reflect the time invested in building, validating, and correcting commodity and advertising data sets essential to the evaluation effort. Our purpose in this section is to review briefly some of the more important data problems and sources. Data issues can be discussed in the framework of four major areas: data sources; timing and tabulations; quality variations and adjustments; and indexing.

Data Sources

In the discussions of postprogram evaluations, two types of general models were noted that were dependent on the data base. Data represented the responses from individual consumers in one case, and market-clearing data in the other. In both cases, the data must be collected in a statistically consistent and systematic way.

Government Sources. For many commodities, market-clearing data are published periodically through federal and state governmental agencies. Although finding the numerous sources can sometimes be frustrating, a significant benefit of government reporting of selected commodities is that the data are collected on a systematic basis and can be obtained at a minimum cost. Data on U.S. disappearance of beef, pork, poultry, and dairy products are good examples where the information is reported and updated on a periodic and reliable basis; the coverage is national and data reported at least quarterly. Researchers needing such data, however, are by definition limited to the periods and product classes included in the data releases. Overall, uses of these types of data have proven invaluable to evaluation efforts.

Information on fresh produce in the U.S. is considerably weaker. Federal government unload data for selected U.S. cities provide information on quantities and prices at the wholesale markets for those cities. These data are reported periodically and are generally considered the best available. A major limitation, though, is that they apply to a select set of cities and not the total United States. Also, within each city, only the volume passing through the wholesale market is accounted for. These limitations may or may not be important, depending on the commodity being studied. Often, federal statistics can be augmented by using state reports for selected commodities. These latter publications are usually reported periodically but may be more difficult to acquire. Sometimes comparing state and federal data for a particular commodity is a reasonable way to judge the quality of the information; however, it is not always clear which one is correct when a discrepancy is observed.

When starting the postprogram evaluation, the model $D = f(z, CK)$, along with the definitions of D and z, will determine the data needs. Usually, a first stage in the research process is to identify the data sources for both D and z. If the commodity analysis is to be based on market-clearing data, then U.S. Department of Agriculture federal disappearance and unload data are the best starting points (USDA, 1981). There is never a case where evaluation modeling can be based on just one data source. Quantities, stocks, and movements are reported in one source; prices are often drawn from another; and income and consumer information still another; and advertising data are nearly always obtained from the commodity groups. There is no systematic effort at the federal level to report marketing-enhancement expenditures on a periodic basis.

These mixtures of data sources can become an important problem, both empirically and statistically. A working example can illustrate the point. In Ward and Dixon's study (1989) of fluid milk advertising, milk consumption was reported through the federal and state milk market order systems and represented by milk utilization records of fluid milk processing plants. Data were available from twelve of the regions, representing approximately 40 percent of the U.S. population. Income and demographic data were drawn from separate data sources that did not initially match up with the milk market order regions. Furthermore, the reporting times for the demographics did not correspond with those of the volume data. Careful procedures had to be devised to make sure that the data sources could be matched and used in a consistent manner. Such problems are real but are often not discussed sufficiently in written reports.

The problems can become even more complicated when data sets from different types of data are merged. For example, sometimes it is useful to incorporate information from consumer panel data into a time series model using national market-clearing data. An example would be the inclusion of consumer panel data on health concerns into the national beef checkoff model developed by Ward (1992). There is not a comprehensive national index adequately reflecting consumers' health profile and concerns, whereas there are several consumer panel sources of data from which a sample health profile can be determined. At issue is whether or not these panel results are representative enough to be included in the national models drawing primarily on time series data. Often the merging of such data, while not preferable, is the only alternative to the researcher.

Private Sources. In contrast to sources of market-clearing data, there are a number of private companies whose business is collecting and selling consumer behavior data. These data sources are usually based on consumer reports, sales monitoring, or various forms of store audits. Consumer reports are most often based on a consumer panel data base where periodic purchasing diaries are maintained. A representative cross section of consumers is usually included in the panel, and each participant reports his or her purchasing activities for certain product categories. Such panel data have proven extremely useful in many evaluation efforts, primarily because they provide a data source on consumer behavior and do not confound supply and demand factors.

The most important pitfall is that information is only reported about a product when it is consumed. One knows nothing about the products that are not reported by a consumer. Did the consumer choose not to buy the advertised good, was it not available, or was the price simply too high? When one considers all of the potential ramifications of panel data, the question can be raised as to exactly what has been measured. Considerable care must be taken in knowing your data bases, their strengths and weaknesses, how they were collected, and how they can be used. Without this knowledge, statistical inferences based on their use is suspect.

Practical Data Issues. As a practical caveat, it should be noted that most evaluations must be completed with what is available. From our experiences, however, there is almost always another way to address the problem, another way to look at the data, and another way to express the information. What is important is that one finally reaches definitive conclusions that are robust across the various ways of addressing the same issue.

In contrast to panel data or period reporting, several data services collect market information through store monitoring and audits. Companies such as A.C. Nielsen have been important leaders in this field. Historically, store audits of one or more major brands for a particular product have been used as the collection point. Auditors collect invoices and record prices for selected products; from these audits, data bases of product prices and movements are developed. Another type of audit has been to record the product as it enters warehouses. Warehouse disappearance data may capture product entering markets beyond the retail outlets but may not reflect the price at the final point of consumption. The SAMI data base was one of the better-known warehouse disappearance databases.

In addition to store audits, the advent of computer scanning has created a new avenue for collecting in-store data (Capps, 1988; Jensen and Schroeter, 1992). Scanner data include quantity, prices, discounts, and possibly information about the consumer. Consumer information is not always assured, however, especially when the transaction is with customers that do not provide any type of identification that is precoded into the store's computer system. Somewhat like panel data, scanning information is based on actual purchases by the consumer. In contrast to panel data, however, both the product price and product availability can be reported along with the consumer purchases. Also, the scanner is based on actual purchases and does not depend on consumer recall about their purchases. A major weakness is that not all purchases are made using scanners; thus, not all transactions by one consumer are necessarily recorded. In principle, with the panel, all transactions are recorded regardless of how the products are purchased. As with market-clearing data, the evaluator must be aware of the data base's strengths and weaknesses and the limits to its use.

Product Characteristics, Quality, and Data Base Issues

Much of our discussion of advertising and promotion theory has been based on product attributes and quality. The U.S. food system is probably the safest and most consistent in the world; even so, there can be quality changes, randomness in certain attributes, and spoilage. These all influence consumer choices and most certainly have a direct bearing on the responses achieved with advertising and promotion. Although U.S. standards are generally well established, most data bases are quite weak in reflecting quality scores and in weighing product attributes. Frequently, the only way to score quality in large data sets is by brand and type of store. For fresh produce that is usually subject to quality variation and spoilage, such information can be of profound importance, yet it is usually impossible to collect this type of information on a systematic reporting basis.

Equally important are the purchases of different product grades and packaging. Both disappearance data (that is, market-clearing data) and consumer response data most often do not account for purchases across grades and/or packaging. For many products this is not a particularly important issue because there is little variation in product quality. Marketing of fluid milk with freshness dates, for example, has generally led to a distribution with minimal quality variation. Some commodities such as beef (which is moving toward a leaner product), however, are in a state of transition. Most reported data bases do not reflect such changes in the underlying characteristics of the product. Thus, when we measure q for beef in 1970, for example, the same level of q in 1992 may not the be same product. This clearly creates data problems that must be dealt with either in the collection process or with the statistical procedures. As discussed earlier, parameter stability in some models can be traced back to improvements (or changes) in the product being reported.

Mandatory product labeling with the information included in the UPC codes will probably provide the most detailed information about product characteristics. Such labels should include the product characteristics, freshness and purchasing dates, packaging type, and storage requirements. From such data sources information on prices, quantities, product attributes, and buyer profiles could be reported. Also, the characteristics of the outlet, stocks, and store prices could be included. The most apparent problem is with the proliferation of products and the massive amount of information that can be generated by even one outlet. Another weakness is that even with the consumer information and profile, there still are not data on whether or not a particular consumer was exposed to specific advertising messages. Part of the consumer profile may reflect how much time is spent watching television or other media; from this, one may make some linkage of purchases with new advertising and promotional campaigns. For example, in our model $D = f(z, CK)$, total expenditures by the checkoff program might be included for each consumer and weighted by the reported hours watching television in a typical week ($D = f(z, CK, $ tv time$)$). This would at least give some index of the potential exposure by the consumer whose purchases are being scanned.

Cross-Sectional and Time Series Data

Data bases can be cross-sectional, time series, or a combination of both. A *cross-sectional* data base is a slice across a point in time where information is recorded over defined groups, whereas *time series* are the reported data over time, with the data usually aggregated over cross sections. For example, scanner data for one day are cross-sectional, whereas federal disappearance data are time series. Occasionally, information can be obtained in both cross-sectional and time series forms. In some analyses it is useful to use both types of data; this calls for pooling cross-sectional and time series procedures (Dielman, 1989).

For many commodities, pooling these two data sources offers some unique opportunities for evaluating commodity advertising and promotional programs. The major advantage exists because of cross-sectional variations in the data, as well as changes over time. The pooled data allow for measuring potential structural changes that occur over time and at the same moment capture differences among the units in the cross section. Some checkoff programs may have variation across regions but much less variation from season to season; thus, the cross-sectional dimension facilitates measurement of the advertising effect because of regional differences more than chronological differences. There may be more variation in both D and z among cross-sectional units than over time. For example, U.S. unload data for many types of fresh produce include cross sections of selected cities, with the information tabulated monthly. Using these data may call for pooling procedures, depending on the problem of interest. Sometimes media use differs by regions, cities, or other cross-sectional units, and their effectiveness can possibly be measured using the pooled data approach. Pooled data can generally be used with any of the models described earlier in this chapter. An example of pooled cross-sectional and time series data is presented in Chapter 7 in the section on milk.

Although exceptions can be found, usually data collected for preprogram evaluations are cross sectional only; that is, the information is for one point in time. Costs and timing often prevent collecting both cross-sectional and time series data on a preprogram basis. Nothing can be learned about the dynamics of the programs (such as the advertising carryover effect) with just cross-sectional data. One cannot measure seasonal differences, and issues relating to optimal timing of programs cannot be dealt with. In contrast, the importance of demographics and how advertising and promotion may interact with demographics can usually be better addressed with cross-sectional data.

Pooling these data offers the advantages of dealing with both dynamics (lagged advertising effects) and demographic differences. Even so, there are problems inherent with such data. The most apparent one is accounting for differences in the cross-sectional units in the pooled model. Increased variation in the explanatory variables comes at a cost of having more to explain, because the performance criteria (for example, demand) vary both over time and across units. Researchers often find it more difficult to model these problems successfully, since so many more factors are involved.

When considering the evaluation process and the available data, one should usually opt for cross-sectional and time series data when it is available. As a rule, you can aggregate over the cross sections and use time series methods of analysis or simply take each point in time as a separate point for analyses. The only difficulty in aggregating across units is in establishing the appropriate weights for the aggregation (Ward and Dixon, 1989).

Checkoff Data Scaling and Indexing

As a final data issue, the units of advertising and promotion must be clearly defined. Criteria for judging checkoff programs include defining the units of measurement. For most econometric studies, checkoff programs are expressed in terms of expenditures. Expenditures are probably the best measure, but using it comes with its own set of problems. The problems can be grouped in four areas: (1) dealing with zero advertising expenditures; (2) accounting for media cost, coverage, and inflation; (3) differentiating among programs with correlated expenditures; and (4) media scheduling, timing, and reporting. Each of these is discussed without ranking the importance of one issue over the other, for in most cases, one or more of the problems occur simultaneously.

Advertising and Zero Values. Most commodity programs have periods where no expenditures are made on programs. Thus, there are periods with zero observations. The importance of the zero expenditures depends on the model specification, that is, $f(z, CK)$. If the model is strictly linear, such as $D = \alpha_0 + \alpha_1 z + \alpha_2 CK + v$, then the issue of zero values is trivial. Yet, as emphasized throughout this text, the role of advertising is most certainly not linear, especially if one accepts the four criteria at the start of this chapter. If the nature of the modeling entails a nonlinear transformation of CK, such as log (CK) or $1/CK$, then the model is not defined when CK is equal to zero. If the modeling specified in equation 6–1 is used, then the zero observations are of no consequences, since when CK approaches zero, the advertising impact multiplier equals one. Many models discussed in the postprogram section, however, incorporate advertising into the model using log (CK) or a similar form. Clearly, log (CK) is not defined when CK approaches zero. One procedure is to include an ad hoc scaler in the log function such that the function will always have some positive element: $\log(\kappa + CK)$. This κ is sometimes referred to as an index of goodwill (see Ward and Dixon, 1989), where even without expenditures there exists some effect of the effort because of the knowledge base or goodwill that has been created. Kappa (κ) can be selected using various search procedures. Unlike the parameters in equation 6–1, however, the researcher seldom has prior knowledge about the appropriate magnitude of κ. Using equation 6–1 is a better approach than imposing κ on the specification. In our review of many of the published works on advertising, it is not at all clear how the zero-value issue was handled.

Missing values entail a different issue from zero expenditure levels. There are several ways for dealing with this problem, but they are all ad hoc. The mean advertising value can be included, or one can interpolate between adjacent values. If seasonal expenditures are apparent, then some type of seasonal adjustment consistent with reported data can be used where the missing value is forecast using a seasonal index model and the nearby reported expenditures. Or the entire observation can be dropped from the analysis; this is usually an unacceptable option, because other valid information is being discarded. When alternative data points are substituted into the model for missing expenditure values, it is important that one test the robustness of the results by using slight deviations from the assumed value. If the results are robust, then one does not have to be as concerned with the artificially imposed expenditure level.

Media Cost, Coverage, and Inflation. Checkoff expenditures involve the purchase of copy, media, and coverage. The cost of each increases over time and is generally thought to be in accord with the overall inflation in the economy. Optimally, any expenditures should be indexed to the changing costs over time and across media. Cost will differ by media and extent of coverage; however, it is nearly impossible to acquire meaningful indices of media costs on a systematically reported basis. In Ward and Dixon's study of the fluid milk market, they used a media index of inflation for radio versus television and then expressed the expenditures on a per capita basis. The per capita basis was based on the reported population in the defined media viewing area. Thus, their expenditure index was real expenditures per capita viewing audience. Such data for indexing is hard to obtain and is not tabulated in a consistent format over time. Clearly, it is as important to have a reliably calculated index as it is to be using the correct index. Most studies have deflated advertising with the consumer price index and expressed it on a national or regional per capita basis. Over long periods, using the consumer price index versus media index will probably not make much difference. For shorter periods, however, there may be a substantial difference between the results using a media index versus the consumer price index.

Correlated Expenditures. Another type of data problem that often occurs is when there is considerable correlation among variables within the data set. The correlations may be between z and CK in the function $f(z, CK)$ or between $CK1$, $CK2$, and $CK3$ when expenditures are broken down by program area. For illustration purposes, suppose that the problem is with correlations among the types of program areas (that is, $CK1$, $CK2$, $CK3$, and so forth. If $CK = CK1 + CK2 + CK3 + \ldots$ but interest is in the effects of each program area, then each program expenditure must be included in the model as discussed in an earlier section of this chapter. Furthermore, if the data and programming are such that each expenditure is a fixed share of the total, then it is impossible to estimated the separate gains from each (that is, the program expenditures *CK1*, *CK2*, and *CK3* are perfectly correlated). If instead the program expenditures were correlated, but not perfectly, the problem becomes one of dealing with multicollinearity. The basic consequence of this problem is that meaningful tests using standard t distributions cannot be made, because the multicollinearity problem causes some variances of the estimated coefficients to become excessively large. The reader should always look at the conditional index for a strong test of the potential problem of multicollinearity (Gujarati, 1988).

One procedure for dealing with this data problem is a principal components procedure. This procedure is based on the conditions that a new set of variables (*C*'s) are to be created from the initial set (*CK*'s), but the new variables are not correlated. Principal components are weights of the original vectors, with these weights noted as loading factors. Weights are derived so that the new variables are not correlated, but at the same time the principal components include most of the informational content that was in the original data.

For illustration purposes, we use three types of beef promotion programs: checkoff advertising and promotion (*CK1*), consumer information (*CK2*), and industry information programs (*CK3*); these expenditures are correlated but not perfectly. With the principal-components techniques, three new vectors are calculated as illustrated below.

$$C1 = \omega_{11} \, CK1 + \omega_{12} \, CK2 + \omega_{13} \, CK3$$
$$C2 = \omega_{21} \, CK1 + \omega_{22} \, CK2 + \omega_{23} \, CK3 \qquad (6.6)$$
$$C3 = \omega_{31} \, CK1 + \omega_{32} \, CK2 + \omega_{33} \, CK3$$

Vectors *C1*, *C2*, and *C3* have all the information that was in the original data set, but they are also uncorrelated. The weights or loading factors are ω_{ij}, a way for weighing the original information. The procedure is well documented in the statistics literature and has been used over a wide range of problems.

Often, the first principal component will account for most of the variability found in the original data set. In many cases, the first two components will represent more than 95 percent of the original information. Thus, the evaluation procedure is to use the variable *C1* and possibly *C2* in place of CK1, *CK2*, and *CK3* in the regression models. To further our illustration, let the original model be linear, where $D = \alpha_0 + \alpha_1 z + \alpha_2 CK1 + \alpha_3 CK2 + \alpha_4 CK3$, but assume that data problems exist with *CK1*, *CK2* and *CK3*. If the first and second principal components accounted for, say, 95 percent of the information in the original data set, them the model is estimated as shown below.

$$D = \xi_0 + \xi_1 C1 + \xi_2 C2 + \nu \qquad (6.7)$$

After estimating equation 6–7, the original coefficients (α's) immediately follow where:

$$\begin{aligned}
\alpha_0 &= \xi_0 \\
\alpha_1 &= \xi_1 \omega_{11} + \xi_2 \omega_{12} \\
\alpha_2 &= \xi_1 \omega_{21} + \xi_2 \omega_{22} \\
\alpha_3 &= \xi_1 \omega_{31} + \xi_2 \omega_{32}
\end{aligned} \qquad (6.8)$$

Given the values of the α's, it is again possible to draw the appropriate statistical inferences using the α's estimated with equation 6–8. Again, the linear model was used for illustration convenience; other functional forms can be used equally well.

Media Scheduling, Timing, and Reporting. Another very practical data problem is when there is a difference between the reported expenditures for a program and the actual implementation of a program. During the evaluation exercise, it is absolutely essential that expenditures reflect when actual programs took place, not when they were planned or when invoices were paid. Timing and reporting of expenditures are primarily important when modeling the lagged effects of advertising and promotion. The performance from checkoff programs should be linked to when the programs were taking place. If the recorded expenditures do not correspond with the exact program schedule, then it is possible to measure erroneously (or to fail to measure) a lagged advertising response. Using the model to make allocation decisions thus would be incorrect, and coordinating optimal timing of programs could be in error. This is not a statistical or modeling problem; it is simply a recording problem that must be carefully handled to assure the maximum quality to the evaluation effort. It is at this point that the researcher must be in close touch with those who know the "ins and outs" of the promotional programs for the particular commodity.

Summary

Commodity evaluation is an integral part of the total process of promoting agricultural commodities. It is at this stage that data bases, consistency in recording program activities, and appropriateness of statistical techniques become important. Problems with any of these can lead to misleading (or no) conclusions about program effectiveness. In this chapter, we have identified a cadre of problems and methods for dealing with them. The process of evaluation entails first and foremost the delineation of the performance criteria and acceptable definitions of the programs. For this, methods are devised to either judge performance and draw inferences about the potential success of planned programs.

Our intent in this chapter was not to give a detailed description of each and every empirical tool that can be relevant to particular evaluation problems. There are simply too many topics even to attempt detailed essays on each potentially important quantitative tool. Instead, we have noted the issues and suggested methods appropriate for the problems. With new developments in computer technology and quantitative techniques, the ability to address evaluation issues has greatly expanded. Furthermore, recognition of the importance of good research techniques by those responsible for checkoff programs makes evaluation efforts even more exciting and meaningful. Researchers have the responsibility to know the industry being evaluated. One cannot draw meaningful inferences without knowing the limits of the data used, the unique aspects of each checkoff program, and the ways programs are implemented and recorded.

The quantitative tools and computer programs are only as good as the user. One must know the limits of their problem sets and what can and cannot be addressed with quantitative tools. There are problems that simply do not lend themselves to econometrics. Policymakers must have realistic expectations of what is to be learned with such quantitative methods and how they can be used. Of all methods available for addressing parts of the performance issue, econometrics probably offers the most insight if presented in an informative narrative; it is a complex field of analysis and can often be expressed in such a way that the general reader sees no value in the results. Researchers must be rigorous with their analysis and equally rigorous with their efforts to show the results in a way that can be easily applied to policy issues. In the next chapter, we will turn to several case studies that apply and/or deal with many of the issues addressed in this chapter.

7

Selected Case Studies of Commodity Advertising Program Evaluations

Are advertising programs effective in achieving their goals? What do we know about the current state of economic evaluation? Are there commonalities among the programs in terms of their effectiveness? What methods of analysis have been used, and what have been the data requirements? In this chapter, our intent is to review several studies to demonstrate types of evaluation efforts, drawing heavily (but not exclusively) on our own research. Most of the evaluations are based on empirical methods where computer modeling is an essential element to the evaluation. Econometric estimation techniques are found within each case study. Each study provides insight into the economics of commodity advertising.

While each case stands alone, the reader should be particularly cognizant of the economic theory, empirical methodologies, and results in terms of their applications to other advertising problem sets. That is, can we conclude from these studies that generic advertising and promotion have a measurable impact? Similarly, do we see evaluation strategies that could assist in the review of newer programs as well as continuing programs?

For many readers, econometrics is well understood, as are the associated problems. We also recognize, though, that many readers will not be familiar with econometrics. Hence, we have tried to reach a balance between the rigor of econometrics and communicating what can be learned about advertising effectiveness with the tool. Econometrics is simply an empirical tool that facilitates measuring the impact of factors contributing to changes in the variables of interest (see Chapter 6). For example, how do we go about measuring the effects of price, income, inflation, and advertising on the demand for milk? With econometrics, models can be specified that are representative of the demand for specific commodities such as milk, beef, or other products. In writing this chapter, we have tried to include enough information about the modeling effects and techniques to satisfy the curiosity of the professional economist, yet not so much that it will subtract from the

196

importance and value of econometrics to the casual reader and readers more interested in the implications.

In economic modeling, the reliability of the estimates can be assessed and the model's ability for forecasting determined. Econometric models can be used to evaluate different policy alternatives, such as projecting the gains from increased assessments and expanded generic programs. Econometric models draw on both time series and cross sectional data, representing actual market conditions in a historical setting. The data represent the market experiment; the experiment is real and occurring daily in the marketplace. The task is to take these data and sort out the major elements contributing to change, including advertising as one element. Rather than having controlled experiments (see Chapter 6) such as focus groups or in-store controlled programs, we are using econometrics to analyze the real events that have taken place. Of course, econometrics can play an important role in analyzing experimental data, but our primary focus is on cases where the data are taken from the marketplace. Each case is not given the same level of treatment because of differences in program size, importance, research knowledge, and need for explanation.

Advertising Case Studies

Each case reviewed in this chapter draws on several statistical procedures. For each study we will note the problem, detail the data needs and methodology, and then review the conclusions. There is no implied ranking in the order that the cases are reviewed. Rather, the cases are used to illustrate several different approaches to evaluation and to demonstrate the complexity of the evaluation process. The importance of maintaining data bases of consistent quality will be apparent as we progress through the cases. Furthermore, the types of advertising and promotional efforts will differ among the studies, and the appropriate methods of analysis should be evident. Notation consistent with the published research will be used; hence, notation in one case should not be carried over to the next case. The cases included are programs for fluid milk, beef, apples, cheese, wool, catfish, orange juice, coupons, soybeans, oils, and tomatoes.

Fluid Milk Advertising

Perhaps the most ambitious promotion campaign for agricultural products has been undertaken by the U.S. dairy industry. Under the 1983 National Dairy and Tobacco Adjustment Act, legal authority was established for the dairy industry to implement a mandatory assessment on all dairy producers in order to underwrite a national dairy advertising program. The act explicitly required an annual evaluation of the programs.

The dairy industry has a long history of evaluation efforts. Much of the early analysis can be found with research from Cornell University dealing with the New York milk promotion programs (Forker and Liu, 1989). Subsequent modeling efforts for the United Dairy Industry Association have been the antecedent to much of the current research for the national fluid milk program. Since the start of the national programs, much of the economic analysis of the national milk advertising program has been completed by Ward and Dixon (1989) and Blaylock and Blisard (1988). Operations of the national dairy programs were described in Chapter 5, and we will not repeat those details here; rather, we will concentrate on the evaluation efforts. Although a number of papers exist that show the effects of regional dairy advertising, Ward and Dixon's published model is the first to address the national program. Hence, our review will emphasize the methods and results of that study. The results of some other dairy studies will be briefly presented.

The national dairy programs started with existing regional programs already in place. Regional programs were operated, for the most part, under state and federal milk market orders. Voluntary and state orders preceded the federal orders and were always bigger; the New York state program preceded the federal orders, as did those of several other states. Hence, the fundamental evaluation question was to measure the economic impact of the national efforts recognizing the role of existing regional activities. The National Dairy Board was established to administer the programs, yet existing organizations (such as the United Dairy Industry Association) were expected to play a major role in the program implementation and evaluation. State programs, including those in California, New York, and Wisconsin, and several regional programs accounted for almost two-thirds of the generic dairy advertising budget.

What methodology is appropriate when national programs are overlaid on existing regional efforts? Ward and Dixon (1989) developed an econometric model where monthly data collected from the regions could be used to address the advertising evaluation questions. Their methodology is one of pooling cross-sectional and time series data, with the cross sections being selected milk market order areas and time being continuous monthly sales and price data. Through the pooling procedures, one can gain experiences from changes over time and differences across the regions. As an example, most of the price variability in fluid milk is found among the regions rather than through time. Given the price behavior of the dairy industry, meaningful price responses are difficult to measure by viewing time adjustments alone. Studies of the New York state markets provide some exceptions.

Cross-Sectional–Time Series Dairy Model. Ward and Dixon's model includes three underlying theoretical premises. Advertising does enter the demand functions, as initially discussed in Chapter 2, and there is likely to be some carryover effect of the advertising. Also, the effectiveness of the advertising is most likely to have changed after the start of the nationally coordinated efforts. This change is reflected through direct increases in advertising effectiveness (that is, increases in the return per dollar spent) and through more longer-term changes in consumers preferences for dairy products. Though advertising may be effective in changing the demand for fluid milk, the gains are not expected to be proportional to continued increases in the program expenditures.

Ward and Dixon's model further shows consumer demographic effects on fluid milk consumption. Their model measures differences attributed to race, age, family size, education, and urbanization of the population; effects of income, inflation, substitutes, and seasonality in demand are accounted for. The complete model is specified below in equation 7–1. The model was estimated allowing for first-order autocorrelation within each cross section and contemporaneous correlation in the errors across the regions. (This estimation procedure is sometimes referred to as the "Parks method" for dealing with pooled data.) Table 7–1 gives the variable definitions for equation 7–1.

$$
\begin{aligned}
LNPCADS_{it} = {}& \beta_0 + \beta_1 LNMAPR_{it} + \beta_2 LNOJPR_{it} + \beta_3 LNDPCIN_{it} + \\
& \beta_4 LNNU18_{it} \\
& + \beta_5 LNFEM_{it} + \beta_6 LNBLK_{it} + \beta_7 LNRUR_{it} + \beta_8 LNHOUS_{it} + \\
& \beta_9 LNSCHL_{it} + \beta_{10} LNADVER_{it} + \beta_{11} ADV1_{it} \\
& + \beta_{12} ADV2_{it} + \beta_{13} ADV3_{it} + \beta_{14} ADV4_{it} + {}_{15} LNTIME_{it} + \\
& \beta_{16} TT1_{it} + \beta_{17} TT2_{it} \\
& + \beta_{18} TT3_{it} + \beta_{19} TT4_{it} + \beta_{19} DJAN_{it} + \beta_{21} DFEB_{it} + \beta_{22} DMAR_{it} + \\
& \beta_{23} DAPR_{it} + \beta_{24} DMAY_{it} + \beta_{25} DJUN_{it} \\
& + \beta_{26} DJLY_{it} + \beta_{27} DAUG_{it} + \beta_{28} DSEP_{it} + \beta_{29} DOCT_{it} + \\
& \beta_{30} DNOV_{it} + \varepsilon_{it}
\end{aligned}
\tag{7.1}
$$

The error term ε_{it} is hypothesized to follow a first-order autoregressive pattern, as displayed in the following equation:

$$
\begin{aligned}
& \varepsilon_{it} = \rho_i \varepsilon_{i(t-1)} + \mu_{it} \\
& E(\mu_{it}\, \mu_{jt'}) = \sigma_{ij} \text{ if } t = t', \text{ or } 0 \text{ otherwise}
\end{aligned}
\tag{7.1a}
$$

Our interest in this pooled model is primarily to show how advertising is incorporated. Data used in Ward and Dixon's analysis included advertising expenditures for twelve milk market order regions; these regions represented approximately 40 percent of the U.S. population. Before September 1984, the regional expenditures accounted for the total fluid milk advertising effort. The national programs started in September and included both direct fluid milk media advertising and advertising of calcium. Before the national programs started, advertising was expressed in deflated media expenditures

Table 7–1
Variable Definitions and Notation for the Pooled Cross-Section–Time Series Model for Fluid Milk Advertising

Variables	Description
LNPCADS	Log of the average daily ounces consumed per capita by regions and months.
LNMAPR	Log of the deflated fluid milk price per half gallon with price reported by the market administrator for selected U.S. cities.
LNOJPR	Log of deflated price of frozen orange juice concentrate
LNDPCIN	Log of the deflated per capita income across regions and over time.
LNNU18	Log of the percentage of a region's population under 18 years of age.
LNBLK	Log of the percentage of a region's population that is black.
LNRUR	Log of the percentage of a region's population that lives in rural areas.
LNFEM	Log of the percentage of a region's population that is female.
LNHOUS	Log of the percentage of a region's households that are single-member families.
LNSCHL	Log of the median number of years of education for individuals over 25 years of age.
LNADVER	The advertising variable expressed as a restricted polynomial lagged model with advertising measured in real per capita advertising expenditures.
LNTIME	Log of the variable TIME
T1	Equal one when $116 < \text{TIME} <= 128$
T2	Equal one when $128 < \text{TIME} <= 141$
T3	Equal one when $141 < \text{TIME} <= 153$
T4	Equal one when $153 < \text{TIME} <= 165$
ADV1	LNADVER * T1
ADV2	LNADVER * T2
ADV3	LNADVER * T3
ADV4	LNADVER * T4
TT1	LNTIME * T1
TT2	LNTIME * T2
TT3	LNTIME * T3
TT4	LNTIME * T4
DJAN	Seasonal dummy variable for January
DFEB	Seasonal dummy variable for February
DMAR	Seasonal dummy variable for March
DAPR	Seasonal dummy variable for April
DMAY	Seasonal dummy variable for May
DJUN	Seasonal dummy variable for June
DJLY	Seasonal dummy variable for July
DAUG	Seasonal dummy variable for August
DSEP	Seasonal dummy variable for September
DOCT	Seasonal dummy variable for October
DNOV	Seasonal dummy variable for November

Source: Ward and Dixon (1989).

per capita according to the population in each region. After September 1984, national expenditures were expressed in real per capita dollars based on the total U.S. population. These national per capita values were then added to each region's per capita expenditure levels. This total, then, represents the advertising intensity within each region. The national intensity would be the same for each region, but the regional programs would differ, thus giving regional differences in the programs. This total regional advertising effort was then included in the fluid milk model as illustrated in equation 7–1.

Given that advertising is expected to have some carryover or lagged impact on fluid milk sales, a distributive lag specification of the advertising expenditures was used. A second-degree polynomial lag with endpoint restrictions was finally adopted as the appropriate specification. Ward and Dixon concluded that the best specification occurred with a twelve-month lagged model using the endpoint restrictions. Before adopting the lagged structure, advertising was expressed in log form with the incorporation of a goodwill index, noted with kappa values in the analysis (see Chapter 6). The kappa value also simply captures the situation where, even with zero advertising in one month, there always exists some level of information about the product from other sources. The kappa value represents a practical way for dealing with log transformations in the advertising data when in some months actual expenditures are zero.

Ward and Dixon further hypothesized that the effectiveness of fluid milk advertising was likely to have changed after the start of the nationally coordinated efforts: advertising copies and messages were better coordinated, and a wider audience was reached. To accommodate this potential improvement, they used varying parameter models where the advertising effectiveness measure was allowed to change over time. A hypothesis in their model was that during the first year of the national effort, there might be little difference between pre- and postadvertising effectiveness. During the second and subsequent years, however, the effectiveness of the same advertising intensity might show considerable improvement. Their model provides a direct test of this hypothesis. Using the pooled model and the resulting estimated effects of advertising and other variables, Ward and Dixon then developed simulations to show the impact of advertising for periods before and after the start of the national programs.

Gains from the National Dairy Programs. Figure 7–1 provides initial insight into the dynamics of the advertising effects. The solid bars in this figure show the measured effect of fluid milk advertising in terms of the estimated parameters. For example, the first solid bar is for the pre-act period. After the first year of the national programs (September 1984 to July 1985), the effectiveness of advertising is shown to have increased slightly. In the second year, the results indicate a major increase, as reflected with the third solid bar. Finally, the last two solid bars point to some leveling off by the October

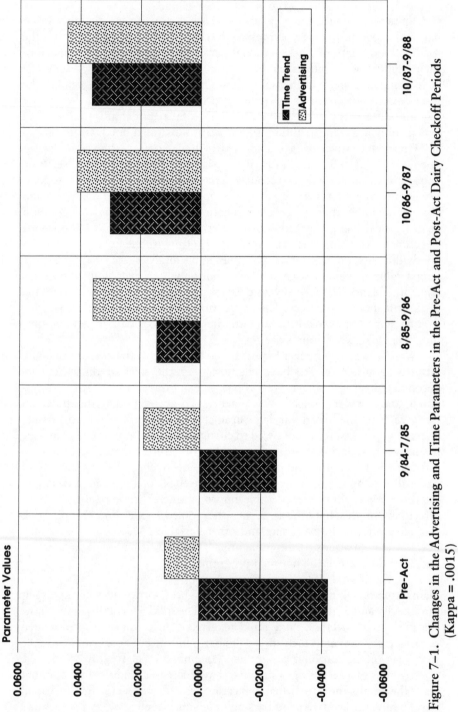

Figure 7–1. Changes in the Advertising and Time Parameters in the Pre-Act and Post-Act Dairy Checkoff Periods (Kappa = .0015)

1987–September 1988 period. It appears from the figure that fluid milk advertising effectiveness improved with the national efforts and approached a new plateau.

The pooled model also included a time shifter to capture the long-term downward trend in fluid milk consumption that has been observed for some time. Such trends reflect habit persistence (see Chapter 1) that is usually difficult to change. A question of interest was to determine if any evidence existed to suggest that the habit persistence toward lower milk consumption had been reversed after the new programs began. Ward and Dixon allowed their time trend also to change in much the same manner that they dealt with shifts in advertising effectiveness. Their conclusions are also illustrated in Figure 7–1 with the shaded bars. The first large shaded bar indicates a negative value consistent with a downward trend in milk consumption after accounting for all other factors. The negative trend persists in the first year of the national programs, whereas comparing the shaded bars in the months after August 1985 shows a complete reversal, with the time trend being positive. Empirical results point to a strengthening of fluid milk demand during the latter years of the analysis.

Table 7–2 provides a summary of the impact of fluid milk advertising as derived with the Ward and Dixon model. During the pre-act months, total advertising was $90.4 million for the twelve regions. For the same regions, post-act advertising totaled $104.8 million, including the share of the national total prorated to the twelve regions. Pre-act expenditures produced a 3.37 percent increase in fluid milk sales over what would have existed without any advertising. These gains translated into 44.13 pounds per dollar of expenditures on average. For the post-act months (column 4 in Table 7–2), sales gains from all advertising yielded a 7.8 percent increase in fluid milk sales relative to no advertising beyond that reflected with the goodwill index. Each advertising dollar for the post-act programs produced an average increase of 62.54 pounds in fluid milk sales; this latter gain reflects both regional and national efforts.

The last column in Table 7–2 shows the gains attributed to the national advertising after subtracting out a level of regional expenditures that it was assumed would have occurred if the national programs had not developed. The simulations give an overall increase of 3.25 percent in fluid milk sales above what would have occurred if the national programs had not existed. The significant improvement in advertising effectiveness is seen with the average gain of 96.93 pounds per advertising dollar (column 5). Finally, the model was extended to show the marginal gains from increasing assessments beyond the current levels.

Results of this study confirm a statistically significant relationship between fluid milk consumption and generic milk advertising. This study indicates that increases in consumption from advertising are more a function of a national campaign, as opposed to regional efforts, than of an increase in

Table 7–2
Estimated Gains in Fluid Milk Sales for the Pre- and Post-Act Periods

Total Effect (1)	Units (2)	Pre-Act (3)	Post-Act (4)	Post-Act Simulated (5)
Advertising expenditures	dollar	$90,442,848	$104,793,833	$29,421,683
Sales gains due to advertising	Millions of pounds	3,991.3	6,553.7	2,851.8
Gains as a share of total sales	Percent	3.37%	7.80%	3.25%
Average gains per advertising dollar	Pounds per dollar	62.54	96.93	

Source: Ward and Dixon (1989).

total advertising expenditures (Ward and Dixon, 1989). Their conclusion is supported by the significant shifts in both the advertising and time-trend coefficients and the increases in the average return per dollar of advertising in the post-act periods compared to the pre-act years. Recent updates of the Ward and Dixon model by Blaylock and Blisard in their report to Congress suggest that these shifts in the advertising coefficients have peaked and declined slightly in the 1990–91 analysis (U.S. Department of Agriculture, 1992).

New York Milk Markets Studies. There are several studies dealing with the New York milk markets that are similar in their use of single-equation models of the regional demand for fluid milk. These models use market-specific time series (not cross-sectional) data and incorporate some form of a lagged advertising effect. A number of different ways for measuring these lagged responses are included. Thompson, Eiler, and Forker (1976) provide much of the details found in the studies of the New York milk markets, using linear models for the New York City, Albany, and Syracuse markets. Their models include the normal explanatory variables, along with lagged advertising effects. In an early study, advertising was shown to be significant in the New York City market, but not so in the Albany and Syracuse markets. Estimates for New York City showed the greatest impact after two months, with the effect fully realized within seven months. Using their model and the increase in the New York promotion order expenditures in 1973, Thompson, Eiler, and Forker concluded that per capita milk sales increased 94 ounces in New York City; 46 ounces in Albany, and 13 ounces in Syracuse. Their estimates of producer returns for the same period and markets was $0.104 per person for New York City, $0.028 per person for Albany, and -$0.031 for Syracuse. It was emphasized that the results for Albany and Syracuse were based on statistically insignificant estimates. Finally, Thompson, Eiler, and Forker extended their model to consider supply responses. Thompson and Eiler (1977), using the New York City estimates, considered the importance of the Class I–Class II price differential to the evaluation of the measured effectiveness of the advertising in the New York City market.

Kinnucan's study (1987) of the Buffalo, New York, market is one of the series of regional analyses where the impact of the Ontario Milk Marketing Board has been evaluated. His study demonstrates some of the common estimation problems that can be experienced with single-market studies conducted over relatively short time periods. In particular, Kinnucan acknowledges the difficulties associated with limited variability in some of the important variables and problems associated with correlations among some explanatory variables. Furthermore, estimation problems are encountered when the advertising data tends to follow seasonal consumption patterns. This study also provides an applied example of using Hadar's "discount-equivalent" index. Discount-equivalent is the price reduction required to maintain the same sales level if advertising were reduced to zero (Kinnucan, 1987).

Liu and Forker (1990), in a later study of the New York City, Albany, and Syracuse markets, observed that the response to advertising had strengthened in Syracuse relative to the other two New York markets. Using an optimal control model, they concluded that greater economic returns could be realized by reallocating media expenditures. Based on their results, expenditures were tripled in Syracuse. In another study of the New York City market, Kinnucan and Forker (1986) noted that responses to advertising followed a seasonal pattern. These kinds of analyses can provide useful information in deciding how to allocate advertising expenditures both spatially and seasonally.

Most of the dairy models are quantity dependent; it is hypothesized that the advertising efforts have a direct influence on the quantity demanded. This is logical for fluid milk, since the price of fluid milk is regulated and the supply of milk for fluid uses is readily available at the regulated price.

A National Dairy Industry Model. To go beyond the single-equation time series models, Liu, Kaiser, Forker, and Mount (1989) developed a multiproduct, multitrade-level model that concurrently accounts for the market impact of the nation's generic fluid milk advertising program and the generic manufactured dairy product advertising program. The model also concurrently accounts for the price and volume behavior of processors and of milk producers to the advertising-induced stronger demand. By using this kind of a complete industry model, the analyst can determine the relationship between manufactured product and fluid milk advertising. This relationship, in turn, can be used to provide insight into the proper allocation of advertising funds between the two groups of products. The model can also be used to determine the extent to which dairy producers share the benefits of the generic advertising program with fluid milk and manufactured dairy product processors. Because the model simultaneously estimates the impact of advertising on the price of milk, the quantity demanded, and the quantity supplied, the results can be used to estimate the impact of a larger or smaller amount of money being spent on the advertising of both fluid milk and manufactured products. It can also be used to determine the best allocation of advertising funds between the two product categories given a fixed budget.

Although tentative results do indicate a positive response to both advertising efforts, the fluid milk advertising appears to have had a greater benefit than the manufactured product advertising at the level of expenditure during the period studied. The model as estimated provides an estimate of the quantity and price impacts for both products at the consumer, wholesale, and producer levels. Generic advertising is incorporated into the retail fluid and the retail manufactured product demand equations to determine the impact on the demand for the two groups of products. The model provides an estimate of the effect of the advertising effort on the government price support program. Such a model can be used to simulate the effects of alternative advertising expenditure levels and program allocations; it can also be used to address policy issues about who benefits and provide insight concerning questions about the appropriate assessment level.

Beef Checkoff Promotion Programs

Beef checkoff programs have been in place since late 1986, and the programs have been ongoing since the first quarter of 1987. Starting in 1989, the first efforts to evaluate the economic gains directly attributed to the checkoff were completed by Ward (1992a.) Evaluations using empirical computer models were again used for the quarters extending from 1979 through the second quarter of 1991. The evaluation issue of major importance to the beef industry was to determine if the substantial checkoff expenditures were having a measurable impact on consumers' preferences for beef.

Beef checkoff activities are administered under the Beef Research and Promotion Board authorized in the 1985 act. Programs are funded under an assessment of one dollar per head each time a bovine animal is sold in the United States, along with an assessment on imports. National programs include direct advertising and other promotion, informational and educational programs, and research. Informational programs are grouped into consumer information, industry information, and producer communication programs. Producer programs are designed to keep producers informed about a broad range of board and industry activities, whereas promotion, consumer information, and industry information programs are demand-enhancing activities.

From the start of the beef checkoff through the second quarter of 1991, assessments totaled $382 million (Ward, 1992a; Ward and Lambert, forthcoming). The national programs are consistent in their theme and design, and the expenditures are readily tracked according to programs funded. For the first quarter of 1987 (shown as 87:1) through the second quarter of 1991 (91:2), approximately 76.5 percent of the national funds were used for advertising and promotion; consumer information programs accounted for 8.99 percent, and industry information programs 4.96 percent. Producer communication programs equaled 4.01 percent of total expenditures. Advertising and promotion, along with consumer and industry information programs, represent the most direct methods for reaching potential beef consumers. Although the other programs provide an underpinning to the total checkoff effort, the promotion and information programs are the most likely to have registered a direct and most immediate impact on consumer behavior.

Theoretically, beef demand should be related to the checkoff programs consistent with those properties developed in Chapter 6. Ward noted several important properties of the beef model that must hold (Ward, 1992a):

- Beef demand should continue at some positive level.
- Beef demand is likely to approach some upward limit.
- The rate of response to the checkoff effort can differ.
- Even with significant expenditures, there may be some time delay between the advertising or information exposure and the response.
- Over time, effectiveness of the same program may change because of consumer perception levels and changes in product knowledge.

Demand (initially illustrated in Figure 6–3) is modeled using a specification where beef price is a function of beef supplies, supplies of beef substitutes, beef checkoff expenditures, and other variables. Beef demand should also be influenced by consumer incomes, inflation, population, and any seasonality in the consumption patterns for beef. In addition, beef checkoff expenditures can be directly included in the demand model, as represented with θ_3 below. The combined effects of the three categories of demand variables are represented with

$$P_b = (\theta_1)(\theta_2)(\theta_3)\, u \qquad (7.2)$$

where P_b is the beef price at one of the market levels. Beef checkoff programs represent major demand-enhancing efforts by the U.S. beef industry. Checkoff efforts are measured by the amount of expenditures in each quarter, incorporated into the demand model through θ_3, and expressed as follows:

$$\hat{\theta}_3 = CK_t^{\delta_1} CK_{t-1}^{\delta_2} \qquad (7.3)$$

CK is a specific form of the checkoff expenditures that has all of the desired economic properties set forth above and in Chapter 6. *CK* is expressed with the subscripts t and $t-1$, denoting the immediate impact from checkoff expenditures in the same quarter and one quarter later (that is, a one-quarter lag). CK_{t-1} is representative of the advertising and promotion carryover effect seen in most commodity advertising programs and is illustrated in Chapter 6 (see Figure 6–4.) The δ's are checkoff parameters showing the impact of the programs, with the magnitude and significance of δ_1 and δ_2 providing the most direct evidence of the impact. Letting *BRD* represent the program expenditures as defined in Ward (1992a), the beef model represents an application of the functional form set forth in Chapter 6. (This functional form was developed by Ward, 1992a, in the course of studying the beef case. Also, *CK* in this chapter does not correspond to *CK* as used in Chapter 6.)

$$CK = \left(1 + \exp^{\left(\frac{-\Gamma_1}{BRD_t}\right)}\right) \qquad (7.4)$$

$$CK_{t-1} = \left(1 + \exp^{\left(\frac{-\Gamma_1}{BRD_{t-1}}\right)}\right)$$

Table 7–3 includes the coefficients for *CK* corresponding to the δ's, along with the other components in the model. The *CK* weights in the bottom portion of the table correspond to the Γ's. Ward (1992a) estimated the model for data ranging from the second quarter of 1979 through the second quarter of 1991. In Table 7–3, the upper half includes the estimated coefficients and related tests for reliability and the lower portion provides statistics useful for judging the quality of the total model. Estimated coefficients are shown for the live weight, boxed beef, and retail market levels.

For each market level, Γ (as developed in equation 7–4) is approximately 0.50; recall from Chapter 6 that $\Gamma < 1.0$ implies a rapid advertising response. Parameter estimates for δ are in the upper portion of Table 7.3 in the rows for current and lag checkoffs. An estimate for the current checkoff program is not significantly different from zero, but the second coefficient corresponding to lag checkoff is positive and highly significant.

One way to illustrate the patterns of response from the checkoff coefficients reported in Table 7–3 is to plot each response against simulated expenditure levels, with expenditures being deflated by the consumer price index. Each response is illustrated in Figure 7–2. The upper curve is the live weight demand response to increases in the beef checkoff expenditures; note that live weight shifts in demand could not be expected to exceed the approximate 7 percent level. Middle and bottom curves in Figure 7.2 portray the response for boxed beef and retail beef prices to different levels of checkoff expenditures. Responses should decrease when comparing the live,

Table 7–3
Estimated Beef Checkoff Model, 79:2–91:2

| Variables | Live Weight | | Boxed Beef | | Retail Beef | |
	Coef.	t test	Coef.	t test	Coef.	t test
Intercept	10.2865	9.8812	9.3705	9.8135	9.7346	15.0130
Beef disappearance	-1.1410	-4.8888	-0.7974	-3.7098	-0.9220	-7.6033
Pork disappearance	-0.3075	-2.6416	-0.2093	-1.9598	-0.0567	-0.7716
Poultry disappearance	-0.1233	-0.5410	0.0356	0.1706	-0.2766	-1.8557
Time	-0.6414	-5.0802	-0.7390	-6.3843	-0.8817	-9.4674
Time adjustment	0.0290	1.3666	0.0412	2.1224	0.0495	3.7769
Income	0.3811	1.5429	0.4418	1.9574	0.2975	1.7432
Current checkoff	-0.0178	-0.4661	-0.0209	-0.5801	-0.0305	-1.2742
Lag checkoff	0.1109	2.8609	0.0971	2.6777	0.0535	2.2547
Season S1	-0.0266	-1.6970	-0.0224	-1.5562	-0.0389	-3.1033
Season S2	0.0159	0.7387	0.0119	0.6036	0.0083	0.5908
Season S3	-0.0164	-0.7370	0.0014	0.0694	0.0201	1.4253
Feeder steer ratio	—	—	—	—	1.7669	3.9913

Statistics	Live Weight	Boxed Beef	Retail Beef
Checkoff Γ	.4500	.5000	.4000
Mean of dep. var.	3.1421	3.7037	4.3485
Std. dev. of dep. var.	0.0718	0.0695	0.1201
SS residuals	0.0358	0.0302	0.0128
Var. of residuals	0.0010	0.0008	0.0004
Std. error of reg.	0.0311	0.0285	0.0188
R^2	0.8553	0.8698	0.9816
Adj. R^2	0.8123	0.8311	0.9754
DW statistic	1.7690	1.8134	1.6633
F statistic	19.8821	22.4722	159.4600
Schwarz-Bayes. crit.	-6.2684	-6.4401	-7.2200
Log of likelihood	107.3990	111.6050	132.6590
Observations	49	49	49

Source: Ward (1992).

boxed, and retail beef levels, since the absolute magnitude of the price levels increase from live to retail market levels. For example, a 3 percent increase in the retail prices may approximate a 7 percent increase in the live weight price level.

With these empirical results, Ward (1992a) concludes that:

- Beef checkoff programs have caused a measurable and significant shift in the demand for beef at each market level.

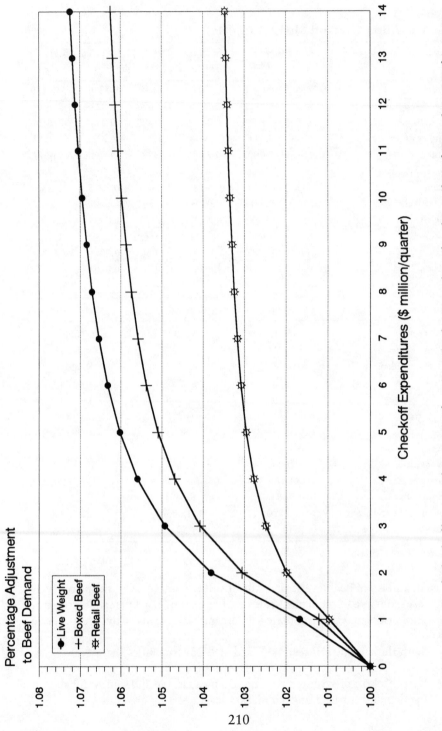

Figure 7–2. Beef Checkoff Demand Response for Live Weight, Boxed Beef and Retail Beef (Based on CPI for 91:2)

- Responses to the checkoff programs indicate that for any one period there is a maximum impact that could be expected (that is, there is an upper limit to the expected gain).
- Although the checkoff programs are targeted to the retail and trade markets, the model clearly shows that gains are registered at the producer level.

Beef Checkoff Gains. Using the checkoff model, the benefit derived with the model are estimated as reported in Table 7–4. In Table 7–4, the first column provides a description of specific calculations, column 2 gives the units, and columns 3 and 4 give the appropriate values for the quarters 87:1–90:1 and 87:1–91:2. The first row gives the estimated live weight revenues while accounting for beef checkoff dollars. Because total assessments must be collected in order to support checkoff programs, the most conservative way to calculate a rate of return to the checkoff programs is to divide the estimated gains by the total beef checkoff assessments. Using this procedure, the gross rate of return for the period 87:1–91:2 is 6.710 (see row 8, Table 7–4). If assessments are first subtracted from the revenues (Row 1 – Row 3 – Row 7), the rate of return is 5.714. That is, on average, the checkoff programs yielded a live weight return of 5.714 net dollars for each dollar of assessments. This gain is directly attributed to the checkoff and represents a significant positive impact for producers.

Empirical results from the analysis point to a possible reversal or leveling out in the downward shift in beef demand observed throughout the last decade. Using the beef model, Ward and Lambert (forthcoming) further show that with the checkoff in place, beef demand in 89:4 was approximately 75 percent of the 79:2 level. This value increased to 78 percent in the

Table 7–4
Estimated Rate of Return to the National Beef Checkoff Programs

Descriptions (1)	Units (2)	87:1–90:1 (3)	87:1–91:2 (4)
1. Revenue with checkoff	($ bil)	$81.067	$114.795
2. Revenue without checkoff	($ bil)	$77.065	$108.939
3. Revenue with $1.5 million per quarter	($ bil)	$79.507	$112.229
4. Gain over no programs (Row 1 – Row 2)	($ bil)	$4.002	$5.856
5. Gain over $1.5 million (Row 1 – Row 3)	($ bil)	$1.560	$2.566
6. Promotions and information	($ mil)	$110.990	$161.340
7. Assessments	($ mil)	$283.890	$382.180
8. Gross Rate of Return: (Row 5)/(Row 7)		5.490	6.710
9. Net Rate of Return: (Row 5 – Row 7)/(Row 7)		4.495	5.714

Source: Ward (1992).

last quarter of the analysis (91:2). If the checkoff had not been in place, demand would have been below the 75 percent level measured with the checkoff expenditures. Although beef demand has declined through most of the quarters, the industry would have been worse off if the checkoff programs had not been in place.

Beef Model Conclusion. At this point in the economic evaluation of the beef checkoff, the evidence is clear that the checkoff has had an important positive effect on consumers' preference for beef. The returns have been substantial. It is equally important, however, to put the checkoff program's impact in perspective to all other factors influencing the demand and prices for beef. Both the dairy and beef models are cases illustrating the issues and methods discussed in Chapter 6. In both instances, the significant investment shows a positive economic impact. With the econometric models used to study both commodities, a number of direct activity and promotion policies are addressed.

Washington State Apple Advertising Model

Ward and Forker (1991) completed a detailed study of the Washington State apple programs. The Washington Apple Commission has used various forms of apple advertising for several years. Programs have been both local and national, using several media. Washington apples face strong competition from other apple-producing regions and potentially from other fruits. Given an adequate distribution of product, a fundamental question is whether apple advertising efforts influence the demand for Washington apples. In Ward and Forker's analysis, the variables considered important were the volume of apple sales in the market in which the advertising occurred, the price of apples at the point of sale, the amount and type of advertising effort, and other factors determined to have an important influence on consumers' decisions to buy Washington apples. They used price and arrival data published by the U.S. Department of Agriculture (USDA) for most fruits for sixteen major U.S. cities. Arrival data provide an estimate of the volume of fresh apples arriving in selected markets; shipment data measure the volume of apples shipped from production areas.

Total advertising expenditures over the period of the Ward and Forker study amounted to almost $34 million. The distribution and level of expenditures varied substantially from year to year. Cable television and spot radio advertising were dominant in the early years, with magazines becoming dominant in 1986–87. In more recent years, spot radio and television provided the major emphasis. These different combinations over time provide the basis for obtaining estimates of the extent to which each contributed to demand expansion.

Washington Apple Advertising Model Specification. Ward and Forker assumed Washington's apple supplies, like many annual crops produced in the United States, to be predetermined by acreage, yields, management practices, and environmental and biological conditions. The final apple model was based on the following conditions:

- The model was estimated using monthly wholesale market arrival data as reported by the USDA. Monthly data extending from January 1984 through December 1990 were used.

- Shipping-point volumes were reported for each producing area. The shipping-point data are used later in the analysis to deal with the linkage between the wholesale demand and shipping-point changes in terms of market shares and price linkages. Note that all demand estimates are at the wholesale level and not at the shipping point.

- Apple prices at the wholesale market are measured using the "red delicious" variety price expressed in dollars per 42-pound carton.

- Aggregate arrival data for the selected cities were used to represent consumption and sales. These cities account for approximately 40 percent of the U.S. population.

- Several potential substitutes for apples were included in the model: oranges, grapefruit, peaches, pears, strawberries, and bananas. Substitute goods (other than non-Washington apples) were based on shipping-point records rather than arrival data.

- All advertising and promotion data were supplied by the Washington Apple Commission. These data show monthly expenditures by media (radio, television, and magazine) and according to spot versus national (cable for television) coverage. Spot expenditures correspond to the arrival cities noted above.

- Income, populations, and other data were tabulated from public sources, primarily using the Department of Commerce Survey of Current Business.

Ward and Forker's model, shown in Table 7–5, was based on a mathematical specification similar to that developed in Chapter 6. Their model has three basic components: the nonadvertising variables (θ_1), the advertising expenditure variables (θ_2), and the media coverage adjustments (θ_3). The full model is set forth below in both its linear and nonlinear forms, with p_t being the wholesale market price.

$$p_t = \theta_1 \, \theta_2 \, \theta_3 \tag{7.5}$$

$$\log(P_t) = \log(\theta_1) + \log(\theta_2) + \log(\theta_3) \tag{7.6}$$

Table 7–5
Econometric Estimates for the Washington Apple Advertising Model

Description	Variable Code	Coefficient	T-Statistic
Intercept	C	68.80250	5.23368
Total U.S. apples	LWQTOT_C	-0.36825	-3.59636
Washington market share	MSWAS	-1.00993	-3.85532
Per capita income	LDINC_D	-6.88371	-4.95172
Time trend	LTM	0.26695	4.07104
Oranges	ORG_C	0.09210	2.32451
Grapefruit	GRP_C	0.26247	3.39088
Peaches	PCH_C	-0.02804	-0.21070
Pears	PER_C	-0.27199	-0.82432
Strawberries	STW_C	0.09235	1.29872
Bananas	BAN_C	0.04591	1.26735
Television (0 lag)	FTOTTV	-0.54254	-4.29832
Television (1 lag)	FTOTTV(−1)	-0.50318	-5.57278
Television (2 lag)	FTOTTV(−2)	-0.46382	-6.03991
Television (3 lag)	FTOTTV(−3)	-0.42446	-4.43374
Television (4 lag)	FTOTTV(−4)	-0.38510	-2.87383
Radio (0 lag)	FTOTRD	-0.03670	-0.11884
Radio (1 lag)	FTOTRD(−1)	-0.22899	-1.07785
Radio (2 lag)	FTOTRD(−2)	-0.42127	-2.64542
Radio (3 lag)	FTOTRD(−3)	-0.61355	-3.23100
Radio (4 lag)	FTOTRD(−4)	-0.80583	-2.89956
Cable television (0 lag)	RRTVNA	1.30751	4.15869
Cable television (1 lag)	RRTVNA(−1)	1.08332	5.21190
Cable television (2 lag)	RRTVNA(−2)	0.85914	5.32652
Cable television (3 lag)	RRTVNA(−3)	0.63495	2.91996
Cable television (4 lag)	RRTVNA(−4)	0.41076	1.25566
Spot radio (0 lag)	RRRDSP	6.12844	0.55750
Spot radio (1 lag)	RRRDSP(−1)	12.20170	1.62448
Spot radio (2 lag)	RRRDSP(−2)	18.27500	3.10014
Spot radio (3 lag)	RRRDSP(−3)	24.34820	3.25841
Spot radio (4 lag)	RRRDSP(−4)	30.42150	2.78080

Number of observations = 80 R^2 = .8523
Mean of Dep. Var = 2.7160   DW = 1.3986
Adj. R^2 = 0.8087   F test = 19.5579

Source: Ward and Forker (1991).

$$\log(\theta_1) = \beta_0 + \beta_1 LWQTOT_C + \beta_2 MSWAS + \beta_3 LDINC_D \qquad (7.7)$$
$$+ \beta_4 LTM + \beta_5 ORG_C + \beta_6 GRP_C + \beta_7 PCH_C + \beta_8 PER_C$$
$$+ \beta_9 STW_C + \beta_{10} BAN_C$$

Television conversion:[48]

$$\log(\theta_2) = \sum_{i-1}^{k} \left(\left(\delta_{1i} + \delta_{2i} \log \left(1 + \exp^{\left(\frac{-\alpha_1}{TVNA_{t-i}} \right)} \right) \right) \log \left(1 + \exp^{\left(\frac{-\alpha_2}{TV_{t-i}} \right)} \right) \right) \qquad (7.8)$$

Radio conversion:

$$\log(\theta_3) = \sum_{i-1}^{k} \left(\left(\delta_{3i} + \delta_{4i} \log \left(1 + \exp^{\left(\frac{-\alpha_3}{RDSP_{t-i}} \right)} \right) \right) \log \left(1 + \exp^{\left(\frac{-\alpha_4}{RD_{t-i}} \right)} \right) \right) \qquad (7.9)$$

In equations 7–8 and 7–9, two types of parameters are recorded: δ and α. The summations are over the lagged values from 0 to 4, and the δ's corresponding to the parameter estimates for television and radio and were estimated using ordinary least squares. The α's were estimated by searching over values and selecting those values that maximize the likelihood function, giving the resulting coefficients:

Television: $\quad \alpha_1 = -6.5$ and $\alpha_2 = -0.13$
Radio: $\qquad \alpha_3 = -1.0$ and $\alpha_4 = -3.5$

Econometric Estimates of the Apple Model. The demand model for Washington apples at the wholesale market was estimated using monthly data from January 1984 through December 1990. Arrivals, as defined above, were aggregated over the selected cities. The resulting econometric estimates are reported in Table 7–5. Column 1 identifies each variable. Column 2 provides the variable code as noted above. Column 3 includes the estimated coefficient for each demand driver, while column 4 gives a statistical test (a t test) for judging the confidence that can be placed on each estimate. From these estimates, Ward and Forker showed that the effects of Washington advertising programs can be measured with the results revealing a significant positive factor influencing the demand for Washington apples. This model specifically shows the separate effects of radio versus television as well as the gains from spot versus national media.

Apple Advertising Media, Type, and Lags. Ward and Forker's primary interest with this model was to determine if the effects of apple advertising could be measured. Further, they were interesting in separating the effects of television versus radio and spot versus national (cable) coverage. The results from their modeling are reported in Table 7–5. Coefficients are reported in four groups of parameters: FTOTTV–FTOTTV(–4) correspond to the television expenditure function for the current through four-month lags; FTOTRD–FTOTRD(–4) correspond to the radio expenditure function; RRTVNA–RRTVNA(—4) correspond to the adjustment in television effectiveness depending on the share of television expenditures allocated to national cable coverage versus spot; RRRDSP–RRRDSP(–4) are the adjustments in radio effectiveness attributed to spot versus national radio. The first and most important result from the modeling effort is that apple advertising influences the demand for Washington apples. Almost every advertising coefficient in Table 7–5 is statistically significant; that is, the apple advertising effects are statistically significant, and the effects differ by media and coverage. Estimates differ between radio and television, thus indicating differences between the two media. Lagged coefficients are statistically significant and appear reasonable according to prior expectations.

Advertising Impact on Apple Prices. Table 7–6 includes the estimated gains directly attributed to the Washington apple advertising programs. All gains are expressed at the shipping-point level. The first column in Table 7–6 represents the crop years 1984–85 through 1989–90. Column 2 is the estimated revenue from the sixteen cities expressed at the shipping point. This is accomplished by estimating the wholesale market prices without advertising; these wholesale prices are adjusted back to the shipping point with a linkage equation. Shipping-point prices are then multiplied by the volume of sales reported within the selected cities.

Table 7–6 illustrates Ward and Forker's calculations of the gains from apple advertising, with column 4 showing an average rate of return of 6.7 to 1 for 1989–90. Clearly, the average rate varies by year, but overall the results

Table 7–6
Rate of Gains to Washington Apple Advertising Programs

Crop Year	Revenue Without Advertising ($ mil.)	Revenue Gains ($ mil.)	Rate of Return	Shipping Price Without Advertising	Price Gain ($/crt)	Demand Growth	Washington Apple Advertising ($)
(1)	(2)	(3)	(4)	(5)	(6	(7)	(8)
1984–85	$217.389	$20.089	5.18	$12.66	$1.170	.092	$3,248,628
1985–86	$216.884	$00.000	0.00	$14.48	$0.000	.000	$526,003
1986–87	$226.448	$34.249	24.44	$11.11	$1.680	.151	$1,346,170
1987–88	$215.654	$39.724	8.87	$ 9.89	$1.821	.184	$4,025,450
1988–89	$229.398	$33.247	9.43	$10.77	$1.560	.145	$3,186,625
1989–90	$265.457	$38.510	6.74	$ 9.90	$1.436	.145	$4,972,848

Source: Ward and Forker (1991).

Note: Calculated at shipping point using gains estimated with the wholesale market demand model.

point to programs that have generated substantial gains for the Washington apple industry. If program intensities were increased further, then total revenue from the advertising would continue to increase, but the average rates of return would be below the 6.7 level shown for 1989–90. Additional analysis for the 1989–90 years shows that if expenditures were doubled, the rate of return would remain large, even though it decreases to 3. A tripling of the 1989–90 expenditures provides an approximate 2 to 1 rate of return, still an impressive ratio for this industry. Obviously, when discussing such increases, one must be extremely careful, since the conclusions are drawn on values far beyond the historical data range used in the modeling of the apple advertising.

Simulated Gains Due to Advertising Policies. Apple advertising gains were calculated based on actual expenditures for the months May 1984 through December 1990. Econometric estimates and subsequent calculated gains were based on actual experiences for those years; those results are most useful to determine whether the programs created a measurable demand response. Given that the estimated models were reasonable and statistically significant, Ward and Forker then used the model to simulate responses to alternative advertising expenditure patterns. Simulations are designed to provide signals for addressing policy issues in a proactive setting. In their simulations, the purpose was twofold: (1) to show the usefulness of the model for addressing a range of what-if questions; and (2) to illustrate the relative responses of the model to different expenditure and allocation schemes.

Each simulation follows the format illustrated with Figure 7–3. The bottom axis includes apple advertising expenditures, with the range extending from zero to $900,000 in one month. Population and other required data for this simulation are for 1991. The left axis shows the simulation adjustment in demand where, for example, 1.06 equals a 6 percent increase in apple prices. Figure 7–3 includes advertising allocations to all radio, all television, and various combinations. The radio response curve shows a rapid increase, then a leveling out as larger expenditures are considered. The all-television advertising response is zero at low expenditure levels; as television expenditures increase, the rate of gain from the television efforts also increases. The impact, assuming all funds channelled through television, is consistently below that of all radio.

Figure 7–3 also shows the simulated gains when expenditures are allocated to both radio and television and for different coverage. The line marked with pluses assumes all television, with 50 percent cable and 50 percent spot. Some improvement is registered, but the gains are still substantially under those for all radio. Finally, a combination of radio and television, with 50 percent of the television being through the spot media, is simulated. The line marked by triangles assumes that 70 percent of the funds are

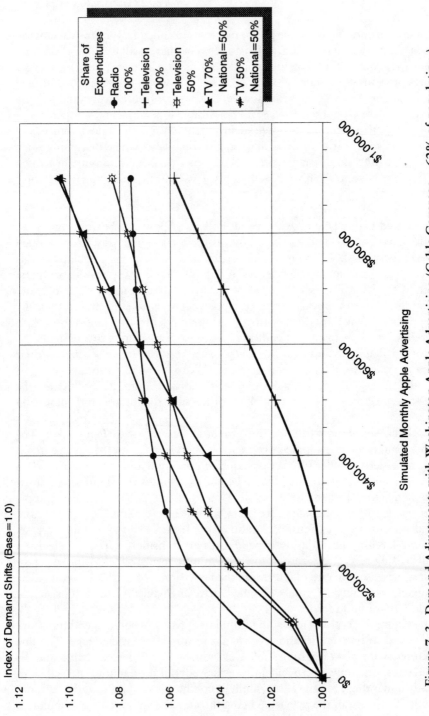

Figure 7–3. Demand Adjustments with Washington Apple Advertising (Cable Coverage = 62% of population.)

allocated to television, whereas the line marked by diamonds assumes that 50 percent of the funds are for television. Their simulations show overall improvements with some combination of radio and television activities. Similarly, the gains from having some share of the television in the spot versus the cable medium are apparent. The model further points to the gains from all radio where funds are in the lower ranges of the analyses.

Advertising Allocation Signals. As a final simulation, it is useful to provide more insight into the potential gains from combinations for radio and television activities. Figure 7–4 shows the simulated shifts in apple demand at wholesale under different allocation schemes and expenditure levels. The bottom axis reports the percentage of funds allocated to television; 50 percent of the television funds are assumed to be spent nationally.

Each line in the figure represents a different expenditure level. Note that for programs of less that $500,000 per month, the rate of gain consistently declines as the share allocated to television increases. In fact, at the $100,000 level, all funds going to television yield a zero response. The upper two curves portray an entirely different picture. These two curves represent $700,000 and $900,000, respectively, and in both cases considerable improvement is seen with some combination of radio and television. Tracing across the graph horizontally shows the peak gain for both the $700,000 and $900,000 to be where approximately 70 percent of expenditures are for television.

Apple Model Conclusions. Using the Washington apple demand model, Ward and Forker (1991) drew the following conclusions:

- Washington's apple advertising is influencing the demand for Washington apples.
- There are measurable differences in the economic impact of radio versus television advertising of apples.
- Media effectiveness differs by the coverage. Radio is most effective through spot coverage, while a combination of spot and cable television coverage is more effective.
- Apple advertising is shown to have some carryover effect extending up to two months beyond the initial efforts.
- Rates of return for apple advertising were calculated for each crop year from 1984–85 through 1989–90. The rates differ for each crop year. By the 1989–90 crop year, the analysis shows that apple advertising led to a 14.5 percent increase in Washington apple demand.
- When comparing the revenue gains to actual program expenditures, the calculations show that by 1990, Washington advertising yielded a 1 to 6.7 effectiveness ratio.

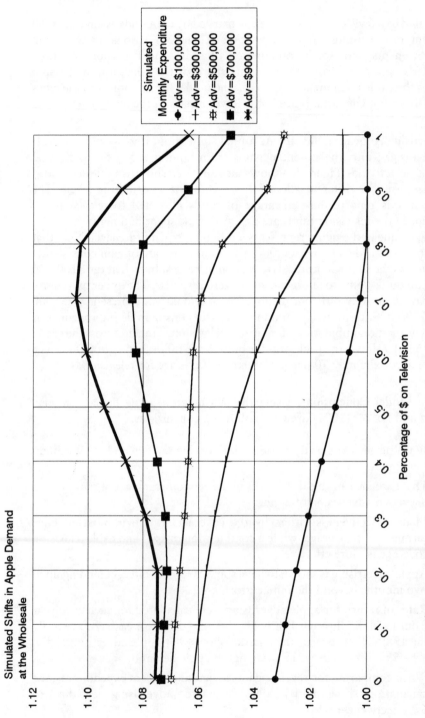

Figure 7–4. Washington Apple Advertising Effectiveness According to TV Share of Expenditures (Cable TV Coverage = 62% of population, National TV Allocation = 50% of expenditures)

- The model clearly shows declining marginal returns to the programs. That is, for each addition advertising dollar, the incremental gains (while positive) are less than the previous gain.

Wool Advertising

The United States is a major market for the exports of Australian wool. In 1983, the International Wood Secretariat doubled its promotion of wool products in the United States. Dewbre, Richardson, and Beare (1987) provide a unique analysis of this promotion effort and draw on several important econometric techniques in dealing with modeling the world wool markets. The wool case is of particular interest because the product goes through considerable transformation before consumption (that is, wool apparels), yet the raw product can still be identified in its transformed state. The two major objectives of the analysis were to measure the effects of apparel wool promotion on the U.S. household demand for wool and to derive the effects of expanded demand for wool on the raw wool prices and subsequent returns to Australian producers (Dewbre, Richardson, and Beare, 1987).

Dewbre, Richardson, and Beare approached the problem in two phases. First they estimated the household demand for wool, incorporating the influence of wool promotions. Then they simulated the impact of the extra wool promotions, using a model of the world apparel and total wool markets (p. 4). Their analysis was based on household apparel purchase records tabulated by the Market Research Corporation of America and the National Purchase Diary Corporation. Purchase records included information on each transaction and considerable details about the exact apparel products purchased.

Using the household data, the researchers' objective was to estimate the demand for wool apparels. Given the infrequency of purchases in wool apparel products, one observes periods with price changes, income adjustments, and so forth but no wool consumption by some households. Stimulates may increase the desirability of wool, yet actual consumption might not change. Dewbre, Richardson, and Beare recognize the concept of notional demand (that is, increased desirability) in contrast to effective demand (where purchases actually take place). Notional demand translates into observed purchases when the notional demand exceeds some purchase threshold.

Their model of the household demand is shown by the following equations:

$$q_{it}^* = B_0 + B_1 P_{jt} + B_2 Y_{it} + B_3 A_{jt} \\ + B_4 q_{(i,\, t-1)} + C'Z_{it} + u_{it}. \tag{7.10}$$

$$q_{it} = \begin{Bmatrix} q_{ij}^*, \text{ if } q_{ij}^* > 0 \\ 0, \text{ if } q_{ij}^* < 0 \end{Bmatrix} \qquad (7.11)$$

where P is the real price of wool, Y is real income, A is real promotion in region j during year t, Z is a vector of demographic variables for household i in year t (including household size, presence of children, and region), q^* is the notional demand, and q is actual demand.

These equations define a demand system and represent a classic econometric problem of censored data. That is, within the sample, there will exist a distribution of households with and without observed purchases. Nonpurchases occur even with meaningful prices, incomes, and other variables that affect the demand for wool. This type of data problem is often dealt with using a Tobit estimation procedure, in which the data are censored such that at some point, zero consumption experiences are observed. Hence, for the wool model, this lower value presents a threshold level where at least an A_{ij} level of advertising or the other variable values must exist before desired consumption equals actual consumption. The threshold is the minimum strength of the desirability needed to lead to action in terms of making purchases.

Ultimately, the question of interest is whether wool promotions have a measurable impact on the household demand for wool apparels. The researchers' first-stage estimates give the probability of making wool apparel purchases: a 10 percent increase in real promotion expenditures produces a 0.0018 increase in the average probability of making a purchase (Dewbre, Richardson, and Beare, 1987). Finally, the censored data estimation techniques lend them to calculate short- and long-term elasticities of demand, as reported in Table 7–7. The promotion elasticity indicates that a 1 percent increase in real expenditures on wool promotions produces a 0.07 percent increase in average household consumption of wool, with the percentage based at the average consumption level.

In addition, the authors of the study measured the impact on total U.S. demand. They simulated the total promotional impact by taking the percentage impact of the increased promotions on the average household purchase and then applying that percentage to estimates of the total market size. Their

Table 7–7
Estimates of Mean Elasticities of Demand for Wool in Apparels

Variables	Short-Run Mean Elasticity	Long-Run Mean Elasticity
Income	0.431	0.527
Promotion	0.070	0.086
Wool price	-1.104	-1.349

Source: Dewbre, Richardson, and Beare (1987).

simulations indicate that total U.S. apparel wool demand increased by 6.5 million kilograms in 1983–84, by 7.6 million kilograms in 1984–85, and by 7.8 million kilograms in 1985–86 as a result of the wool promotions.

Given that wool materials may be supplied by several sources beyond Australia and that there exists a world demand for total wool and apparel wool, the authors developed a partial model of the world demand system for wool products. The primary reason for this extension was to recognize that demand shifts in the United States might stimulate world price increases as well as adjustments by competing suppliers. A world model would account for the more significant adjustments when attempting to calculate the returns to Australian producers.

We will not provide the details of this world demand system, but rather will present the final conclusions. Benefits were calculated for a five-year period and for a longer term period for both apparel wool and total wool. Drawing from the econometric models, the authors indicated that for each dollar spent on promotional efforts in the United States, Australian growers realized $1.94 in returns. When viewing the total wool market, the yield was somewhat lower, with a benefit-cost ratio of 1.03 to 1. Note that the former benefit-cost ratio (1.94 to 1) is appropriate to Australia, since nearly all of their production is for apparel wool.

This case study is useful it that it deals with many empirical as well as data problems. Furthermore, returns back to the producers are calculated while recognizing the world scope of the market being analyzed.

Catfish Advertising

Most of the econometric studies of advertising make a direct link between program expenditures and consumer purchasing behavior. Conceptually, this linkage entails a complex process of exposure, awareness, beliefs, and attitudes that leads to changes in behavior and consumption patterns. Kinnucan and Venkateswaran (1990) provide insight into this problem with their analysis of the U.S. catfish industry. Catfish advertising programs have only a short history, hence providing little historical data for the researcher to use. Therefore, Kinnucan and Venkateswaran turned to a consumer survey to gain an understanding of consumers' response to catfish advertising. They used a nationwide telephone survey that resulted in 3,600 useful interviews. Their survey data included demographics, advertising awareness, and consumer beliefs, attitudes, and consumption activities. Using these data, an eight-equation model was developed that incorporated exposure and awareness; beliefs about the product, including nutrition, flavor, and odor; attitudes about catfish; and purchasing frequencies, both at home and in restaurants.

Although we will not give the model's details, the essence of the authors' conclusions was that advertising changed awareness and exposure, which in turn changed beliefs and attitudes about catfish. Consumption of catfish was then dependent on these attitudes and beliefs (Kinnucan and Venkateswaran, 1990). Because many of the authors' variables took discrete values, methods dealing with limited dependent variables for some of their equations were appropriate. In particular, the awareness and exposure equations were based on probit models (see Chapter 6), since these two variables were scaled as either yes or no.

This study provides insight into additional ways to deal with evaluating promotional programs. The analysis shows an approximate 15 percent increase in consumer awareness of catfish attributed to the advertising campaign. Also, at-home consumption and restaurant consumption increased by nearly 13 percent. One aspect of the model is particularly interesting in that the authors showed that flavor was considerably more important than nutrition and odor in setting attitudes. This is important not only for copy design, but for emphasizing the role of quality controls through grades and standards. It also points out the importance of awareness as a response measure.

Generic and Brand Citrus Advertising

Of all U.S. commodities, the Florida citrus industry probably has the longest history of dealing with the evaluation of its national advertising programs. Florida's programs have been diverse and have evolved through time. The range of studies have paralleled the diversity in programs. Studies by Lee and Brown (1992), and Ward (1988a, 1988b) all provide examples of the use of a number of econometric techniques for measuring the impact of citrus advertising. Space limits our ability to review all of the citrus studies; thus, in this section we will provide an overview of research experiences with this commodity (Ward, 1988a).

Florida citrus advertising efforts are unique in that strong brand advertising exists along with major generic efforts. Given the product characteristics of orange juice and the range of ways the product can be differentiated, one would expect the product to lie somewhere between the classification of cooperative and predatory goods (see Chapter 2). In fact, at one time the Florida Department of Citrus funded cooperative efforts via a brand advertising rebate program (see the discussion in Chapter 5). This program was conceived as a way of stimulating additional brand advertising and for the industry to have some input into the copy design of brand messages. As a result of these recent programs, the industry became more interested in knowing the relative productivity of both types of advertising. At issue was whether brand advertising simply shifted market shares, or whether it expanded the product category. Similarly, it was asked what impact generic advertising had on total demand.

An orange juice model by Ward (1988a) included both generic and

Table 7–8
Estimated Orange Juice Advertising Model

Variable	Estimated Coefficient	t Statistic
Constant	–2.0227	–1.9226
Price	–0.46894	–12.568
Price Adjustment	–0.07884	–6.2932
Income	0.41595	3.2719
D2	0.00669	0.8206
D4	–0.015	–1.9677
D6	–0.04486	–5.6275
D8	–0.03436	–4.3819
D10	–0.01785	–2.7201
LG1 (Generic)	0.0034	2.4789
LG2 (Generic)	0.00393	2.0447
LB1 (Brand)	0.00774	2.5756

	Generic			Brand	
Lag		tStatistic	Lag		t Statistic
0	0.0034	2.4789	0	0.0077	2.5756
1	0.004	3.247	1	0.0066	2.5756
2	0.0042	2.7816	2	0.0055	2.5756
3	0.0042	2.3304	3	0.0044	2.5756
4	0.0039	2.0447	4	0.0033	2.5756
5	0.0034	1.8593	5	0.0022	2.5756
6	0.0025	1.7318	6	0.0011	2.5756
7	0.0014	1.6395			
Sum	0.027			0.031	

Sum of squared residuals =	0.0103
Standard error of the Reg. =	0.016047
Mean of dependent variable =	0.57835
Standard deviation =	0.036941
R^2 =	0.852
Adjusted R^2 =	0.8113
Durbin–Watson statistic =	1.3378
F statistic (11, 40) =	20.9337
Log of likelihood function =	147.913
Number of observations =	52

brand advertising, using distributed lag functions for both. Nielsen bi-monthly time series data were used for 1978 through 1988; estimated results are reported in Table 7–8, along with the lagged structures. The analyses show both generic and brand advertising to have a positive impact on total orange juice consumption. Furthermore, the generic and brand effects differ in their immediate and long-term impacts. Figure 7.5 illustrates the differences between generic and brand advertising effects in terms of the estimated parameters: partially shaded bars represent brand advertising, and the solid bars correspond to generic advertising.

It is apparent from these values that the immediate impact of brand advertising exceeds that of generic. The brand impact peaks at the outset and declines in all subsequent periods. In contrast, generic advertising's initial impact is low relative to brand advertising and peaks after several periods. The impact of both types of citrus advertising decays to near zero after the seventh bimonthly period. Note in Figure 7–5 that the carryover effect of generic generally exceeds that of brand. Summing the current and lagged estimates for generic and brand advertising in Table 7–8 gives estimates of the long-term advertising effectiveness. These sums point to a slightly larger brand effect, with a value of 0.031 versus the generic value of 0.027. The citrus model was further used to show the total gains in sales resulting from advertising and to devise a method for pointing to optimal combinations of generic and brand advertising. Figure 7–6 shows the estimated sales gains attributed to generic and brand advertising.

An analysis of the imposition of an import advertising equalization tax provides a good example of using econometric advertising models to address specific policy issues. Lee's model (1984) and a subsequent paper by Fairchild, Gunter, and Lee (1987) used a single-equation specification that included the separate effects of generic and brand advertising on the demand for orange juice. Both generic and brand advertising were shown to have positive impacts on total demand. The model did not account for lagged effects that have been observed with monthly data in other citrus studies. It is also worth noting that the brand effect was significant, even though brand advertising was relatively small before 1983. That is, even during periods of low brand expenditure, the model showed that brand advertising contributed to growth in the total orange juice demand. Comparing these results to those of Ward (1988 and 1988b) again confirms that both generic and brand citrus advertising can add to growth in the product category (Lee, 1984; Fairchild, Gunter, and Lee, 1987; Brown and Lee, 1992).

Although we do not have space to review other studies dealing with citrus, one can find a range of applications of econometric techniques. Hochman, Regev, and Ward (1974) were the first to analyze long-term allocation of advertising funds using optimal control theory; a recent paper by Lui and Forker (1990) adapts this optimal control framework to the dairy promotion issue. A study by Ward and Myers (1979) addressed the issue of stability in the advertising parameters. When programs are evolving through time and significant copy changes are taking place, it is reasonable to expect potential adjustments in the advertising coefficients. Citrus advertising coefficients were estimated by Ward and Myers using time-varying parameter

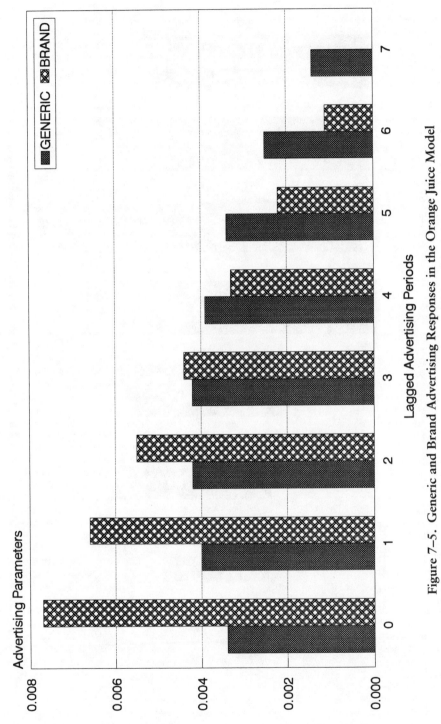

Figure 7–5. Generic and Brand Advertising Responses in the Orange Juice Model

227

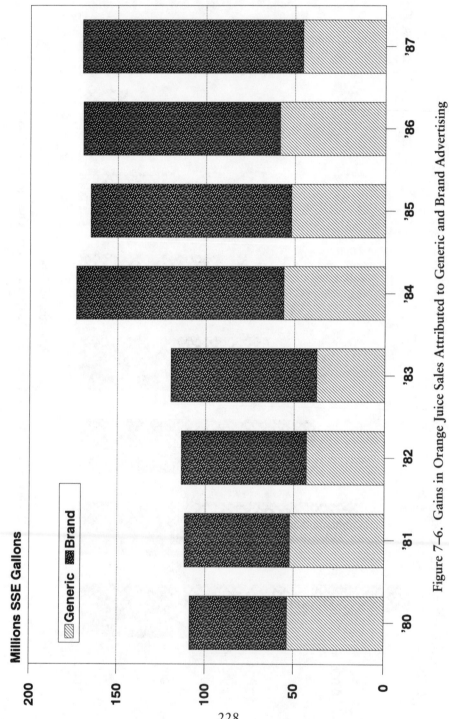

Figure 7–6. Gains in Orange Juice Sales Attributed to Generic and Brand Advertising

techniques (see Chapter 6), and specifically the Cooley-Prescott model. Over the period of the study, the citrus advertising coefficients were shown to have increased: the effectiveness of the advertising improved for the immediate period and as well as for the longer carryover effect (Ward and Myers, 1979).

Cheese and Yogurt Generic and Brand Advertising

Kinnucan and Fearon (1986) provide another case study of the impact of generic and brand advertising with their study of the demand for cheese in New York City. Using monthly time series for the years 1979 through 1981, they estimated a single-equation model of cheese including both generic and brand advertising. Their model was specified assuming declining marginal returns to advertising and potentially different advertising carryover effects for generic and brand efforts. Given the relative short time period for estimation and the lagged advertising structure, Kinnucan and Fearson collected advertising data for two years prior to the period used for estimation; in this way they could maintain the maximum degrees of freedom possible for their model. Corrections for serial correlation were made, and two alternative specifications of their model were presented.

As evident with the variables G (generic) and B (brand) in Table 7–9, both generic and brand advertising are significant and have the correct estimated signs. The model points to a carryover effect with 90 percent of the generic effect occurring within sixteen months. The long-term brand effect

Table 7–9
Regression Results for Alternative Functional Forms of the Cheese Demand Equation, New York City Area, Monthly Data, 1979–81

Independent Variable	Log Model		Log-Inverse Model	
	Estimates	*t ratio*	*Estimates*	*t ratio*
Intercept	−7.276	−1.02	−9.92	−1.42
Cos 1	0.044	5.76	0.043	5.55
Sine 2	−0.03	−4.404	−0.029	−3.91
Cos 4	0.025	2.56	0.025	2.54
Income	0.97	1.4	1.14	1.71
Cheese price	−0.065	−0.16	−0.15	−0.38
Generic	0.0593	2.74	0.000023	2.75
Brand	0.2021	1.85	0.0018	2.01
R^2	0.862	0.86		
DW	1.96	1.94		
Rho	−0.33	−0.318		
F	32.3	31.6		

Source: Kinnucan and Fearon (1986).

on cheese demand decays much more slowly than the estimates for generic, with up to fifty-four months required for the full impact to be realized. This longer brand carryover effect is the opposite from that shown for citrus.

Kinnucan concluded that with the log-linear model, increasing brand advertising by 0.1 cent per capita each month would increase sales by 0.7 percent, while the same increase in generic advertising would increase cheese sales by 1.98 percent. Thus, at the margin, spending an extra dollar on generic advertising would be 2.8 times more effective than the same dollar spent on brand advertising. These marginal differences must be interpreted while recognizing that brand advertising was generally fifteen times greater than generic in the New York market (Kinnucan and Fearon, 1986).

Kinnucan and Fearon concluded that generic advertising had enhanced cheese sales in the New York market by nearly 8 percent. Furthermore, the results point to a significant interaction between generic and brand advertising. The effectiveness of generic advertising was shown to be enhanced by nearly 18 percent when large brand efforts existed, whereas the effectiveness of brand advertising showed much less sensitivity to the levels of generic advertising of cheese.

Research by Blaylock and Blisard (1988) provides additional insight into national models for natural and processed cheeses; their models include both generic and brand cheese advertising. Using monthly consumer panel data for the period from 1982 through the first half of 1987, they estimated cheese models showing generic advertising of natural cheese to be positive and significant. The effects of brand advertising on natural cheese was statistically insignificant. The authors concluded that generic advertising has a significant impact on natural cheese only in the same month of the advertisements. When considered separately, generic and brand advertising of processed cheese were insignificant. With the two types of advertising combined,

Table 7–10
Summary of Model Simulation Results on the Effect of Regional and National Generic Cheese Advertising on National At-Home Consumption, September 1984 to June 1987

	Units	Natural Cheese	Processed Cheese
Total sales	Millions of pounds	3,200.3	2,103.3
Increase in generic advertising	Millions of dollars	$145.6	
Gains due to advertising	Millions of pounds	16	98.4
Gain as share of sales		0.5	4.7
Gain per advertising dollars	Pounds	0.1	0.7

Source: Blaylock and Blisard (1988).

however, advertising estimates resulted in a positive significant effect on processed cheese, and the carryover effect extended beyond 12 months.

With the estimated models, Blaylock and Blisard then simulated the impact from cheese advertising after the start of the national dairy checkoff programs. Their simulation results are summarized in Table 7–10 for both types of cheese. Natural cheese sales increased by 16 million pounds between September 1984 and June 1987; processed cheese sales increased by 98 million pounds for the same period. Finally, Blaylock and Blisard concluded that generic advertising influences households not normally purchasing natural cheese to make such purchases. It does not, however, influence households that normally buy natural cheese to increase their consumption (Blaylock and Blisard, 1988).

In another processed dairy study, Hall and Foik (1982) observed that generic and brand yogurt advertising combined in California was much more effective than generic alone in expanding demand for the category. Furthermore, returns to generic yogurt advertising were small compared to returns from generic fluid milk advertising.

National Potato Programs

Jones and Ward's study (1989) of the U.S. potato industry offers another example where generic and brand advertising are incorporated into the modeling efforts. The Potato Research and Promotion Act of 1971 provided checkoff assessments intended for advertising, research, market development, and promotion of fresh and processed potatoes. Generic advertising generally accounted for 75 percent of the expenditures.

This analysis was intended to estimate the returns to potato producers from generic and brand advertising while considering the interproduct relationships between fresh and processed potatoes. There are considerable differences in potato product forms, including fresh potatoes, chips, and frozen and dehydrated potatoes. Given this diversity in products, would one expect brand advertising to be more effective than generic where the former is more focused on specific product forms?

The methodology used to evaluate advertising was an econometric model of the demand and supply forces characterizing each sector of the potato industry. A fifteen-equation system was estimated, with demand equations for potato chips and fresh, frozen, and dehydrated potatoes. Jones and Ward adopted a simultaneous model using annual data from the period 1970–85, estimated using three-stage least squares. Their first two equations in their system reflect total production of potatoes, whereas other equations represented demands for the fresh and processed groups. Current and lagged generic and brand advertising entered the demand equations, and equations were specified for linking retail, wholesale, and farm prices. The system was placed in equilibrium with the final equations.

Generic advertising expenditures are not included in the demand for potato chips, because little or no generic funds were used to promote chips during the study period. Considerable funds were allocated to potato chips by brand manufacturers, and this is captured with current and lagged chip advertising expenditures in the model. The importance of advertising in each equation was pretested by running regressions that excluded these variables. The pretests pointed to fairly constant estimates for the included variables, but a pronounced decline in the explanatory power of the equations when the advertising variables were excluded from the estimation.

This is a complicated model, with a full systems approach being used. The parameter estimates are of interest, as well as the reduced forms after all parameters are known. Recall that the parameters show the effects of advertising on each equation where advertising is included, whereas the reduced form represents the full impact of the advertising, recognizing that advertising has both a direct and indirect effect on everyone. That is, one can interpret the parameters directly but also show the full effects of advertising after recognizing the linkages among the product forms.

What can be concluded from this approach to advertising evaluation? Jones and Ward's estimates fail to show any direct significant impact of generic advertising of fresh potatoes. This result was unexpected, because most of the generic expenditures had gone to promote fresh potatoes. Jones and Ward suggested that inclusion of the generic expenditures in the fresh equation assumes a well-defined linkage between advertising and fresh consumption. In the complete system, this time linkage may not have been fully specified, since generic advertising is a relative new addition to the total marketing efforts for potatoes. Similarly, it could be that the generic expenditure levels were simply too low to reach a needed threshold before gains could be measured, or it may be true that generic advertising of fresh potatoes simply failed to stimulate significant increases in fresh consumption. It is often hard for researchers and policymakers to accept negative results, but one must be prepared to do so after critically reviewing the research.

This model does show significant positive gains from brand advertising for chips. A 1 percent increase in brand chip advertising points to a 0.14 percent gain in chip consumption. Both generic and brand advertising are shown to have significant positive impacts on the consumption of frozen potatoes, primarily french fries. Compared with chips, brand advertising elasticities are smaller for the frozen potatoes. Likewise, a 1 percent increase in generic advertising generates a smaller response in the frozen market than a corresponding increase in brand expenditures. Consumption of dehydrated potato products is also influenced by generic and brand advertising. The long-run elasticity of brand advertising is smaller for dehydrated potatoes than for chips or frozen products. Also, relative to frozen potatoes, generic advertising of dehydrated potatoes is more effective.

Jones and Ward suggest that the marketing of many of these products through institutional outlets may be a contributing factor for the observed differences in effectiveness. They conclude that both brand and generic advertising are quite effective in stimulating demand for all processed potato products. Yet fresh potatoes, the primary product of emphasis for generic advertising, were not positively affected, at least as measured for the annual model over the period considered.

This model extends the research scope beyond the single-equation approach. The system is more complicated, and the data requirements increased considerably. Modeling flexibility is sometimes limited when trying to deal with the total system, yet gains can be realized in that the interrelationship among commodity forms are present and must be considered.

Coupon Effectiveness in Citrus Promotion

Coupons represent a unique aspect of advertising and promotion that has not yet been discussed in our case studies. Coupons inform, and they also entice consumers to respond to the price discount inherent in their redemption (see Chapter 3). Coupons permit direct marketing efforts to be accomplished with greater consumer selectivity and without changing consumers' perception of the product's shelf price (Ward and Davis 1978a). Ward and Davis dealt with the economic effectiveness of citrus coupons in two phases. An econometric model of coupon redemption was first developed to address questions relating to the national distribution of coupons, then the researchers determined if the use of coupons contributed to increased consumption of the good being promoted. We will review both models, since they provide examples of unique problems addressed with econometric modeling.

What level of coupon effort must be used to achieve a particular level of consumer redemption? Is the medium used likely to influence the rate of redemption? What is the lagged response to an initial coupon drop? Ward and Davis's coupon redemption model provides empirical estimates useful for answering these questions. Theoretically, coupon redemption should vary with the total coupon drop, the media used to distribute the coupons, the face value, and the time period since the drop took place (Ward and Davis, 1978b). The authors noted that accounting for media use may capture much of the demographic differences among consumers, since various media (such as newspaper versus magazine) may reach different demographic cross sections.

Their model is nonlinear in the variables but is intrinsically linear in the parameters, as illustrated in equation 7–12. The model shows a direct link between redemption and the level of the initial coupon drop, with this linkage differing by face value and with the drop medium, which is the interaction term between the coupon drop (CR) and the variables for medium

(M) and value (V). The model was estimated with ordinary least squares, and the results are reported in Table 7–11. Note in the model that the media are expressed with discrete dummy variables, using newspapers as the base. Hence, the estimated media parameters in the table are being measured relative to newspapers.

$$\log(CR) = \left[\left(\sum_{i=1}^{6} \alpha_i M_i\right) + a_7 V\right][\log(C)] + \beta_0 + \beta_1 T^{-1} \qquad (7.12)$$

The redemption model is specified such that direct redemption elasticities are estimated and shown to be conditional on the media and coupon value. For a selected medium and value, the models are such that the redemption elasticities are fixed. Elasticities of coupon redemption and a ranking of the effectiveness across distribution methods are included in Table 7–11.

Coupons distributed by direct mail far exceed the other methods in terms of redemption, whereas on-package coupons are the least effective. The column labeled "Relative Effectiveness" demonstrates the redemption rates achieved, normalized to direct mail effect; for example, on-package redemption is only 13 percent as effective as direct mail in achieving redemptions. Redemption elasticities further show that for all media,

Table 7.11
OLS Estimates of the Coupon Redemption Model

	Estimated Coefficient	t Test		Elasticity	Relative Effectiveness
Variables					
Constant	0.0539	0.0809			
Coupon effort	0.6854	10.3736	Newspaper	0.7087	0.2110
Media					
Direct mail	0.1492	7.8450	Direct mail	0.8546	1.0000
Magazine, on page	0.0004	0.0239	Magazine, on page	0.7090	0.2160
Magazine, pop-up	0.0528	2.4512	Magazine, pop-up	0.7614	0.3700
Sunday supplement	0.0220	1.3737	Sunday supplement	0.7307	0.2690
On package	−0.0489	−2.5636	On package	0.6598	0.1300
Coupon value	0.0233	2.1034			
Time span	−3.5736	−10.7045			
R_2 =	.8246				
F (8,81) =	47.5900				
No. of Obs. =	90.0000				

Source: Ward and Davis (1978a).

increases in redemption cannot be expected to be proportional to the increases in the coupon drops. All redemption elasticities are less than one, thus indicating marginally declining redemption rates with larger coupon drops. Finally, the estimates show a significant positive response to the use of fifteen-cent coupon versus ten-cent coupons. All elasticities are increased by 0.023 with the use of the higher-valued coupons. As a rule, Ward and Davis concluded that the redemption rate of fifteen-cent coupons can be expected to be 25 percent greater than for the ten-cent coupons.

Figure 7–7 provides an overview of the results from the econometric redemption model. Coupon drops are on the bottom axis, and redemptions on the left axis; each plot compares ten- and fifteen-cent coupons distributed through three selected media types. The pronounced difference achieved with direct mail is apparent, as are the gains associated with higher valued coupons. Likewise, the declining redemption rates with increases in the total drop are clearly evident. The model was also used to show the lag redemption response as estimated in Table 7–11. It shows that maximum redemption rate occurs in the second month after the initial drop. Redemptions continue after the second month, but at a decreasing rate: A 30 percent redemption rate is achieved by the third month, a 50 percent rate occurs by the fifth month, and nearly three years are required to achieve 90 percent of the realized redemption.

To our knowledge, this is the only published econometric model providing the direct linkage between redemptions and coupon drops for generic promotions. The empirical results are convincing. Whether they can be generalized to other programs is, however, another issue. Although the empirical application was to citrus products, we see little that is unique about citrus coupons that would prevent these results from being generalized to (at least) the broader class of food goods. Goodwin (1992) estimated a model of consumer use of grocery coupons and found that coupon usage was closely tied to household demographics, shopping practices, and size and composition of grocery transaction. Goodwin's approach measured whether or not consumers used coupons but does not identified the intensity of coupon drop as used in the specific citrus case. The Goodwin model is not commodity specific.

As indicated above, the second phase of the coupon analysis was to determine if consumers' demand for citrus was influenced by the use of coupons. Because redemption represents individual uses of coupons, changes in individual consumption behavior must be the focal point in order to measure the coupon impact on demand (Ward and Davis, 1978a). Coupons are expected to influence consumption through both their redemptive value and informational effects. The redemptive value represents reductions in the purchasing price depending on the face value of the coupon; the informational value results from exposure to the coupons. Ward and Davis's model measured both effects.

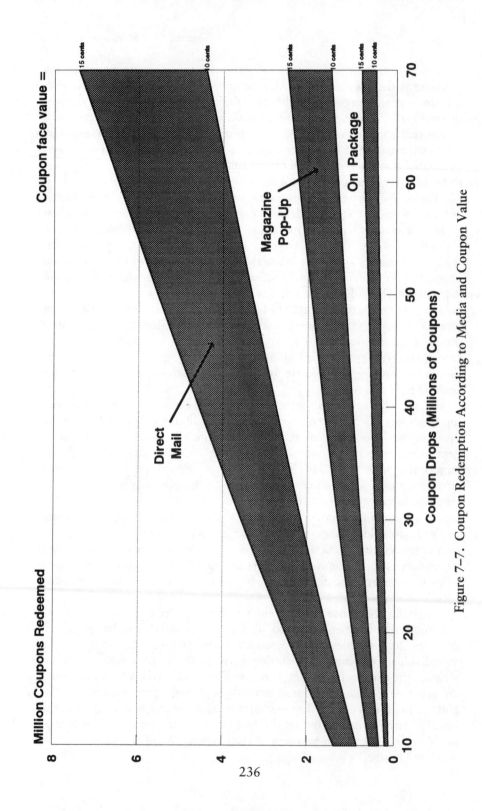

Figure 7-7. Coupon Redemption According to Media and Coupon Value

Although we will not present the econometric aspects of this model, the overall effectiveness of coupons from this model is illustrated in Figure 7–8. The demand for the average consumer is plotted assuming different face values of the coupons and for no coupons. Consumers facing higher prices respond less to the use of coupons in terms of additional consumption. Also, coupons show a declining marginal rate of return. At a price of 0.5 cents per ounce, for example, coupons valued at 20 cents, 5 cents, and 15 cents yield an increase in demand of 137.4 ounces, (as shown by points (a) and (b) in this figure.) Nearly 47 percent of this increase could have been achieved with 5-cent coupons, 72 percent with 10 cents' worth of coupons, and 88 percent with coupons equaling 15 cents. Their result also indicate that coupons have an informational effect; for example, for 5 cents worth of coupons and a container price of 0.6 cents per ounce, 87 percent of the gain in consumption is attributed to the informational effect. At higher prices, the informational components decrease relative to the total effect. At higher prices it is clearly more difficult to stimulate consumers using the new information found within the coupon, as is seen in Figure 7–8, where the curves are nearly equal for the higher prices (Ward and Davis, 1978a).

Lee and Brown (1985) extended the coupon model by allowing for the data to include both users and nonusers of coupons. They concluded that the Florida Department of Citrus coupon programs had a positive impact on consumers of orange juice but had little impact on those nonusers. Scratch-off magazine coupons tend to have a greater impact on the demand for frozen orange juice among users.

U.S. Soybean Exports

The U.S. soybean industry has a long history of international promotion activities designed to expand the foreign demand for its product. The American Soybean Association and the Foreign Agricultural Service, along with importers, have jointly funded several efforts over the years. Recently, the promotional effects shifted from promotion of soybeans to soybean products. Williams (1985) has addressed the question of the economic effectiveness of these programs using a large econometric model of the world soybean complex.

Though the scope of our presentation prevents us from detailing the model in depth, it is important to give an overview. The analysis is based on a ninety-six-equation, annual econometric simultaneous model that estimates supplies, demands, prices, and trade of soybeans and soybean products in eight major trading regions of the world: the United States, Brazil, the European Community (nine members), Canada, Japan, Other Asia and Oceania, Africa, and a Rest-of-the-World region. Market development expenditures are incorporated into the demand equation for Europe, Japan, the remainder of Asia, Africa, and the composite region. Furthermore, the model

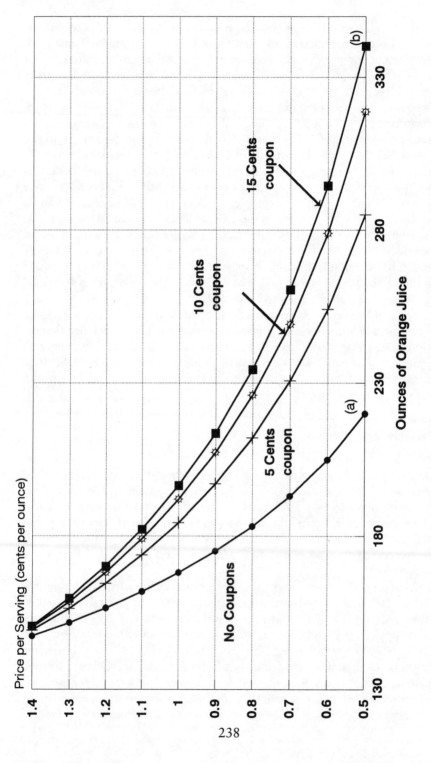

Figure 7–8. Coupon Effect on the Average Household Demand for Orange Juice

attempts to account for lagged promotional effects (note that we are dealing with an annual model, in contrast to earlier monthly models). Williams's initial estimates for the promotional effects with such lagged structures were generally unsuccessful; hence, he derived an alternative using a three-year-moving-average series of development expenditures. The full model was estimated with appropriate simultaneous-equation estimation techniques.

Given the fully specified and estimated model, Williams then used simulation techniques to deal with the evaluation of the soybean promotion programs. The procedure entailed first forecasting all endogenous variables in the model using the full data set, including the development expenditures. This gave a benchmark for subsequent comparisons. Then, using the same model, he simulated the endogenous variable values after restricting the promotion expenditures in total and for selected regions.

Given the model and simulation techniques, what do we know about the returns for the international promotion of soybeans and soybean products? It is important to note that his model shows the impact not only on soybeans but on other sectors closely tied to the soybean industry. Between 1970 and 1980, the model indicates that market development efforts led to increases in U.S. production, demand, and prices by an annual average of 1 to 2 percent (Williams, 1985, p. 254). Soybean cash receipts increased 4 percent, and soybean product revenues increased by 7.5 percent. Export returns to all contributors averaged $62 per dollar invested and $58 per investment dollar by growers. Although the model showed some impact on other agricultural sectors, the impact was generally quite small, being usually less than 1 percent (p. 255). Furthermore, the simulations pointed to only a very small gain to Brazil as a result of the U.S. effort, indicating that the free-rider benefits did not appear to be substantial.

This type of evaluation deals with a more realistic setting, where the interactions among various parts of the world markets are recognized; clearly, most of the single-equation models considered earlier do not do this. These complex models are often difficult to estimate and are subject to considerable specification and estimation problems. One loses flexibility in modeling the advertising dimension to the problem as other factors are considered concurrently. Data requirements expand, and the potential for error that can influence the entire system is greatly increased. Also, the ability to simulate specific advertising policies is sometimes compromised because of the complexity of the model. In defense of these systems, they are much closer to representing actual market interactions, given the global importance of many of the commodities having checkoff programs. Our purpose in reviewing this model (and others) is to demonstrate what can and has been utilized to deal with evaluation. Whether or not the precise rates of return are reasonable is another issue.

Canadian Fats and Oils

Canadian advertising of butter via generic efforts and brand advertising of margarine, shortening, and vegetable oils provides an example of promoting a class of goods that clearly should be highly substitutable. Goddard and Amuah (1989) address the issue of measuring the impact of all advertising on the total demand for Canadian fats and oils and then the specific effects of advertising on each of the four categories. They noted that to determine the effect of fats and oils advertising, one must deal with the cross-commodity effects among the four commodities. The issue, then, is to devise methods for testing the aggregate effects, the effects on each commodity, and the cross effects among the commodities.

Goddard and Amuah estimate linear expenditure models, rather than the demand models reviewed in most of the other case studies. Given the appropriate assumptions regarding a consumer utility function, one can easily specify expenditure-share equations. Each equation represents the share of total expenditures on one of the four types of fats and oils (butter, shortening, margarine, and vegetable oils).

Although we will not repeat the theory found in the paper, it is worth presenting their final equations to be estimated, since the analysis is somewhat different from our other case studies. First, the aggregate expenditures for fats and oils is specified to be some function of a weighted average price (P^*), lagged consumption of each good, and the total advertising efforts (see the section on demand systems in Chapter 6). Equation 7–13 reflects the aggregate model. Second, the expenditure for each good is shown to be affected by lagged consumption of that good, relative prices of all oils and fats, and the advertising of each type of oils and fats, as shown in equation 7–14. The share equations are then defined as the ratios of the individual good to the total expenditure equation.

$$TEXP = \sum_i a_i + \sum_i d_i X_{i(t-1)} + \sum_i \sum_j \beta_{ij} \log(P_j^*) + \sum_i \sum_j c_{ij} \log(A_j) \quad (7.13)$$

$$P_i X_i = a_i + d_i X_{i(t-1)} + \sum_j \beta_{ij} \log(P_j^*) + \sum_j c_{ij} \log(A_j) \quad (7.14)$$

$$W_i = \frac{P_i X_i}{TEXP}$$

The econometric problem entails a standard two-stage estimation procedure. The aggregate-expenditures equation is first estimated using ordinary least squares, and then the expenditure-share equations are estimated. Because the error terms across equations are likely related, seemingly unrelated regression procedures were used for this second-stage estimation.

As with the other models, we will concentrate on the advertising results and not the full model and its implications. Goddard and Amuah's estimates for the aggregate-expenditure equation showed no significant effect of fats and oils advertising on the total. This would imply that the total fats and oil market is not expanded with advertising; rather, the advertising may create some redistribution of consumption patterns among the goods within the category (Goddard and Amuah, 1989, p. 744). In contrast, the estimated impacts of advertising on each good were quite different. All own-advertising elasticities were positive, with vegetable oil having the largest coefficient (0.07 percent) and butter the smallest (0.01 percent).

The model further shows the advertising cross effects among the four goods. Margarine advertising has a negative effect on butter, shortening, and vegetable oils demand. Interestingly, the effect of butter advertising on margarine is much stronger than the effects of margarine advertising on butter. Although the negative cross effects are theoretically correct, the model also indicates some positive cross effects that are more difficult to rationalize.

Given their empirical estimates, Goddard and Amuah then simulated the impact of changing various advertising expenditure levels. Their final conclusion is that advertising of fats and oils does not expand the total demand for the category, but does affect the goods separately. In particular, the results show a return to butter of approximately 1.11 to 1 and to margarine of 1.31 to 1 (Goddard and Amuah, 1989, p. 748). Cox (1989) completed a study of the same group of products using a Rotterdam demand model. Using different data sets and modeling techniques, he did not show any significant effect of advertising for this commodity group.

Fresh Tomato Promotions

Fresh tomatoes are probably the most perishable of the commodities reviewed in this chapter. This commodity is unique in that it is generally distributed to the wholesale and retail outlet in an unripened state; tomatoes will continue to ripen in the home or other places for final consumption. Consumers' perception of the quality of the product is closely tied to the stage of ripening when consumed. The tomato industry has for years faced a problem where consumers purchase tomatoes and then refrigerate them, which stops or at least gently alters the normal ripening process. Through educational and promotional efforts, the Florida tomato industry has attempted to encourage consumers to adopt room-temperature storage practices. The argument is that improved storage leads to improved in-house quality and thus increased consumption. In the early 1980s, the industry increased its educational and promotional expenditures in an effort to increase the percentage of tomatoes being stored at room temperatures.

Degner (1985) used an extensive telephone survey to quantify consumers' purchases of tomatoes and their awareness of the promotional and information activities by the tomato industry. The intent of the survey was to determine if any relationship existed between the media advertising for fresh tomatoes and the adoption of correct ripening and storage practices. Degner's analysis of these cross-sectional data provide numerous insights into consumption habits and buyer characteristics; of interest to our review, however, is how the linkage between advertising and storage behavior was measured.

One quantifiable unit was whether or not consumers had switched their storage practices in the last three years. This is a classic limited dependent variable problem, since the response is either yes or no (see Chapter 6). Degner adopted a probit model to this analysis, with the variable of interest being the adoption of room-temperature storage. The model and empirical results are shown in Table 7–12. Note that the model includes demographics, region (by city), and several measures to determine if the consumer recalled seeing or hearing any tomato advertising or publicity for fresh tomatoes, as well as the number of magazine subscriptions that could have contained tomato advertising.

The probit model results in Table 7–12 can be used to calculate the probability of switching to room-temperature storage (RTS) with respect to a one-unit change in the appropriate variables. Estimates for magazine subscriptions are positive and significant at the 90 percent level. With a one-unit increase in subscriptions, the probability of switching to RTS increases by .016. Recalling television commercials was also likely to contribute to switching to RTS, whereas the use of other media did not show a significant role. Television commercials led to a probability increase of .14 in switching, and television shows yielded a .07 probability of switching to RTS.

Degner (1985) concludes that TV commercials and publicity have the greatest impact on switching behavior. While the number of magazines the respondents subscribed to that contained FTE ads was statistically significant, this variable may be reflecting attributes of the respondents (such as intelligence, inquisitiveness, etc.) rather than actual influence of an ad. Degner also concludes that with both the descriptive analysis and the econometric approaches, all elements of the Florida Tomato Exchange promotional programs have influenced consumers to adopt room-temperature storage. The results are strong and reasonable.

Overview of Econometric Studies

Can any conclusions be generalized from the array of promotion evaluations? Are there commonalities and points of departure? Does the methodology lend itself to the types of questions being asked? As one would expect,

Table 7–12
Probit Model Estimates for Switching of Storage Method for
Fresh Tomatoes

Explanatory Variables	Parameter Estimates	t Ratio	Marginal Probability
Intercept	−1.0549	3.9728	−0.3960
Number of magazines	0.0419	1.5553	0.0157
Education	−0.4520	0.4184	−0.0170
Age	0.0095	2.4559	0.0036
Income	0.0041	1.0872	0.0015
Race	0.1286	0.8196	0.0483
Sex	0.3018	2.5236	0.1133
Boston	−0.1046	0.6532	−0.0393
Philadelphia	0.3493	2.0724	0.1312
New York	0.2518	1.5072	0.0945
Pittsburgh	0.1599	0.9856	0.0600
TV commercial	0.3624	2.6594	0.1361
TV show	0.1954	1.2551	0.0734
Newspaper	−0.0764	0.5215	−0.0287
Radio	−0.0923	0.7530	−0.0346
Posters	0.1010	0.8700	0.0379
Leaflets	0.0611	0.2317	0.0229
Observations	653		
% wrong	0.3911		
Akaike information criterion	444.24		

Source: Degner (1985).

the first and foremost question most often asked is whether consumers are responding to investment in commodity advertising. Other questions posed relate to the allocation of funds to programs, media use, message content, market orientation, and product form—in other words, where the monies should be invested. This latter issue is an allocation question for which econometric analysis is especially well suited.

Promotion evaluations can be viewed in two major ways: (1) what the results are and how they apply, and (2) what the quality of the research is in view of the theory, data, and methods of analysis. Advertising and promotion is a marketing tool that can potentially influence consumer behavior and demand. It can be the tool used to achieve product differentiation and to inform potential consumers about new products, their attributes, and their uses. Without commodity advertising, producers must depend on others to disseminate information about their products. With commodity checkoff programs, they may at least have some control over the information agenda.

Our selected case studies are by no means exhaustive, and they have been purposely limited to agricultural markets. As a rule, most if not all of the published commodity advertising studies deal with industry-level evaluations. The impact on consumer behavior is measured with respect to the sales of all firms; this is reasonable, since the programs represent the total industry and not just some of the firms. Also, most of the costs are born by the producers. What we know empirically applies most directly to the industry level, with inferences and logical arguments applied to the other levels. The theoretical issues have been discussed at some length in the literature for all levels, but the empirical counterparts are mostly focused at the industry level. As noted earlier, sometimes firm-level analysis does not appear in the literature because of the proprietary nature of the analysis. When reviewing the growing volume of literature on commodity advertising, as a rule the research addresses real applied problems and usually provides insight into program strategies for the industry. Obviously, there are questions that cannot be addressed with any of these studies, but they do seem to be more oriented to dealing with real problems than studies of noncommodity advertising research.

Before turning to specific conclusions, several general observations are appropriate, some of which are subjective observations on our part. The theory of advertising at the firm level is reasonably well developed, with much of it found in advanced microeconomics texts. The theory for generic advertising is less well developed in the literature, but we have tried to advance this area in Chapter 2 and 3. In reviewing the many cases (only some of which are reviewed in this chapter), one generally sees greater attention given to new empirical methodologies and ways to deal with data problems and less to theoretical advertising issues. The former are essential to reaching some closure on a particular problem. Yet the underpinning to commodity (generic) advertising and promotion must have a theoretical base, and this theoretical base deserves further consideration (see Ward, Chang, and Thompson, 1985). Attention to this, however, should not be at the cost of continuing the applied work.

The research points to considerable innovations in developing, adopting, and applying a spectrum of empirical tools. Similarly, issues associated with data problems have generally been handled. Details in the various studies almost consistently show data problems in measurement, availability, and reporting consistency. These important issues are sometimes passed over while still applying sophisticated research methods; data are sometimes accepted without giving the necessary accuracy and reliability tests. In defense of this process, though, one must work with what is available. Data problems are a major reason that researchers and the various commodity program coordinators must work together to deal with data collection and related issues.

Economic analysis of commodity programs, although not new, is still evolving. The first important questions were raised at the industry level. As the history of these programs increases, the importance of generic efforts to changing market structure will likely receive more attention. For example, can the national beef programs have any impact on the concentration in the beef processing industry? At the national level, have commodity advertising programs altered our diets, and if so, are we better or worse off? We clearly have not been able to deal with such issues here, but we will offer some insight in the next chapter.

Econometric Results

Two initial conclusions generally stand out among the cases reviewed. First, existing econometric techniques provide meaningful results and have been applied to real questions about allocation and implementation policies. Second, the rates of return are generally positive but are considerably different across commodity groups. This should not be surprising, since in Chapter 2 we emphasized the role of commodity characteristics as a major factor leading to differences in effectiveness among programs. It is, however, essential that the calculated rates come from programs and commodity differences and not the tools used. While our empirical tools are developing, we must be extremely careful that our generalizations are not "tool" specific.

Most of the econometric models have been single-equation studies with various forms of advertising included in the specifications. Usually the demand function is specified to allow for lagged promotional effects. There are several ways for dealing with the lag structure and no one procedure appears to be optimal, nor should it necessarily be. In fact, one is struck by the different methods used and how the results seem to be quite sensitive to the lagged specification. Also, there are a few cases of inconsistency in the use of lagged effects within the same commodity group. In all cases, the lagged structure adopted should be driven by the theory and empirical results and not the preference of the researcher.

Even with the variations in methods used for dealing with lagged structure, it is clear that commodity advertising programs do have a positive lagged effect for most commodities. Although the length of the lags can differ, the fact that some consistency in empirically showing the lags is of more importance for policy purposes. Most checkoff policies are not based on whether the program has a six-, eight-, or twelve-month lag; rather, programs are designed according to whether a lagged structure does or does not exist. The analyses point to positive gains and some measured carryover effect at the industry level. Having some insight into when the peak advertising effect occurs is important, and many of the commodity studies show when the maximum advertising effect occurs.

The use of larger systems models have been shown for several commodities. These models allow for gaining a better empirical understanding of the full impact of promotion on an industry as well as across industries. As a general rule, however, most of the large models have been adopted at a cost of using simplistic specifications of the advertising components. The complexity of large systems and the increased data requirements sometime dictate using ad hoc procedures for including the advertising components. As such, uses of the model for policy purposes become diluted and more difficult for policymakers to use and understand. For example, in large regional models, advertising data for every region may simply not be available; hence, there are data gaps in the analysis for which something must be done to operationalize the model. Whatever procedure is used, it ultimately affects the entire system by the very nature of the systems modeling. This is clearly a major drawback to using full-systems modeling. Most of the studies we have reviewed do not provide sufficient sensitivity analysis to show the implications from using proxy measures for advertising in the system. Full-systems analysis does, however, provide a wider perspective to policy analysis.

The Use of Simulation in Evaluations and in Allocation Policy

Once an econometric model is developed, simulations are often used to derive conclusions about rates of return and alternative allocation policies. Simulation applications can fall within the following categories:

- Using the historical data, one can simulate demand assuming no advertising and promotion over the historical data period. These predicted gains provide a base for judging the returns from all advertising and promotion expenditures included in the model. The base does not necessarily have to be against a zero expenditure level, but can be against some level assuming that the checkoff programs never existed. Taking this difference gives the estimated total effect and provides the numbers for calculating a rate of return.

- Simulations can be used to show how much of a price increase would be required to offset the calculated gains from the advertising and promotion. This price increase is another way to derive the implicit economic value of the advertising and promotion.

- Simulations can be used to estimate the economic gains expected from changes in expenditure levels and expenditures across programs. Usually, a fixed period is set, and then alternative advertising policies are explored and the gains shown. This procedure is particularly useful for showing the marginal gains from advertising and how best to utilize limited funds. Such policies include media allocations, adjustments in total expenditures, and others depending on the nature of the advertising model.

- Simulations can be used to forecast future crop years and to explore what would be needed to achieve specific industry (or firm) targets. For example, how much advertising would it take to sustain a 1 percent real growth in demand for beef? Is it feasible? Similarly, how much adjustment in expenditures would be needed just to keep up with inflation?

- Simulations are often used to deal with the economic cost of new government policies, changes in crop sizes, or other economic factors having a bearing on the supply and demand pictures. It is useful for illustrating the potential benefits (or cost) from increasing (or decreasing) checkoff assessments.

No commodity advertising study is complete until it has dealt with the what-if questions. It is at this point where economic analysis provides the real value to policymakers.

Only a few of the models deal with more detailed allocation questions, that is, how funds should be allocated across media and programs. For many checkoff programs, it is still too early in the life of the program to address those issues. One can look at commodity programs that have been ongoing for some time (such as citrus), however, and there still is limited empirical evidence about the appropriate allocations across program areas and commodity forms. For example, the Florida citrus industry still does not know how to allocate funds optimally between fresh and processed products. In defense of that industry, we have cited studies of generic and brand activities and between types of coupon programs to illustrate how econometrics can and has been used to assist in the allocation decision-making process. As with most commodity groups, economics is but one of several factors influencing advertising policies. The apple case probably comes the closest to suggesting allocation policy; the dairy study of three New York markets also provides an example dealing with spatial allocation (Liu and Forker, 1990).

Almost every study has been limited by inconsistency in the data collection process. Record keeping has improved over time, yet this in and of itself creates problems. There are potential recording inconsistencies embedded in the data that may not be apparent to the user. Most often, aggregate expenditures are available, but more detailed program allocation, copy changes, and related adjustments are not well documented.

As a rule, most of the econometric models deal with inflation adjustments in a very ad hoc way. Generally, advertising is deflated by the consumer price index or some other nationally published index. This is the only alternative available. Given the strong seasonal adjustments in some of the media rates, though, one could argue that a media deflation index should be used. Ward and Dixon's model (1989) of fluid milk provides one example where separate radio and television deflators by region were used. At this juncture, it is not clear how sensitive all the reported results across the case studies are to the deflators used.

New developments in econometrics offer several potential solutions to some of the estimation problems. Limited dependent variables and censored data examples were discussed, and several cases were illustrated. Given the nature of consumer decision making, these relatively new tools offer considerable opportunity for measurement. Similarly, methods for measuring parameter adjustments provide a way to "back into" the issues of embedded changes in the advertising programs. For example, if copy and messages have improved over time, then the effectiveness as measured with advertising expenditures should have also improved. Time-varying parameters will at least allow for adjustments in the advertising coefficients while using the aggregate expenditure data; increased computer capabilities make these types of analyses readily accessible. Incorporating some of the techniques into the systems approach provides a good example of the difficulties associated with trying to capture the advertising response in a more fully specified market model.

Finally, few of the studies dealt with measurement error. Measurement error can be addressed in econometric models if one has some understanding of the nature of the errors. Errors occur in timing and quality: timing errors relate to precise documentation of when advertising took place (that is, which month or other period), whereas quality errors relate to the precise measurement of the event. Most of the studies dealt with expenditures as the unit of measurement. Whether expenditures are correctly recorded and, equally important, are the appropriate measurement of program activities are major issues. Possibly, program intensity should be measured with recall data, as were used in Degner's tomato study (1985). A rich set of data on consumer recall and awareness data exist that generally have not been integrated into the econometric approach to advertising evaluation. Almost none of the studies cited dealt with the questions of appropriateness of their measure of advertising activity. As a rule, the researcher has little choice in what to use; hence, there was little to be gained empirically by dealing with the measurement issues.

The Minimum Criteria for Evaluation

Evaluation is an important element to the total checkoff effort. We have discussed several cases and presented a wide range of conclusions about the effectiveness of programs across commodities. As one synthesizes these cases and the descriptive materials, there are several criteria for successful evaluation that become apparent. We state these as being minimum criteria, simply because that is precisely what they are. The list below should represent the starting point for developing an effective evaluation program.

From this list, one must tailor the evaluation effort according to the unique aspects of the commodity under scrutiny.

1. There should be a list of minimum acceptable *indicators for program performance*. The acceptability should be from the policymakers' perspective. Performance indicators could include message awareness, programming timing and coordination, gross rating points, market growth, index of consumer entry, and demand shifts. Good measures of demand shifts are the most useful, but also the most difficult to determine accurately. The type of acceptable indicators will determine the amount of investment that must be made in the evaluation effort.

2. There must be a precise, agreed-upon *definition and description of the programming effort* and how it is to be measured. Some examples include print space, air time, coverage, exposure, and expenditures. Most often, expenditures are used in the modeling efforts as the appropriate measure of program intensity. The definition must include allowances for different media and changes in copy. Copy changes have generally been one of the more difficult measurement problems of ongoing evaluation efforts.

3. The *time dimension for evaluation* must be established so that the evaluation efforts correspond with the types of program allocation decisions. For example, if experience decisions are made monthly and the evaluation model is based on annual data, then most likely the analysis will be of little assistance to the monthly decision-making process.

4. *Data needs* must be articulated, and the data must be tabulated systematically and continuously. Usually, if the data were not collected at the outset, it is nearly impossible to go back and generate the historical data retroactively. Hence, it is essential that the appropriate mechanisms be put in place early on to assure that appropriate data are being collected. Minimum data requirements for modeling purposes include quantifying the advertising and promotion efforts and the program objectives.

5. The evaluation must be put in *context with other economic dimensions* important to the industry under consideration. Evaluation modeling cannot be adequately dealt with in the absence of a good understanding of the other driving economic and noneconomic forces in the industry.

6. There must be *adequate resources* devoted to the evaluation effort to assure research quality and continuity. Yet, there must also be a time to bring issues to closure.

7. There must be in place a *staff or other administrative vehicle* whereby evaluation results can be used. Otherwise, the evaluation becomes meaningless.

8. The *expected report content* (not results) must be established, as well as a *plan to disseminate the results*. In particular, a method for communicating evaluation results to producers is essential.

9. The evaluation must *satisfy the rules of scientific inquiry* and the rules of reasonableness. The analysis must be based on the appropriate economic principles and empirical techniques.

10. The evaluation efforts must be *free of any political influence* or other pressures that could influence or be perceived to influence the outcome.

11. The evaluation should be *designed in scope* to address the issues of importance in some type of rank order. Likewise, the design should allow the decision maker to ask what-if questions, as covered in the simulation discussion above.

12. The evaluation efforts should be *integrated as a contributing element* in the total decision-making process. This also implies that the evaluation results be put in the proper perspective to noneconomic factors that affect the expenditure decisions.

13. Evaluation results must be *presented in a clear format* that can be easily interpreted and used by those less familiar with the empirical techniques.

Summary

We will conclude this chapter by noting that modeling efforts have been successful in measuring the impacts of commodity advertising. Econometrics is the one tool that provides explicit parameter estimates from which one can develop consumer models for dealing with an array of advertising policy issues. Furthermore, from our perspective, there appears to be an increasing mutual appreciation of what can be gained through cooperation among researchers, commodity groups, and advertising agencies. Without this co-operation, much of the research will have limited usefulness, and many of the important data problems will not be solved.

Commodity advertising research brings the researcher, commodity groups, and the advertising agency closer together in addressing the issues. This interchange provides a rich perspective from which we can all learn. Within these case studies, much of this interaction takes place but is not always apparent in the writings. Such interchange is the way that empirical research gets extended.

8

Conclusions and Promotion Policy Issues

I n this chapter we conclude the presentation on the economics of commodity advertising and promotion. We draw conclusions about the checkoff programs, discuss policy issues (public and private) associated with the existence and operation of commodity promotion programs, and provide a summary. The costs and benefits of commodity advertising and promotion programs are considered from the perspective of producers that fund the programs and consumers who respond; for this, we have used a few concepts from welfare economics.[49]

Are such programs in the public interest? Most commodity promotion programs are supported by mandatory assessment against the income of producers. Some argue that the programs are unconstitutional. What does the evidence show about public interest and constitutionality? Since a mandatory assessment is similar to an excise tax and in effect increases costs, who really pays? Even though it has been shown that generic advertising can increase sales, are producers better off, or are they merely reallocating markets among different farmers and commodity groups without a real gain to society or to the agricultural sector? What are the appropriate methods for evaluating the programs to decide if they are in the public interest? Are the programs justified on economic grounds? For some involved in commodity advertising activities, the issues encompass political and organizational concerns in addition to economics; hence, one should not expect economic analyses to provide all the relevant input for dealing with allocation and policy issues.

Even if the programs are constitutional and in the public interest, to what extent does advertising and promotion solve the income problems of farmers? If other means of government intervention are used to influence producer income, how do they affect the impact of generic advertising? Producers who fund the commodity promotion efforts have particular

251

objectives in mind. What policies do their representatives (board members) need to establish to make sure that the objectives are being met?

The Public Interest

Are the legislated commodity promotion programs really in the public interest? How can we tell? To the economist, aside from legal issues, the answer to this question has two dimensions. First, do the programs provide the potential for an increase in the welfare of producers? Second, do the programs have the potential for increasing consumer welfare? Concerning the former, are the producers of the commodity as a group better off with the program than they would have been without it? Concerning the latter, are there welfare gains and is consumer satisfaction greater than it would have been without the advertising and promotion efforts?

Welfare economics provides a framework for analysis. From the research that has been done, we know that commodity advertising can increase the demand for a commodity. A discussion of how this results in higher prices and increased volumes has been presented in Chapters 3 and 6; empirical measures were presented in Chapter 7. In welfare economics, the measure of consumer welfare is referred to as *consumer surplus*, and the measure of producer welfare is referred to as *producer surplus*. To provide a basis for discussion of the welfare issues, we will provide a simple presentation of how producer and consumer surplus are measured.

The supply curve (S) in Figure 8–1 represents the willingness of producers to supply and the costs of supplying various quantities of a commodity. The demand curve (D) represents the willingness of consumers to pay for various quantities of a commodity. PBQ is total revenue received by producers and the total expenditures of consumers. The area ABQ represents producers' costs, while the area ABP is the excess of revenue over costs. This area is called producer surplus. The area PBC is consumer surplus. That is, some consumers would have been willing to pay more for smaller quantities, but only have to pay P for the total amount Q.

If advertising increases demand to D_a, producer surplus increases by the amount in area $PBdP_a$. The consumer surplus increase is the amount in area $EdFC$ less the additional cost $PBdP_a$. In the discussions that follow, we will use increases or decreases in "welfare" (instead of the more technically correct *surplus*) as measures of economic benefits of commodity advertising.

As demonstrated in earlier chapters, advertising can cause the demand curve to shift upward and to the right. But advertising can also cause the curve to change slope. Conceptually, it can also cause demand to become more stable; that is, commodity advertising might influence consumers to chance preference patterns and become more habit persistent. Changes in the level, slope, and variability will all affect the magnitude of the measures of

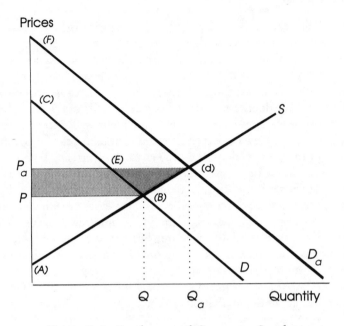

Figure 8–1. Producer and Consumer Surplus

producer and consumer benefits. Most of the studies in Chapter 7 concluded that commodity advertising increased the demand for the advertised commodity. Most of the econometric models were specified in such a way that they measured the extent to which the demand curve was moved to the right. Some of the models measured the extent to which there was an offsetting supply response.

Consumer and producer surplus provide a criteria for judging societal gains. This measure, however, does not capture the benefit from promoting good health and nutrition. Likewise, the welfare scale is static in that it does not reflect improvement in quality. For example, we draw a shift from D to D_a and attribute that shift to advertising. This assumes that demand is for more of the same-quality product. The inherent attributes of the good may differ, though, and if the change is enough, the shift may be for an entirely different product. Calculating consumer surplus with the shift from D to D_a may underestimate (or, in some instances, overestimate) its value with these changes in attributes. Basically, part of the argument is that generic programs can facilitate product innovation. The consumer-producer surplus measure is not a good way to capture these kinds of benefits, and yet these changes may have real value to individuals and to society.

Producer Benefits

In the previous chapter, it was demonstrated empirically that generic advertising can increase demand and that revenue increases sometimes exceed the cost of the advertising effort. In other words, the demand has been shifted to the right enough to provide a positive increase in producer welfare. Will producer welfare be increased in all cases? No. Just because it is possible to provide empirical evidence that the producer benefits are positive for some commodities does not necessarily mean that benefits will exceed costs for all commodities, for any level of expenditures, or for all types of programs. The magnitude of the benefits depend on the level of advertising investment, the nature of other kinds of promotion programs associated with it, the nature and extent of the research effort, the quality of the advertising and promotion effort, the nature of the commodity, and the extent to which consumers and producers respond. Generic commodity promotion programs have the potential to enhance producer welfare, but whether the enhancement is positive for a particular commodity can only be answered empirically. If the increase does more than cover the cost of the program, the increase in producer welfare translates into a stronger, healthier industry. The industry will thus make greater contributions to the economy.

Consumer Benefits

Whether consumers are better off with commodity advertising and promotion efforts has been and will continue to be debated. From commodity advertising, consumers obtain information about commodity attributes. Information that has potential value is information that reduces search costs, improves understanding of the quality and nature of the product (including its nutritional content) or notifies about availability and presence of new products. If this information increases the value of the commodity, the consumer will either consume more or be willing to pay a higher price. The combined effects will translate into increased demand for the commodity. If this increase is large enough to offset the welfare loss due to higher prices, we conclude that consumers have a welfare gain. Given a fixed budget, however, this means that they will have transferred some of their expenditure budget to the purchase of this commodity at the expense of some other commodity, good, or service or of savings. Of course, budgets or incomes may increase or decrease over time. But if consumers do make these switches in purchase patterns, this means that they now have a higher level of satisfaction; otherwise, they would not have shifted their expenditure pattern in this way. Based on empirical work and the welfare arguments, legislated commodity promotion programs have the potential of increasing producer welfare and consumer welfare and thus have the potential of being of benefit to both consumers and producers.

Processor Benefits

Processors of a commodity will also be affected by successful commodity advertising even though they do not pay for it directly. Several scenarios are possible. If the programs increase consumer demand, the demand for processing and distribution services will expand along with the demand for the commodity. The extent to which processors benefit will depend on the degree of processor competition. Producers will benefit more than processors if perfect competition exists among the latter. On the other hand, if processors have monopsony or monopoly power, processors are likely to benefit more than producers. We know that the processing sector for most commodities is neither perfectly competitive nor perfectly monopolistic. It is therefore likely that processors as a group will benefit to some extent if the program expands demand. Also, the benefits to processors will be closely tied to the types of vertical linkages between processors (in this case, first handlers) and producers. Some contractual relations provide for a sharing of profits of the processor with the producer.

If processors benefit, do they also share in the costs? In most programs, the assessments represent direct costs to the producers of the commodity. Indirectly, though, everyone—consumers, processors, and producers—pays for the assessment, because the assessment is similar to an excise tax. Processor welfare is influenced, then, by the degree of competition and vertical market arrangements, the extent of demand expansion, and the impact of the assessment as an excise tax. In addition, first handlers of the commodity, since they usually are responsible for collecting the assessment, incur the administrative costs of collection and record keeping.

Contrary Views

Although there is evidence to support the view that commodity promotion programs increase producer and consumer welfare, there are also contrary views about whether the programs are in the public interest. If one assumes that the advertising and promotion programs contain no information of value to message recipients, it follows that consumers will not respond. If they do not respond, there can be no welfare gain. Thus, proponents must prove that the programs carry information of value to consumers of the advertising and promotion messages. As discussed in Chapter 2, generic programs are more likely than brand advertising to have more informational content about the product attributes.

Some argue that commodity advertising is a zero-sum game; even though one commodity group increases demand for its commodity, the increase is offset by decreases in demand for other commodities. This is the full-stomach argument and has some merit, but it also assumes that the messages have little information of value to the consumer in making purchase decisions. The full-stomach argument ignores health and nutritional education benefits, improvements in market efficiency, and the importance of providing consumers variety. Consumers are dynamic in their consumption behavior, with or without advertising. Advertising provides some direction to this dynamic process. Opponents to generic programs must recognize that consumers move through life-cycle stages, with each stage calling for specific information needs. Consumers will make decisions, experiment, and develop new tastes, and commodity programs can have some input into this process. Competition among competing foods can most likely improve the quality of the food in the food chain; one can simply look at the beef industry's efforts to develop leaner beef, in part as a result of the beef checkoff program. The full-stomach argument is static and does not recognize the dynamics of the marketplace or of consumer tastes. Also, when considering global issues, the full-stomach argument is meaningless. Domestic commodity groups have to compete against producers from other countries, and the information available to foreign consumers about U.S.-produced commodities is usually limited.

The full-stomach argument also assumes a perfectly elastic supply situation for all commodities. If the supply response function for a commodity has a positive slope, as indicated in Figure 8–1, an increase in demand will provide additional welfare to all producers of the commodity. The value of information and the issue of welfare gain or loss can be empirically measured and cannot be written off by assumptions.

Public Policy

In the context of the welfare questions, several policy issues become important. Many policy questions get asked by government policymakers and the directors and staff of the promotion programs as well as the general public.

Are Commodity Promotion Programs Constitutional?

Often the question of constitutionality has surfaced as commodity promotion programs were legislated. According to Frank, "There have been more than 45 challenges at the state level regarding the constitutionality of the checkoff concept. In nearly every instance the state courts have upheld the constitutional validity of the concept and associated market developments" (Armbruster and Myers, 1985 p.5). In 1937, the Florida Supreme Court denied a challenge by the C.V. Floyd Fruit Company against the constitutionality of the 1935 Florida Citrus Advertising Act. The court declared that the advertising tax was an excise or occupational tax and that it was in the public interest. This ruling has been used by many other state courts in upholding the validity of their commodity checkoff programs. The challenger argued that the mandatory assessment constituted a property tax and therefore violated constitutional rules of equity and due process, and that it also was not in the public interest.

A more recent court challenge against the national beef promotion program assessment was denied by the United States Court of Appeals for the Third Circuit. Robert L. Frame, Sr., and Vintage Sales Stables, Inc., as defendants against the United States of America, argued that the Beef Promotion and Research Act of 1985 went beyond the constitutional authority of Congress. The challenge was against the mandatory requirement to participate that is, (pay the assessment) in a promotion program that put forth statements (in advertisements) with which the defendants disagreed or that they found abhorrent. The defendants also argued that they should not be held liable for the collection of the assessment from producers. They argued that this represented a violation of constitutional rights and specific clauses of the First and Fifth Amendments. The appeals court upheld a lower court's ruling that the mandatory assessment and the regulation that a "collecting person" be held responsible for collecting and forwarding the assessment to the government-designated promotion organization were not unconstitutional. It should be noted though that this appeal decision was not unanimous.[50]

The Refund Issue

A major policy concern during the evolution of legislated commodity promotion programs concerned the refund provision. The federal policy until the 1980s leaned toward providing refunds to those producers who disagreed with the idea of commodity research and promotion programs. This created a free-rider problem: if only a portion of the producers of the commodity incurred a cost while all producers shared in the benefits, the benefit-cost ratio would be reduced by the proportion of the volume that was not actually assessed. Although the producers as a group might be enough better off to more than offset the aggregate costs, it was possible that the benefit-cost ratio would not be adequate to justify the investment on the part of those who actually contributed.

Other Free-Rider Issues

This free-rider problem also has other dimensions. Suppose that some states that produce a commodity have mandatory assessments while others do not. If the commodity moves in interstate commerce, a free-rider situation is created. Similarly, the free-rider problem exists if there is a substantial import volume that is not assessed the same as the domestic volume. There can also be a problem if another commodity has some of the same product attributes or is a complementary product. When a commodity group conducts a generic or commodity export promotion effort, they always face a free-rider problem. This problem in export promotion can be resolved only if the commodity being promoted has some unique attributes that have a high value in the target market. This is the reason why it is useful to have the foreign importer participate in the total promotion program.

The free-rider issue will always exist in some form, but the negative effects can be mitigated through nonrefundable mandatory assessments on all of the volume going into the market area in which the demand-expansion program is to be conducted. Thus, the policy of a mandatory assessment on all milk produced within the contiguous United States eliminates the free-rider problem for a nationwide milk promotion program. The free-rider problem is serious, though, for a commodity like Florida orange juice. A large volume of orange juice is imported into the United States from Brazil (Ward and Kilmer, 1989), and the imported volume cannot be assessed if it comes through U.S. ports outside Florida. To counter, every attempt is made to differentiate Florida orange juice from the imported juice.

Who Really Pays?

Most of the promotion programs require that the first handler of the commodity make payment to the promotion board. The regulations authorize the collection of the assessment from the producer by deducting it from the producers' check (thus the term *checkoff*). The producer pays for the program; this results in an increase in the cost of doing business for all producers and is similar to an excise tax. If treated as an excise tax, the actual cost of the promotion program effort is shared by consumers and by the intermediate handlers of the commodity.

Chang and Kinnucan (1991a) demonstrate graphically the effects of an excise tax (or assessment) on price, output, and welfare. The assessment increases the cost of all producers by the amount of the assessment. This will cause the producers as a group to be willing to produce the same amount only at a higher price, or a smaller amount at the same price. This means that the consumers will pay more for the same volume or get less volume for the same amount of total expenditure. If the advertising effort causes the demand to increase, however, then it is possible that consumers will be willing to pay more for the same or even larger volumes. Because of the adjustments in supplies and prices, consumers and the producers, in effect, share in the cost of the promotion effort. The extent to which they share will be determined by the relative elasticities of supply and of demand. For example, if the elasticity of demand is -1.00 and the elasticity of supply is 0.50, the farmers' share would be 51 percent and the consumers' share 49 percent. The shares for other supply and demand elasticities are presented in Table 8–1. While the excess tax argument is of interest, one must clearly recognize the usually small percentage of costs that most checkoffs represent.

Table 8–1
**Farmer's Share of an Advertising Tax for Hypothetical Values of
Farm Supply and Retail Demand Elasticities**

Elasticity	*Elasticity of Demand (E_x)*			
of Supply (E_a)	-.50	-1.00	-1.30	-1.50
0.00	1.00	1.00	1.00	1.00
0.30	0.46	0.63	0.69	0.72
0.50	0.34	0.51	0.57	0.61
1.00	0.20	0.34	0.40	0.44

Source: Chang and Kinnucan (1991a).

The likelihood that the producers can pass on a portion of the cost to consumers provides an additional incentive for producers to support mandatory assessments. But it also creates an incentive for consumers to be concerned about the welfare implications. Unless the generic advertising enhances demand enough to offset the consumer share of the cost, consumers will suffer a welfare loss.

Is It a Zero-Sum Game?

A goal of a commodity promotion effort is to increase the volume of sales or the total value of sales for a particular commodity. If every commodity group is given the same authority to mount an aggressive promotion effort, what will be gained? The full-stomach and fixed-food-expenditure arguments lead to a conclusion that everyone will be worse off. Increases in the sales of one commodity, it is claimed, will be offset by a loss of sales by another. In retaliation, the second commodity group mounts its own generic advertising effort to gain back its market share. After all adjustments occur, it is argued that all commodity groups will have the same market share as before advertising, but the cost of doing business will have increased by the amount of the checkoff.

Some research concludes that this is indeed the situation, when they assume the fixed stomach or fixed food expenditure hypothesis. The zero-sum-game argument overlooks short-run gains that a commodity group can realize by shifting demand for its commodity even when longer term supply shifts occur. It also ignores the concept that advertising and promotion contains information of potential value to consumers and reduces search costs, ignores the role of advertising as a facilitator of competition, and fails to recognize income growth.

The use of single- and multiple-equation models that evaluate the effectiveness of one or even two commodity promotion programs simultaneously does not address the zero-sum-game issue. More complex multicommodity models that are designed to handle the cross-commodity effects so far have been too complex, and often too aggregated, to incorporate the advertising relationships properly. In addition, the checkoff programs provide information and research that can result in changes in product attributes, production and distribution processes, and marketing strategies that provide benefits to consumers, processors, and producers. Measurement of these additional potential benefits needs to be considered for a proper evaluation of the zero-sum-game question. It is an important public policy issue and should be addressed.

A Model for Evaluation

As indicated earlier, the dairy promotion program legislation requires an annual postprogram economic evaluation that is not required in the legislation of other commodities. Whether required or not, a regular periodic economic evaluation is desirable. In Chapters 6 and 7, we provide examples of the kinds of economic evaluations that have been and can be done. Such studies provide an estimate of the linkage between the advertising and promotion effort and the consumers' response. A statistically valid and robust econometric model can be used to provide advertising elasticities and rate of return estimates. They can also be used to answer what-if questions and to provide insight for allocation decisions. The models described for the various industries so far have been used in only limited ways; the potential use is greater. Several promotion organizations are developing data bases and models to provide a method of continual evaluation. The development and maintenance of appropriate data bases are essential before meaningful models can be developed and made operational for continuous use.

Every promotion organization should have an evaluation policy. It is not our role to prescribe one, nor should it be mandatory. A legislated requirement for an economic evaluation can lead to a situation where the evaluation becomes an end unto itself. An appropriate policy would include the maintenance of a proper historical record of all advertising and promotion activities, with the data base designed to support postprogram evaluation efforts. To ensure that this policy is properly implemented, the method of analysis should be designed concurrently with the specification of the advertising and promotion data base. A model to provide an annual evaluation of actual performance would be appropriate; this would provide the means of postprogram evaluation and would provide input for future allocation and program adjustments. Fulfillment of this policy will provide the basis for doing additional types of economic analysis.

Economic evaluation models use actual data from actual program activities. As such, the results provide valid estimates of the effectiveness of advertising programs of the past. It is valid to assume that if the same programs are conducted in the future and that if changes in the other economic forces are accounted for (which they can be and are in the economic modeling), similar economic results will occur. This makes these models appropriate for economic evaluation of past programs and useful for predicting the consequence of expanding or contracting the same or similar program activities. It must be noted, however, that these economic studies do not provide information that can be used to evaluate creative material that does not yet exist. Some brand advertising studies have indicated that the quality of the advertising message is more important and creates more impact variation than results from substantial changes in the level of advertising effort. Not enough research has been conducted on different generic advertising messages to confirm or deny this conclusion. Ward and Dixon's study (1989) of the fluid milk market indirectly deals with the relative effects of increased expenditures versus message content and design.

The Importance of Data Quality

A critical element in economic analysis is the quality of data. First, it is necessary to have valid measures of the advertising and/or promotion efforts. The economic analyses in this book use advertising and promotion expenditures as a measure of promotion effort. Conceptually, gross rating points (GRPs) could be used, as well as line inches or pages of print or seconds of television or radio time. The advertising expenditure measure is convenient because of the ease in making economic inferences. If appropriate economic deflators are used, expenditures should provide the same results as a measure like GRP.

In collecting advertising expenditure data, it is essential that the data be audited. Accounting data are not appropriate, because the expenditure amount is recorded at the time of payment. This might be up to several months after consumers were exposed to the advertising effort. In addition, the amount of advertising time paid for in a particular period is not always the same as the amount actually delivered. If the viewing audience is different in size than expected, debits or credits are made, and additional or fewer advertisement units are delivered at a later date to compensate. Thus, to obtain expenditure estimates that accurately reflect the effort delivered, adjusted data must be obtained. Data that represent other types of promotion efforts (such as in-store demonstrations or coupons) should also coincide with dates of actual exposure.

To be most useful, the expenditure data should represent periods of no longer duration than one month. Quarterly data, however, are better than annual data. In addition, the data should represent clearly defined market areas, such as the media coverage area or the standard metropolitan statistical area. The advertising expenditure data (or comparable measures of effort) are most effectively collected, adjusted, and recorded by the agency that makes the media buys. If meaningful economic analysis is to be conducted, it is essential that measures of the advertising effort be collected and that historical records be maintained and made available to the analyst. The promotion organization might want to require the maintenance of an advertising effort data base as part of its agreement with the advertising agency.

Second, it is necessary to have good measures of consumer behavior toward the commodity in question. Several sources and types of data have been used and are appropriate. Secondary data collected by governmental agencies that represent the volume of the commodity that moves through a specified market (for example, disappearance, arrivals, or shipments) provide useful proxy measures of consumption. One advantage of using this type of data is that it usually covers all uses of the commodity. It is also less costly than the purchase of primary data (because the government pays for it). It is also collected on a consistent schedule and in a consistent manner over time.

Movements through retail outlets, as collected and reported by one or more of the nation's market research companies, provide useful measures of at-home consumption patterns in the areas that the survey sample represents. Some market research companies maintain consumer panels where individual consumers record their purchases or actual consumption. These data are useful to the extent that the volume of the commodity of interest can be identified. For items such as fluid milk or fresh apples, the volume is measured directly. The commodity content of prepared foods, however, has to be derived. How much cheese in purchased pizzas? How many apples in prepared apple pies? How many raisins in cereals? An important shortcoming of consumer panel data or of retail store sales is that the volumes of the commodity used as ingredients in processed food items and the volumes sold through food service establishments are not identified. But panel data do have some important advantages. Panel data in which individual consumer behaviors are recorded permit more in-depth analysis of how different categories of consumers respond to advertising and other economic stimuli.

Third, in economic analysis we must account for the influence of the other forces that affect consumer behavior toward the commodity in question. Necessary and appropriate information includes estimates of the commodity's own price, the availability or price of the important competing goods, the amount of brand advertising of the commodity in question and the amount of brand and generic advertising of competing goods, an estimate of the purchasing power of consumers, and (in some studies) the demographic characteristics of the population in the markets being studied. Much of this last type of data can be obtained from government sources. If one is using primary sales data from consumer panels, much of the price and income information can be collected as part of the collection process.

The nature of the advertising and promotion program, the nature of the commodity, and the economic model for analysis will determine the best and most appropriate data mix. The data mix is likely to be different for each commodity program being evaluated. The important point to make here is that if the analysis is to be valid and useful, the data must be of the highest quality possible. For economic analysis to occur, the promotion organization must assume the responsibility for collecting the data and maintaining a data base. A good policy for a commodity promotion board would be to require the maintenance of a data base from their own records on advertising expenditures and the type of program they represent.

Commodity Advertising and Unreasonable Expectations

Periods of low prices and low farm income have provided the political motivation, at least in part, for the legislative authority for some commodity promotion programs. Some producers and others expect the actions of the commodity promotion boards to solve the farm income problem. They expect the programs to eliminate periods of low commodity prices, completely reverse downward trends in consumption, and secure a reasonable income for everyone producing the commodity. Such expectations are unrealistic. Usually, the low prices result from cyclical overexpansion in production because of favorable prices in previous periods. Supply increases also occur because of the adoption of new technology, which lowers costs and thus sets the stage for production increases. Low farm income problems arise for some because of the inability to keep up with or to manage new technologies that provide some producers with much lower production costs.

Advertising and promotion programs cannot, in and of themselves, solve problems caused by structural adjustments. Commodity promotion programs only have the potential of increasing demand above what it would have been without the program. The promotion and research activities can increase demand enough over time to mitigate, but not solve, the negative impacts of structural adjustments caused by other factors.[51] Forces other than those under the control of a commodity promotion organization will continue to exert influence on the cost of production, supplies of the commodity, farm income levels, competition from other commodities, and the distribution of returns among the producers of the commodity. One therefore should not expect commodity checkoff promotion and research programs to solve the income problems of commodity producers, even though such programs can provide a positive contribution. The only realistic expectation is that sales and incomes to the group might be increased enough to more than cover the checkoff costs of the commodity group. In this appraisal, it is useful to note that the effective economic cost of the advertising tax to the producer is less than the assessment (see the discussion above on "who really pays").

Generic Advertising and the Degree of Competition

As we have discussed, commodity promotion programs are generally funded by the producers of the commodity.[52] As individuals, and usually as a group, they have little control over the market price or volume, the quality of the products, or the distribution system that delivers the products to the final customer. But the degree of competition and the extent and type of government intervention in the pricing of agricultural commodities will influence the extent to which the commodity group benefits from its commodity advertising efforts. Although no market situation in practice will be exactly comparable to theoretical structures of perfect competition, imperfect competition, or specific types of government intervention, the implications can be presented more precisely if we hold to specific theoretical situations.

The Case of Perfect Competition

In perfect competition, all producers of a commodity receive the same price, after adjustments for quality and location differences, regardless of the individual firms' costs of production. An advertising-induced increase in demand at retail will result in an increase in total industry profits from some combination of price and volume increases. If the marketing system is perfectly competitive, total profits at the producer level will increase in proportion to the total increase at retail. Individual producers will share in the increase in proportion to their share of total production. The amount of the increase at the producer level will depend on the extent of the advertising-induced increase in demand and the extent of supply increase resulting from stronger demand. The increase in total producer profit will be greater given larger advertising-induced increases in demand and smaller industry supply responses over time. The more responsive the industry is to higher prices, the less will be the benefit from a given demand increase.

Several commodities that have legislated advertising programs are sold in a market environment that approaches perfect competition, with little or no government intervention. These commodities (including most fresh fruits and vegetables, eggs, beef, and pork) are subject to cyclical movements in price and volume as producers overreact to price changes. In these cases, commodity advertising can reduce risk if it can be directed toward making consumers more responsive to price changes, thus dampening the degree of price volatility. If there is a tendency for the supply to increase over time given any particular price pattern, total revenue can be increased by directing the advertising effort to make demand more responsive to price changes. This would be the appropriate strategy if there is a continuous stream of cost-reducing technology that makes this commodity more competitive in the use of resources. If, on the other hand, there is a tendency for the supply to decrease over time given a particular price pattern, total revenue can be increased by directing the advertising effort to make demand less responsive to price changes.

The lack of control over price, supply, or product quality poses unique challenges to promotion program managers. Knowledge about the size of the potential demand increase, the manner in which consumers respond to price changes, and the nature of the supply response is important to have in designing a promotion strategy.

The Case of Imperfect Competition

Although most commodity groups operate in an environment that approaches perfect competition, there are some situations in which producers can exert some measure of control over price, output, or both. Marketing orders for some fruits and vegetables authorize control over the volume marketed in a particular period or of a particular quality. Minimum prices are established for milk used for fluid milk under federal and state marketing orders. In some countries, commodities are placed under the control of a single marketing agency. For example, in Canada, the fluid milk marketing board has control over supply through production quotas; it also sets prices. It is possible under such circumstances to generate a greater increase in total revenue to the producers than under the conditions of perfect competition. Benefits to farmers will depend on the price and output decisions made by the board managers and on the impact of advertising efforts.

If the commodity group does control both price and quantity, the group has some degree of monopoly power. With monopoly power, there are several rules of thumb about how much should be invested in advertising. For example, Ward (1975) applied the Dorfman-Steiner theorem to grapefruit advertising. The Dorfman-Steiner theorem suggests that the ratio of the advertising elasticity to the own-price elasticity of demand can serve as an indicator of the optimal advertising/sales ratio. That is, if the extent of the advertising response to advertising is known, along with the manner in which consumers respond to price changes, it is possible to determine the level of advertising expenditures that will maximize returns to the commodity group. This rule, however, applies only if the group has monopoly control over price and volume. If it does not have absolute control, then more complex analytical techniques (like some of those presented in Chapters 6 and 7) need to be used to derive optimal levels of investment.

Another issue has to do with the degree of competition in the marketing system. If imperfect competition exists in the marketing system between the commodity producer and the consumer, part of the benefits of the commodity advertising effort will be captured by the group of firms handling the commodity. A study of the linkage between the wholesale and farm-level effects of generic advertising of catfish indicated that the degree of competition does have an impact on the extent to which farmers benefit. The study concludes that "despite industry concentration at the wholesale level, it appears that farmers can benefit from promotion programs aimed at shifting retail demand" (Zidack, Kinnucan, and Hatch, 1992). In reality, consumers help pay for the advertising effort, and they share in the benefits.

Generic Advertising and Farm Policy

Although commodity groups generally operate in a nearly perfect competitive environment, several have been able to obtain some degree of regulatory control over volume and price through government intervention. Government intervention alters the extent to which producers benefit from the advertising-induced increase in demand. The extent to which benefits are altered will depend on the type of intervention. Four types are discussed here: purchase programs, deficiency payments, production control and classified pricing.

Purchase Programs

Purchase programs refer to situations in which the government maintains prices above market-clearing levels by agreeing to purchase enough of the commodity to maintain a target price, referred to as a *support price*. The price support program for dairy products will provide an example. In an attempt to maintain dairy farm income, the government establishes target support prices for milk used in manufacturing. To achieve this price, the government purchases butter, cheese, and nonfat dry milk powder. During most of the past two decades, the government price support for milk has been above the market-clearing price; therefore, during some years, purchase volumes have been substantial.

In this situation, advertising-induced increases in demand will result in fewer purchases by the government, without direct benefit to the producers. Assume, for example, that the government purchased cheese, butter, and powder equivalent to 7 percent of the total milk production. If the advertising program increased effective demand by 5 percent, the benefit will be entirely in the form of reduced government purchases. This translates into lower costs to the government. Total returns to dairy producers will not be increased, however, until the advertising program increases demand more than 7 percent.

Although the dairy farmers might not benefit directly, indirect political benefits could be substantial. Lower government outlays could alleviate the pressure to reduce the level of government price supports. In analyzing the effects of commodity advertising when a purchase program is in place, it is useful to distinguish between the political and economic effects of the advertising effort. The political impacts are likely to be favorable, regardless of the magnitude of the advertising-induced demand increase. For positive economic benefits, however, the demand increase must be large enough to move the market price above the support price and thus take the government out of the market.

Deficiency Payments

Deficiency payments are also designed to increase total returns to the commodity group. The intervention however, is directly on price; the producers are paid the difference between a target price and the market price. This results in lower prices to consumers and enables a commodity to be competitive. As with the purchase program, an advertising-induced demand increase could provide an increase in price and reduce government costs, without direct economic benefit to producers as long as the market price remains below the target price (although the political benefits might be significant). This scheme is popular because the market-clearing price prevails.

With the deficiency payment scheme, it is important to consider whether the advertising effort is designed to make the demand for the commodity more or less responsive to price changes. In addition to increasing demand, an advertising campaign can be designed to make consumers less responsive to price changes by more completely differentiating the advertised commodity from competing products. A program that would make consumers less responsive would result in higher government costs without increasing the benefits to producers, thus adversely affecting political benefits. Conversely, a program that would encourage consumers to be more responsive to price changes could provide positive political benefits by reducing government costs.

Production Controls

Of the four forms of government intervention discussed, production controls are the most important for commodity advertising. This is comparable to the monopoly case. All of the effect of an advertising-induced increase in demand will be on price, and returns to producers will be in direct proportion to the price increase. Because all government costs are administrative and no direct government payments are involved, the advertising will not lower government costs. Therefore, the political benefits will be minimal. In fact, if the increase in consumer price results in political pressure to relax production controls, the initial gains could be dissipated as output expands and prices decrease. The benefit to the advertised commodity will depend on the extent to which the government controls production.

Classified Pricing

Classified pricing refers to the establishment of minimum selling prices for a commodity depending on its use. The basic reason for classified pricing is that returns to producers can be enhanced by setting a higher price for a use where demand is not responsive to price changes and a lower price for a use where the demand is more responsive to price. In this way, the total revenue will be greater for a given supply of the commodity. Classified pricing is a common policy instrument for the dairy industry. The provisions of some marketing orders for fruits and vegetables enable producers to set grades and standards and operate inventory control programs that in effect serve as market discrimination mechanisms; however, the extent of coverage and importance are modest.

The effect of advertising under classified pricing depends on how producers are compensated and on the mechanism used to maintain price differentials. In the dairy industry, returns from the various uses are pooled, and the producer receives a "blend" price. If the advertising results in an increase in the proportion of the total supply used in the higher-priced usage, the blend price will be increased, thus increasing total returns to milk producers. The optimum allocation of advertising effort across the various usages will depend on relative responsiveness to the advertising as well as to price changes. Moreover, an increase in demand for one use will shorten the supply available for the other uses. Therefore, to determine impact, one needs to know the price effect in the market for the other uses of the commodity. A summary of the impacts of market competition and farm policy on advertising effectiveness is presented in Table 8–2.

Summary

It can be argued that mandatory assessments to support commodity promotion programs are in the public interest. They have the potential of enhancing producer and consumer welfare. As an excise tax, the assessment is in reality shared by producers, consumers, and the processors of the commodity. The producer share is determined by the relative elasticities of supply and demand for the commodity. Because the mandatory assessments are authorized by government, government oversight is also in the public interest.

Advertising is viewed as information. Commodity advertising and promotion can provide information that can make consumers more aware of the availability of a commodity and its unique characteristics. This information can alter beliefs and attitudes and change consumer behavior. The value that consumers place on this information can be determined by measuring the extent to which demand for the commodity is increased. This measure in turn will provide an estimate of the producer benefits and the return on the checkoff assessment. Studies reviewed and summarized in Chapter 7 have

Table 8–2
Summary of the Impacts of Market Competition and Farm Policy on Advertising Effectiveness

Competition/Policy	Effects of Advertising	Comments
Perfect competition	Increases price, quantity, or both depending on the slope of the supply schedule. The resulting increase in producer surplus will be larger given (1) larger advertising-induced shifts in the demand schedule and (2) steeper slopes of the supply schedule.	The direction of shifts in the supply schedule has important implications. For example, an advertising campaign designed to make demand *more* elastic is appropriate if the supply schedule is expected to shift to the right over time. If the supply schedule is expected to shift to the left over time, the advertising campaign should be designed to make demand *less* elastic. The lack of control over supply and product quality poses unique management challenges.
Imperfect competition	Increases price, quantity, or both depending on institutional setting, degree of market power, and anticipated responses of rivals. The ability to control price and/or output increases the profit potential of advertising.	The Dorfman-Steiner theorem suggests that the ratio of the advertising elasticity to the own-price elasticity of demand can serve as an indicator of the optimal advertising/sales ratio. Thus, the proportion of revenue spent on advertising, ceteris paribus, is directly related to the advertising elasticity and inversely related to the (absolute value of) demand elasticity.
Government purchase programs	Depends on the magnitude of the shift in the demand curve relative to government inventories of the surplus commodity. The demand shift has to be large enough to deplete government inventories; otherwise, the advertising program will have no effect on prices, quantity, or producer surplus. If demand shifts are modest, they serve to reduce government costs but provide no direct benefit to producers.	Generic advertising tends to reduce the government costs of purchase schemes. In this way, the advertising program might confer political benefits even though direct economic benefits cannot be established.

269

Table 8-2 Continued

Competition/Policy	Effects of Advertising	Comments
Government deficiency payments	Similar to the purchase scheme: unless the demand shift is large enough to move the equilibrium price above the guaranteed price, advertising will have no effect on price, quantity, or producer surplus. However, because advertising reduces government costs, it might confer indirect benefits.	The government cost of deficiency payments is sensitive to the elasticity of demand, becoming more costly as demand becomes less elastic. Thus, in general, elasticity-decreasing ad campaigns should be avoided.
Government production controls	Increases price and producer surplus. The effect on quantity depends on the extent to which the government relaxes production controls in response to rising price.	The most favorable structure for commodity advertising. Producer surplus generated by advertising is dissipated as production controls are loosened.
Government classified pricing	Depends on the mechanism used to maintain price differentials. A blend price scheme is common. Advertising the product *not* subject to surplus removal (e.g., fluid milk) will raise the blend price. Advertising of products subject to removals will lower government costs but have no effect on market prices or output.	Analytical results suggest elasticity-increasing advertising is preferred to elasticity-decreasing advertising. The optimal allocation of advertising funds between the less elastic and the more elastic markets cannot be determined solely on the basis of differing demand elasticities.

Source: Forker and Kinnucan (1992), Table 4.1.

provided measures of producer benefits and of rates of return on some major commodity advertising programs. The econometric models that have been developed to measure consumer and producer benefits can also provide information for allocation decisions.

Conceptually, commodity advertising and promotion programs can alter the behavior response of consumers. Consumers might become more habit persistent. This will decrease the variability of price caused by demand instability and provide positive benefits to producers and consumers. Alternatively, consumers might become less responsive to price changes. This would increase price variability associated with supply adjustments. If the commodity has a tendency to increase production over time, a less elastic demand would likely decrease producer gains from advertising. If, on the other hand, there is a tendency for supplies to decline over time, a less elastic demand will likely increase benefits from advertising. Whether the strategy of an advertising campaign should be to increase or decrease demand elasticity depends on the nature of the industry's cost structure and supply response to changing prices.

The econometric studies reviewed in Chapter 7 provide additional information about the economics of commodity advertising. We close with a list of broad conclusions about the overall performance of generic commodity advertising as deduced from the research that has been completed to date.

- Commodity advertising and promotion programs can have positive impacts on sales. Several empirical studies show these increases have been large enough to benefit producers.

- Producer benefits will be larger the more inelastic the supply.

- In the evaluation of market impacts it is important, even essential, to account for carry over effects of the advertising or promotion program.

- Brand advertising as well as generic advertising can increase aggregate demand for a commodity. Generic and brand advertising can complement each other.

- Advertising responses are likely to differ across markets, and products. Therefore, one cannot predict, a priori, the size of the benefits. Rather, economic studies need to be conducted on a continuing basis.

- The effectiveness of commodity advertising programs can increase over time. The response can also reach some upper limit. This increase might be due to experience and improvements in creative work and in positioning the advertising effort.

- It is not possible to know the true nature of the advertising response function. Econometric modeling can, however, provide a valid estimate. A consensus gained from the review of studies leads us to conclude that it has a shape similar to the theoretical functions presented earlier. Little market impact occurs at low levels of expenditure. As expenditure increases beyond some threshold level, the market response increases, first at an increasing rate and then at a decreasing rate, to some maximum level.

- Advertising expenditures invested in television and radio will have different impacts. Small expenditures are likely to yield greater returns from radio. For large expenditure levels, a mix of television and radio will probably yield optimum results.

- Studies generally fail to show linkages between awareness, beliefs, attitudes, intentions, and behavior. Therefore, most economic studies derive estimates of the direct relationship between advertising effort (expenditure) and consumption. A study of catfish advertising and one of fresh tomato advertising illustrate two exceptions.

- Commodity promotion organizations, in addition to increasing demand directly, have been able to influence the rate of technical change in production and marketing. This kind of collective action has enabled the beef, pork, and cotton industries to improve more rapidly the quality and attributes that are more strongly in demand by consumers.

- Measuring the advertising impact requires high-quality data and econometric models can be used to analyze specific commodity programs.

- A substantial improvement has occurred in modeling and estimation of commodity advertising response functions. Reasonably robust models have been estimated for the generic advertising of fluid milk, orange juice, grapefruit, beef, apples, catfish, cheese, fats and oils, and wool.

- Most of the economic analysis so far has been on domestic advertising and promotion programs. Less has been done on export promotion programs.

- The economic studies completed to date provide some insight into the shape of the advertising response function. Less is known, however about the shape of the response function for other types of promotion programs.

Generic commodity advertising and promotion have become important marketing tools for commodity groups. Mandatory assessments enable producers of a commodity collectively to influence consumer behavior and the rate of technical change in production and marketing. Commodity advertising and promotion, though, is only one of several factors that influence consumer purchases of a particular commodity. Other factors, such as available supplies and supplies of competing commodities, also explain some of the dynamic variation in price and industry revenue. Studies completed to date confirm that commodity advertising and promotion programs can benefit consumers, producers, and processors. They suggest, though, that the market impact can and will vary considerably among commodities, products within commodity groups, different promotion activities, and time periods.

The challenge facing all interested parties is to develop the appropriate policies and management practices that will provide optimum market results. This will require more extensive and in-depth economic analysis. This economic analysis will need to be supported by concurrent enhancement of the theory and measurement of the market impact of generic commodity advertising and promotion. Economic analyses, when properly conducted over time and when used with information from market research and experience, can contribute to a much greater understanding of the consequences of alternative allocation decisions.

Notes

1. Note that the characteristic equation includes the scale factor k. Hence, when $g(A) = 0$, $C = k$. This implies that in the extreme case when $g(A) = 0$, X will yield a fixed amount of the characteristics; for example, we can only consume so much of a particular characteristic, regardless of how much is there. In contrast, when $X, = 0$, then $C = 0$. When advertising is ineffective, the more likely case is that $g(A) = g$ and g is small. Then $C = kX^g$, and C will increase by g with each percentage increase in X. In this case the change in C may be small, but it is positively related with X.

One could also use the argument by L. Nichols (1985) that advertising only influences k and that then there is also a proportional relationship between C and X, regardless of the level of x. This case is, however, much more restrictive.

2. We are not suggesting the success or failure of the raisin programs, but simply emphasizing an example where the entertainment aspects of the commercial are quite high.

3. For a complete mathematical development of these models, see J. Chang (1988).

4. The survey was conduced in 1989 to determine the kind of operational program objectives that commodity promotion organizations establish and to determine the methods of evaluation used to determine whether the objectives were realized (Lenz, Forker, and Hurst, 1991).

5. A few commodity promotion programs are entirely or jointly funded by the processors or distributors of the commodity.

6. This statement holds if the commodity is produced by an increasing-cost industry. If it is a decreasing-cost industry, producers will not benefit.

7. If the industry has substantial economies of scale, a significant advertising-induced demand increase could result in narrower margins and a producer price increase greater than the retail price increase.

8. Bennett, 1988, pp. 230–233; 153–158.

9. Hahn, 1988, pp. 281–285.

10. These costs represent averages for the year, including average rating points per spot, for all viewing times. They were obtained from personal correspondence from the American Dairy Association and Dairy Council and DMB&B, an advertising agency. The large differences result from differences in market size, the

275

degree of competition among broadcasters, and the strength of demand for advertising time.

11. If specific demographic targets are identified, demographic rating points (DRPs) are the measures used to describe the reach and frequency associated with reaching the target audience.

12. For a more complete description of media plan development and strategies, see a modern textbook on advertising.

13. The survey covered most of the agricultural commodity promotion organizations in the United States. There were 116 respondents representing 71 percent of all possible respondents.

14. Listed according to approximate importance in terms of the dollars invested in television advertising.

15. For more detail see Ward and Davis (1978a), and Ward and Davis (1978b).

16. A referendum of all affected parties is usually required. For some commodities, the vote is required before the assessment can begin. For other commodities, the program is put in place and the assessment begun eighteen to twenty-four months before the referendum is conducted.

17. Agricultural Marketing Agreement Act of 1937, Reenacting, Amending, and Supplementing the Agricultural Adjustment Act, as Amended [7 U.S.C. 601, 602, 608a–608c, 610, 612, 614, 624, 671–674].

18. Title VII of the Agricultural Act of 1954, 68 Stat. 910, August 28, 1954, as amended.

19. Pub. L. 89-502, 80 Stat. 279, July 13, 1966. The supplemental assessment rate became effective in 1985.

20. The wheat research and promotion program carried out under Pub. L. 91–430, September 26, 1970, Stat. 885–886 was terminated in June 1977, and the order issued pursuant to Pub. L. 195-113 was terminated on Nov. 1, 1986. The Potato Research and Promotion Act was enacted as Title III of Pub. L. 91-670, 84 Stat. 2041–2047, January 11, 1971. The egg promotion program operates pursuant to Pub. L. 93–428, October 1, 1974, 88 Stat. 1171–1179. Authority for a floral promotion program is Title XVII of Pub. L. 97-98, 95 Stat. 1348–1358, Dec. 22, 1981.

21. The Dairy Research and Promotion Act is Subtitle B, Title I of the Dairy and Tobacco Adjustment Act of 1983, Pub. L. 98–180, 97 Stat. 1136, Nov. 29, 1983.

22. The Honey Research, Promotion, and Consumer Information Act is Pub. L. 98-590, 98 Stat. 3115, Oct. 30, 1984.

23. The Beef Promotion and Research Act is based on earlier legislation but in its final form is in Title XVI, Subtitle A, of the Food Security Act of 1985, Pub. L. 99-198, 99 Stat. 1597, Dec. 23, 1985. The Pork Promotion, Research, and Consumer Information Act of 1985 is Subtitle B, Stat. 1606. The Watermelon Research and Promotion Act is Subtitle C, Stat. 1622.

24. The official title for the 1990 farm bill is the Food, Agriculture, Conservation, and Trade Act of 1990.

25. All promotion order programs established under state or federal legislation have a recall procedure whereby a certain number (usually 10 percent) of the producers of the commodity can ask that hearings be held to consider withdrawal of the order authority and the possibility of a referendum. Also, in most instances, the

secretary of agriculture or the appropriate state commissioner of agriculture can withdraw the authority if it appears that the program in place is not consistent with or fulfilling the purposes as stated in the enabling legislation.

26. This section is based on material in Pamphlet 5 of *Generic Agricultural Commodity Advertising and Promotion: International Programs*, by H. W. Kinnucan and G. W. Williams (1988).

27. Prior to 1992 this was called the Targeted Export Assistance (TEA) program. The use of funds was limited to those countries where trade retaliation was called for.

28. Henneberry, Ackerman and Eshleman (1992) p. 59.

29. Title I, Subtitle B of the Dairy and Tobacco Adjustment Act of 1983, Pub. L. 98-180, 97 Stat. 1136, Nov. 29, 1983.

30. Importers of pork, floral products, and honey are authorized to vote because they will also be assessed under the terms of the orders.

31. This requirement is specified in Title 3, Sec. 301, part 4 of the Dairy and Tobacco Adjustment Act of 1983.

32. In the survey of 116 promotion organizations, Lenz Forker, and Hurst (1991) determined that only 50 percent made specific budget allocations for program evaluations; however, 96 percent indicated some form of program evaluation (p. 25).

33. This amount does not include money appropriated by state governments to promote the agricultural industry in general (such as "Grown in New York" or "New York Seal of Quality").

34. The level of support increased to $200 million for fiscal years 1989 and 1990.

35. Legislative authority was also in place by 1988 for promotion checkoff programs for the floral industries, but the industry has not been able to muster the vote required to implement the legislation. The fluid milk processors had not yet mustered enough industry support in 1992 to proceed with a special fluid milk program as authorized in the 1990 farm bill.

36. ADA & DC, Inc., is affiliated with UDIA and is based in Syracuse, New York. It receives funds, under contract, from the New York State Department of Agriculture and Markets and from dairy producers in New Jersey and Pennsylvania. The New York Milk Promotion Advisory Board, appointed by the New York commissioner of agriculture, makes recommendations to the commissioner relative to the terms of the contract with ADA & DC and other contractees. ADA & DC is incorporated in New York State as a nonprofit corporation. Its board of directors is elected by constituent dairy farmers from the areas that provide the funds.

37. American Dairy Association & Dairy Council, Inc. (NY, PA, NJ), ADA of Illinois, ADA of South Dakota, Associated Milk Producers, Inc. (southern region), Dairy Farmers, Inc. (FL), Maine Dairy Promotion Board, Middle Atlantic Milk Marketing Association, Mid East UDIA, Midland UDIA, Milk Promotion Services, Inc. (New England), MPS of Indiana, Minnesota Dairy Promotion Council, North Dakota Dairy Promotion Commission, Southeast UDIA, UDI of Michigan, United Dairyman of Arizona, UD of Idaho, Utah Dairy Commission.

38. Dairy farmers in Oregon, Washington, and Louisiana also operate independent promotion programs.

39. In 1991 and 1992, a group of dairy farmers were actively soliciting signa-

tures for a "Dump the Dairy Board" campaign to ask the secretary of agriculture to terminate the dairy promotion assessment.

40. *Prairie Farmer*, January 21, 1992, p. 26.

41. The four provisions were (1) a reduction in the price support level, (2) a dairy herd reduction program, (3) a promotion program, and (4) a change in the class price of federal marketing orders.

42. The number of state programs and states involved is changing constantly. The reader will note different number counts in different sections of this book because of different sources of data and different dates of the count.

43. Note that Spatz's table shows only $167 million; the author had entered Florida citrus at $5.8 million rather than $58 million.

44. Imports through non-Florida ports cannot be taxed by Florida, of course. In 1985–86, only 73 percent of the total available supply of orange juice in the United States paid the tax. With increased domestic production, the number was up to 88 percent in 1989–90.

45. Washington Apple Commission, 1987–88 annual report.

46. Because of the nature of demand for some agricultural commodities, the total revenue from the sale of a small crop is often larger than the total revenue from a large crop. Thus, an assessment based on a percentage of total revenue can be low when it is most important to advertise heavily.

47. Data in this section are from the Foreign Agricultural Service of the United States Department of Agriculture and relate to fiscal years 1986–88.

48. The equations for television and radio provide a way for interacting the media (radio and television) with the coverage (national or spot). Note that in these equations we estimate the coefficients δ_{1i} and δ_{2i}, which correspond to the effect of television and radio. δ_{3i} and δ_{4i} correspond to the adjustment in the effect of television and radio, depending on the coverage expressed with *TVNA* (share of television national coverage) and *RDSP* (share of radio with spot coverage). The reader needing more detail on these procedures is referred to Ward and Forker (1991).

49. A rigorous discussion of welfare economics can be found in Just, Hueth, and Schmitz (1982). A discussion of welfare economics and dairy promotion can be found in Forker and Kinnucan (1992).

50. No. 88–1104, United States Court of Appeals for the Third Circuit, September 14, 1989.

51. Ward (1989a) showed that less than 3 percent of the variations in beef prices can be attributed to the beef checkoff. He used this percentage to put the beef checkoff in the proper perspective to all factors affecting that industry.

52. This and the following section follow a presentation made by Forker and Kinnucan (1992) in a review of econometric studies of generic dairy product advertising. The concepts and format for this discussion were originally developed by Kinnucan. The analytical framework follows Tomek and Robinson (1990), pp. 275–281.

References

Albion, M., and P. Ferris. 1981. *The Advertising Controversy: Evidence on the Economic Effects of Advertising.* Auburn House Publishing, Boston.

Armbruster, W. J., and G. Frank. 1988. "Generic Agricultural Commodity Advertising and Promotion: Program Funding, Structure and Characteristics." A.E. Ext.88-3, Northeast Regional Committee on Commodity Promotion Programs (NEC-63), Department of Agricultural Economics, Cornell University, Ithaca, NY.

Armbruster, W. J., and D. R. Henderson, and R. D. Knutson, Eds. 1983. *Federal Marketing Programs in Agriculture: Issues and Options.* Interstate Printers and Publishers, Danville, IL.

Armbruster, W. J., and L. H. Myers, eds. 1985. *Research on Effectiveness of Agricultural Commodity Promotion.* Proceedings from seminar (Arlington, VA, April 9–10, 1985), Farm Foundation, Oak Brook, IL.

Armbruster, W. J., and R. W. Ward. 1988. "Generic Agricultural Commodity Advertising and Promotion: Public Policy Issues." Leaflet #3, A.E. Ext. 88-3, Northeast Regional Committee on Commodity Promotion Programs (NEC-63), Department of Agricultural Economics, Cornell University, Ithaca, NY.

Ball, K., and J. Dewbre. 1989. "An Analysis of the Returns to Generic Advertising of Beef, Lamb and Pork." Discussion Paper 89.4, Australian Bureau of Agriculture and Resource Economics, Canberra, Australia.

Bain, Joe S. 1972. *Essays on Price Theory and Industrial Organization.* Little, Brown & Co., Boston.

Bennett, Wayne. 1988. "Opening New Markets for U.S. Soybeans." *Marketing U.S. Agriculture: 1988 Yearbook of Agriculture.* U.S. Government Printing Office, Washington, DC.

Blaylock, James R., and William N. Blisard. 1988. "Effects of Advertising on the Demand for Cheese." USDA-ERS Technical Bulletin Number 1752, Economic Research Service, U.S. Department of Agriculture, Washington DC.

Blisard, N., and J. R. Blaylock. 1992. "A Double-Hurdle Approach to Advertising: The Case of Cheese." *Agribusiness,* 8(2): 109–20.

Blisard, W. N., T. Sun, and J. R. Blaylock. 1991. "Effects of Advertising on the Demand for Cheese and Fluid Milk." ERS Staff Report No. AGAES 9154,

Commodity Economics Division, Economic Research Service, U.S. Department of Agriculture, Washington, DC.

Brown, D. J., and L. Schrader. 1990. "Cholesterol Information and Shell Egg Consumption." *Amer. J. Agr. Econ.*, 72(3):548–55.

Brown, M. G., and J. L. Lee. 1985. "Subgroup Demand: An Application of Dynamic Linear Expenditure System to a Fruit Juice/Drink Commodity Subgroup." Paper presented at the Souther Agriculture Association winter meetings, Biloxi, AL.

Brown, M. G., and J. Lee. 1992. "Theoretical Overview of Demand Systems Incorporating Advertising Effects." *Commodity Advertising and Promotion.* Iowa State University Press, Ames, IA.

Capps, O. 1988. "Utilizing Scanner Data to Estimate Retail Demand Functions for Meat Products." Technical Article #22976, Texas Agricultural Experiment Station, Texas A & M University, College Station, TX.

Carlton, D. W., and J. M. Perloff. 1990. *Modern Industrial Organization.* Harper-Collins Publishers.

Chang, H., and H. Kinnucan. 1991a. "Economic Effects of An Advertising Excise Tax." *Agribusiness,* 7(2);165–73.

Chang, H., and H. Kinnucan. 1991b. "Advertising, Information, and Product Quality: The Case of Butter." *Amer. J. Agr. Econ.*, 73(4):1195–1203.

Chang, Julis A. 1988. "A Thearetical Model of Generic and Brand Advertising." Ph.D. dissertation, University of Florida, Gainsville.

Connor, J. M., and R. W. Ward, Eds. 1983. "Advertising and the Food System." Proceedings of symposium, Airlie House, VA, November 6–7, 1980. North Central Research Project NC-117, Monograph No. 14.

Cooper Lee G., and Masao Nakanishi. 1990. *Market Share Analysis.* Kluwer Academic Press, Boston.

Cox, Thomas. 1989. "A Demand Systems Approach to the Analysis of Commodity Promotion Programs: The Case of Canadian Oils." Staff Paper No. 305, Department of Agricultural Economics, University of Wisconsin.

Deaton, A., and J. Muellbauer. 1980. *Economic and Consumer Behavior.* Cambridge University Press, Cambridge, MA.

Degner, Robert L. 1985. "An Evaluation of the Promotional and Public Relations Programs for Florida Tomatoes." Florida Agricultural Market Research Center, Industry Report 85-2, University of Florida, Gainesville.

Dewbre, J., B. Richardson, and S. Beare. 1987. "Returns from Wool Promotion in the United States." Occasional Paper #100, Australian Government Publishing Service, Canberra, Australia.

Dielman, T. E. 1989. *Pooled Cross-Sectional and Time Series Data Analysis.* Marcel Dekker, New York.

Dhyrmes, P. J. 1985. *Distributed Lags: Problems of Estimation and Formulation.* North-Holland. Elsevier Publishers, New York.

Ekelund, R. B., and D. S. Saurman. 1988. *Advertising and the Market Process: A Modern Economic View.* Pacific Research Institute for Public Policy, San Francisco, CA.

Fairchild, G., D. Gunter, and J. Lee. 1987. "The Impact of Florida's Import Advertising Equalization Tax on the Florida Orange Juice Industry." *Agribusiness,* 3(2): 179–88.

Forker, O. D., and H. Kinnucan. 1992. *Econometric Measurement of Generic Advertising.* International Dairy Federation Special Issue No. 9202, Brussels, Belgium.

Forker, O. D., and D. J. Liu. 1986. "An Empirical Evaluation of the Effectiveness of Generic Advertising: The Case of Fluid Milk in New York City." A.E. Res. 86-12. Department of Agricultural Economics, Cornell University, Ithaca, NY.

Forker, O. D., and D. J. Liu. 1988. "Generic Agricultural Commodity Advertising and Promotion: Program Evaluation." Leaflet #6, A.E. Ext. 88-3, Northeast Regional Committee on Commodity Advertising Programs (NEC-63), Department of Agricultural Economics, Cornell University, Ithaca, NY

Forker, O. D., and D. J. Liu. 1989. "Generic Dairy Promotion Economic Research: Past, Present and Future." A.E. Staff Paper 89-34, Department of Agricultural Economics, Cornell University, Ithaca, NY.

Forker, O. D., and R. W. Ward. 1988. "Generic Advertising: A Marketing Strategy for Farmer Groups." *Marketing U.S. Agriculture: 1988 Yearbook of Agriculture.* U.S. Government Printing Office, Washington, DC.

Friedman, James. 1983. *Oligopoly and Advertising.* Cambridge University Press, Cambridge, MA.

Goddard, E. W., and A. K. Amuah. 1989. "Demand for Canadian Fats and Oils: A Case Study of Advertising Effectiveness." *Amer. J. of Agr. Econ.,* 71(3)741–49.

Goodwin, Barry K. 1992. "An Analysis of Factors Associated with Consumer Use of Grocery Coupons." *Western J. of Agricultural Economics,* 17:110–20.

Green, Richard. 1985. "Dynamic Utility Functions for Measuring Advertising Response." *Research on Effectiveness of Agricultural Commodity Promotion,* W. Armbruster and L. Myers, eds. Proceedings from seminar (Arlington, VA, April 9–10, 1985) Farm Foundation, Oak Brook, IL.

Green, Richard D., H. F. Carmen, and K. McManus. 1991. "Advertising Effects for Dried Fruit." *J. of the Western Agr. Econ. Assn.,* 16(1):63–71.

Greene, W. H. 1990. *Econometric Analysis.* Macmillan Publishing Co., New York.

Gujarati, Damodar N. 1988. *Basic Econometrics.* 2nd ed. McGraw-Hill Book Co., New York.

Hahn, J. N. 1988. "Consumers 'Take Comfort in Cotton.'" *Marketing U.S. Agriculture: 1988 Yearbook of Agriculture.* U.S. Government Printing Office, Washington, DC.

Hall, L. L., and I. M. Foik. 1982. "Generic Versus Brand Advertising for Manufactured Milk Products—The Case of Yogurt." *North Central J. of Agr. Econ.,* 5(1):19–24.

Harvey, Andrew C. 1989. *Forecasting, Structural Time Series Models and the Kalman Filter.* Cambridge University Press. Cambridge, UK.

Henneberry, S. R., K. Z. Ackerman, and T. Eshleman. 1992. "U.S. Overseas Market Promotion: An Overview of Non-Price Programs and Expenditures." *Agribusiness,* 8(1): 57–58.

Hochman, E., U. Regev, and R. W. Ward. 1974. "Optimal Advertising Signals in the Florida Citrus Industry: A Research Application." *Amer. J. of Agr. Econ.,* 56(4):697–705.

Hollander, Myles, and Douglas Wolfe. 1973. *Nonparametric Statistical Methods.* J. Wiley & Sons, New York.

Holleran, J. M., and M. V. Martin. 1989. "Should States Be in the Agricultural Promotion Business?" *Agribusiness,* 5(1):65–75.

Hurst, Susan, and Olan Forker. 1991. "Annotated Bibliograph of Generic Commodity Promotion Research (Revised)." A.E. Res. 91-7, Department of Agricultural Economics, Cornell University, Ithaca, New York.

Jensen, Helen, and John Schroeter. 1992. "Evaluating Advertising Using Split Cable Scanner Data: Some Methodological Issues." Ch. 4, *Commodity Advertising and Promotion.* Iowa State University Press, Ames, IA.

Jesse, E. V., and A. Johnson, Jr. 1981. "Effectiveness of Federal Marketing Orders for Fruits and Vegetables." Agricultural Economic Report No. 471, Economics and Statistics Service, U.S. Department of Agriculture, Washington, DC.

Jones, E., and R. W. Ward. 1989. "Effectiveness of Generic and Brand Advertising on Fresh and Processed Potato Products." *Agribusiness,* 5(5):523–36.

Just, R. E., D. L. Hueth, and A. Schmitz. 1982. *Applied Welfare Economics and Public Policy.* Prentice-Hall, Englewood Cliffs, NJ.

Kinnucan, Henry. 1987. "Effect of Canadian Advertising on Milk Demand: The Case of the Buffalo, New York Market." *Canadian J. of Agr. Econ.,* 35(1):181–196.

Kinnucan, Henry, and Deborah Fearon. 1986. "Effects of Generic and Brand Advertising on Cheese in New York City with Implications for Allocation of Funds." *North Central J. of Agr. Econ.,* 8(1):93–107.

Kinnucan, Henry, and O. D. Forker. 1986. "Seasonality in the Consumer Response to Milk Advertising with Implications for Milk Promotion Policy." *Amer. J. of Agr. Econ.,* 68(3):563–71.

Kinnucan, H., and O. D. Forker. 1988. "Allocation of Generic Advertising Funds Among Products: A Sales Maximation Approach." *Northeastern J. of Agr. and Resource Econ.,* 17(1):64–71.

Kinnucan, Henry W., Stanley R. Thompson, and Hui-Shung Chang. 1992. *Commodity Advertising and Promotion.* Iowa State University Press, Ames, IA.

Kinnucan, Henry, and Meenskshi Venkateswaran. 1990. "Effects of Generic Advertising on Perceptions and Behavior: The Case of Catfish." *Southern J. of Agr. Econ.,* 22:137–52.

Kinnucan, Henry, and Gary W. Williams. 1988. "Generic Agricultural Commodity Advertising and Promotion: International Programs." Leaflet #5., A.E. Ext. 88-3, Northeast Regional Committee on Commodity Promotion Programs (NEC-63), Department of Agricultural Economics, Cornell University, Ithaca, NY.

Lee, J. Y. 1984. "Demand Interrelationships Among Fruit Beverages." *Southern J. of Agr. Econ.,* 16:135–43.

Lee, J. Y., and M. G. Brown. 1992. "Lag Structures in Commodity Advertising Research." *Agribusiness,* 8(2):143–54.

Lee, Jonq-Ying and M. Brown. 1985. "Coupon Redemption and the Demand for Frozen Concentrate Orange Juice: A Switching Regression Analysis." *Amer. J. Agr. Econ.,* 66(3):647–53.

Lee, J. Y., and G. F. Fairchild. 1988. "Commodity Advertising, Imports, and the Free Rider Problem." *J. of Food Distribution Research,* 19(2):36–42.

Lenz, J., O. D. Forker, and S. Hurst. 1991. "U.S. Commodity Promotion Organizations: Objectives, Activities, and Evaluation Methods." A.E. Res. 91-4, Department of Agricultural Economics, Cornell University, Ithaca, NY.

Little, A. D., Inc. 1985. "Econometric and Statistical Analyses of the Effectiveness of Generic Advertising for Fluid Milk, Cheese and Butter." Report to the National Dairy Promotion and Research Board, Cambridge, MA.

Liu, D. J., and O. D. Forker. 1988. "Generic Fluid Milk Advertising, Demand Expansion, and Supply Response: The Case of New York City." *Amer. J. Agr. Econ.*, 70(2):229–36.

Liu, D. J., and O. D. Forker. 1990. "Optimal Control of Generic Fluid Milk Advertising Expenditures." *Amer. J. of Agr. Econ.*, 72(4):1048–55.

Liu, D. J., H. M. Kaiser, O. D. Forker, and T. D. Mount. 1989. "The Economic Implications of the U.S. Generic Dairy Advertising Program: An Industry Model Approach." *Northeastern J. of Agr. and Resource Econ.*, 19(1):37–48.

Maddala, G. S. 1977. *Econometrics*. McGraw-Hill Book Co., New York.

Mercer, R. L. 1988. "Potatoes—Turnaround in Consumer Attitudes." *Marketing U.S. Agriculture: 1988 Yearbook of Agriculture*. U.S. Government Printing Office, Washington, DC.

Morrison, Rosanna M. 1984. "Generic Advertising of Farm Products." Agr. Inf. Bul. No. 481, Economic Research Service, U.S. Department of Agriculture, Washington, DC.

Nelson, Phillip. 1974. "Advertising as Information." *J. of Political Economy*, 81:729–54.

Nerlove, M., and F. V. Waugh. 1961. "Advertising Without Supply Control: Some Implications of a Study of the Advertising of Oranges." *J. of Farm Economics*, 43(4):813–37.

Nichols, J. P., and H. W. Kinnucan, and K. Z. Ackerman, eds. 1991. *Economic Effects of Generic Promotion Programs for Agricultural Exports*. Agricultural and Food Policy Center, Department of Agricultural Economics, Texas A & M University, College Station, TX.

Nichols, Len M. 1985. "Advertising and Economic Welfare." *Amer. Econ. Rev.*, 75:213–18.

Parket, I. Robert. 1974. *Statistics*. Random House, New York.

Pollak, Robert A., and Terence J. Wales. 1992. *Demand System Specification and Estimation*. Oxford University Press, Oxford, UK.

Porter, M. E. 1976. *Interbrand Choice, Strategy and Bilateral Market Power*. Harvard University Press, Cambridge, MA.

Schultz, R. L, and D. R. Wittink. 1976. "The Measurement of Industry Advertising Effects." *J. of Marketing Research*, 13(1):71–75.

Sheth, J. N., ed. 1974. *Models of Buyer Behavior: Conceptual, Quantitative, and Empirical*. Harper & Row, New York.

Spatz, Karen J. 1989. "Export Market Development by Agricultural Commodity Promotion Programs." ACS Research Report No. 79, Agricultural Cooperative Service, U.S. Department of Agriculture, Washington, DC.

Stigler, G. J., and G. S. Becker. 1977. "De Gustibus Nor Est Disputandum." *Amer. Econ. Rev.*, 67:76–90.

Tauer, J. R. and Forker, O. D. 1987. "Dairy Promotion in the United States 1979-1986: The History and Structure of the National Milk and Dairy Product

Promotion Program with Special Reference to New York." A.E. Res. 87-5, Department of Agricultural Economics, Cornell University, Ithaca, NY.

Thompson, S. R. 1974. "Sales Response to Generic Promotion Efforts and Some Implications of Milk Advertising on Economic Surplus." *J. of the Northeastern Agricultural Economics Council,* 3(2):78–90.

Thompson, S. R., and D. A. Eiler. 1977. "Determinants of Milk Advertising Effectiveness." *Amer. J. of Agr. Econ.,* 59(2):330–35.

Thompson, S. R., D. A. Eiler, and O. D. Forker. 1976. "An Econometric Analysis of Sales Response to Generic Fluid Milk Advertising in New York State." *Search,* 6(3):1–24, Cornell Agricultural Experiment Station, Ithaca, NY.

Tomek, William G., and Kenneth L. Robinson. 1990. *Agricultural Product Prices.* 3rd ed. Cornell University Press, Ithaca, NY.

U.S. Department of Agriculture. 1981. "A Review of Federal Marketing Orders for Fruits, Vegetables, and Specialty Crops: Economic Efficiency and Welfare Implications." Agricultural Economic Report No. 477, Agricultural Marketing Service, Washington, DC.

U.S. Department of Agriculture. 1986. "Compilation of Statutes Relating to the Agricultural Marketing Service and Closely Related Activities: As of December 31, 1986." Agricultural Handbook No. 665, Agricultural Marketing Service, Washington, DC.

U.S. Department of Agriculture. 1991. "USDA Report to Congress on the Dairy Promotion Program." Dairy Division, Agricultural Marketing Service, Washington, DC.

U.S. Department of Agriculture. 1992. "USDA Report to Congress on the Dairy Promotion Program." Dairy Division, Agricultural Marketing Service, Washington, DC.

Ward, Ronald W. 1975. "Revisiting the Dorfman-Steiner Static Advertising Theorem: An Application to the Processed Grapefruit Industry." *Amer. J. of Agr. Econ.,* 57(3):500–504.

Ward, Ronald W. 1982. "Asymmetry in Retail, Wholesale and Shipping Point Prices for Fresh Fruits and Vegetables," *Amer. J. of Agr. Econ.,* 62(2):205–12.

Ward, Ronald W. 1988a. "Evaluation of the Economic Gains from Generic and Brand Advertising of Orange Juice." Comments to the Advertising Committee, Florida Citrus Commission, Lakeland, FL (April).

Ward, Ronald W. 1988b. "Advertising Expenditure Implications from the Generic and Brand Advertising Model for Orange Juice." Comments to the Advertising Committee, Florida Citrus Commission, Lakeland, FL (May).

Ward, Ronald W. 1992a. "The Beef Checkoff: Its Economic Impact and Producer Benefits." University of Florida, Gainesville (January).

Ward, Ronald W. 1992b. "Beef Price Adjustments to Supply and Demand Changes: An Application of the Beef Checkoff Model." Supplement 92:1 to the 1992 Beef Checkoff Report, University of Florida, Gainesville.

Ward, Ronald W., J. Chang, and S. Thompson. 1985, "Commodity Advertising: Theoretical Issues Relating to Generic and Brand Promotions." *Agribusiness,* 1(4):269–76.

Ward, Ronald W., and J. Davis. 1978a. "Coupon Redemption." *J. Adv. Res.,* 81(4):51–58.

Ward, Ronald W., and J. Davis. 1978b. "A Pooled Cross-Section Time Series Model of Coupon Promotion." *Amer. J. of Agr. Econ.*, 60(3):393–401.

Ward, Ronald W., and Bruce L. Dixon. 1989. "Effectiveness of Fluid Milk Advertising Since the Dairy and Tobacco Adjustment Act of 1983." *Amer. J. of Agr. Econ.*, 71(1989):730–40.

Ward, Ronald W., and Olan D. Forker. 1991. "Washington Apple Advertising: An Economic Model of Its Impact." Washington Apple Commission, WAC 91:1, University of Florida, Gainesville.

Ward, Ronald W., and R. L. Kilmer. 1989. *The Citrus Industry: A Domestic and International Perspective.* Iowa State University Press, Ames, IA.

Ward, Ronald W., and Chuck Lambert. Forthcoming. "Generic Promotion of Beef: Measuring the Impact of the U.S. Beef Checkoff." *Journal of Agricultural Economics.*

Ward, Ronald W., and L. H. Myers. 1979. "Advertising Effectiveness and Coefficient Variation Over Time." *Agr. Econ. Research*, 31(1):1–11.

Williams, Gary W. 1985. "Returns to U.S. Soybean Export Market Development." *Agribusiness*, 1:243–61.

Wolf, A. F. 1944. "Measuring the Effects of Agricultural Advertising." *J. of Farm Economics*, 26(2):327–47.

Zidack, W., H. Kinnucan, and U. Hatch. 1992. "Wholesale and Farm-Level Impacts of Generic Advertising: The Case of Catfish." *Applied Economics*, 24(959–68)

Index